CurryEasy Vegetarian

CurryEasy Vegetarian
Madhur Jaffrey

EBURY
PRESS

10 9 8 7 6 5 4 3 2 1

Published in 2014 by Ebury Press,
an imprint of Ebury Publishing
A Random House Group Company

The Random House Group Limited Reg. No. 954009
Addresses for companies within the Random House Group can be found at
www.randomhouse.co.uk

A CIP catalogue record for this book is available from the British Library

The Random House Group Limited supports the Forest Stewardship Council® (FSC®),
the leading international forest-certification organisation. Our books carrying the FSC
label are printed on FSC®-certified paper. FSC is the only forest-certification scheme
supported by the leading environmental organisations, including Greenpeace. Our paper
procurement policy can be found at
www.randomhouse.co.uk/environment

To buy books by your favourite authors and register for offers visit
www.randomhouse.co.uk

Design: Nathan Burton Design Ltd
Photography: Jonathan Gregson
Food stylist: Katie Giovanni
Prop stylist: Liz Belton

Printed and bound by Firmengruppe APPL, aprinta druck, Wemding, Germany

ISBN 9780091949471

Contents

Introduction

Indian vegetarian foods are perhaps the most flavourful, the most nutritionally balanced, and the most varied in the entire world. Many are of ancient origin or inspiration, seasoned with an array of spices carefully blended for both health and taste.

With this book, I want to take you on an adventurous ride through India, tasting the real vegetarian dishes that Indians eat in the privacy of their homes, in their very local cafés and temples, at the parties they throw for each other, and at their wedding banquets and religious festivals. Some may be completely unfamiliar to you, though not to those who have travelled and eaten in homes in Kerala or Tamil Nadu, Karnataka or Kashmir, Delhi or the Punjab. Even if they are unfamiliar, they are easy to put together.

Just imagine crisp okra fries dusted first with chilli powder, turmeric and chickpea flour, or grilled Portobello mushrooms flavoured simply with green chillies, squeezes of lime juice and salt, or a hot, sweet and sour mash of aubergines on toast. You will find all these in the very first chapter – Soups, Appetizers & Snacks.

The vegetable chapter holds more good things. Some of you may, just may, have had the sweet, sour, hot, salty and coconut-enriched Kodava Mushroom Curry that originated with the hunter-gatherers of the forested regions of Coorg in southern Karnataka, though

I doubt it. It is so easy to make, yet is never on any restaurant menu in the West. You will find that recipe here, along with a sublime spinach stir-fried with garlic, cumin and fenugreek seeds, and some potatoes from Goa studded with mustard seeds and refreshed with green chillies and fresh coriander.

Indians eat more dals – dried beans and legumes – than perhaps any other country. From black-eyed peas to lentils, mung beans and even soya granules, we cook them every day and each time in a different manner. For Indians these ingredients are a protein-rich mainstay. In chapter 3 you will find dozens of recipes that might well change the look of your daily meals forever.

An American friend once said that she ate an exquisite poha upma in a hotel in Madhya Pradesh. A what? She too did not know the name or what it was she was eating. She just knew that she has yearned for it ever since. You will find that recipe here in chapter 4. Poha is a version of rice that has been magically cooked, flattened and dried in such a way that it retains all its nutrients. Yet, as it is precooked, it can be combined with spices and vegetables to make poha upma, a spicy pilaf, with great speed. Indians need and love such recipes as they too want to put food on the table as quickly and easily as possible. I want you to get to know this ingredient, as

I am sure you will want to use it frequently.

As I travelled around India for this book, I kept my eyes wide open for vegetarian dishes that are both delicious and easy to make. India has so many of them, and we all need them in our repertoire. But I am going to make you go running to Indian shops to get a few new ingredients to add to your store-cupboard. Poha will be among them, as you will not find it in your local supermarket. At least not yet. Very few Indian ingredients were available when I first started writing cookbooks. But today cardamom and coriander, which I could not find back then, are in every supermarket. What is even better, you can sit comfortably at home and order almost everything you need online. Poha is a great new ingredient to learn about. I just cannot wait to introduce it to you. Indian vegetarians always have it in their larders to make a very quick snack if unexpected guests show up. You should too.

For this book I have collected recipes for Mung Bean Pancakes from Andhra, a Potato Salad from Nepal, a superb Egg Curry in a Spicy Tomato Sauce from the aristocratic families of Hyderabad, and lovely potato dishes from the Marwari business community that originated in the deserts of Rajasthan.

I am equally interested in how different Indian communities eat – their eating habits and their menus – as these offer true glimpses into the different vegetarian worlds within India. You will get to know some of these people as I did. Food, as we all know, does not exist in a vacuum. I always like to know the context and background of the dishes I eat. I hope you do too, and I have done my best to provide both.

In Bombay, I followed two very successful vegetarian jewellers to see what they ate for lunch and how they ate it. Both have shops at the Taj Mahal Hotel in the city. One, who comes from Varanasi in Uttar Pradesh, left his office every day around noon and went home to his family for lunch, the main meal of the day. He spent about 1½ hours eating and then went back to his office. His father, who had replaced him for that time, now took his car and went back to the same home (they all live together) to have his lunch. You will find the details of that meal, as well as the full menu, on page 144.

The second jeweller, whose shop had been shot at during the terrorist attack on the Taj Hotel in the winter of 2008, is a Punjabi from Delhi. His lunch set-up, right in the shop, was entirely different. There are three brothers who work at their various shops and they all eat together. The food, cooked by their wives, comes from home at the last possible minute in a large tiffin-carrier. The top of one of the larger jewellery cases is cleared off. Yes, the mirror for customers to see themselves in the earrings or necklaces they might buy is removed, a tablecloth spread out and the 'table' laid properly. Then the tiffin-carrier is opened and the brothers sit down to a full meal, right in the middle of their shop. Read all about this on page 152.

I was also very curious about the hundreds of ashrams in India. They all serve vegetarian food. What were they like and what did they serve? Did they have certain culinary principles that they followed? The Aurobindo Ashram in Delhi is located in a stunning modern building, where the round, granite dining room, right at its heart, is open to the sky in the centre. Anyone who is hungry is welcome to go in and eat – for free. The food, originating from all over India, is always made with very fresh ingredients, some grown on the premises, and is always mildly spiced and never too oily. See more about this on page 78.

For this book I have also created quite a few 'modern' dishes that use traditional Indian spices and techniques but have Western origins, such as Pan-grilled Courgettes with Spicy Tomato Sauce, and Mangoes Mumtaz, a lovely light, fluffy dessert (see pages 38 and 334).

Perhaps most important of all, none of the recipes in this book are hard to make. They may have many ingredients and take a little time, but do not be put off by that. Indian dishes need their spices and they need to cook at their own pace, but they are all simple to put together. Vegetarians – and even non-vegetarians – will want them in their repertoires. In India's ancient Ayurvedic system of medicine, it is believed that the simple acts of cutting, chopping and stirring are graces than can bring you peace and calm. This is what I wish for you.

A note on ingredients

Here are some notes about a few of the common ingredients and techniques required in this book. More uncommon ingredients have notes within the chapters (see index, page 344).

Chillies, chilli powder and the matter of heat:
How hot should a dish be? When is it too hot? Who decides? All these decisions are very personal. If chilli heat were indicated by the colour red, it would be true to say that Indian food comes in all shades, from a very pale pink to very deep crimson. You could also opt for no heat at all, as some Indians do. For every dish of Indian food you make, you will have to decide just how hot you want it. I have provided a guide by giving a sliding number to the chillies or chilli powder in a recipe. Use more or less, as you desire. Practice and experience will have to be your guides.

To make matters more difficult, however, both green chillies and dried red chillies can have different amounts of heat, even if you buy the same variety each time. You have to leave a certain amount to chance. Use less to start off with, and if you want more heat later, increase it with chilli powder.

Green chillies, fresh:
Indian chillies are thin-skinned, bright green, slim and hot, but nowhere near as hot as the West Indian habañeros. Green chillies are an essential part of the taste of authentic Indian foods, so what kind should you buy? If you have access to an Indian grocer, buy your chillies there. They always carry the small, slim, bird's eye chillies, and a longer chilli somewhat like a cayenne pepper but milder. Buy any of them. If you have no access to an Indian grocer, get small serrano chillies. Their skin is thicker and they are fatter, but they will do. As serranos are larger, use fewer of them.

If whole green chillies are called for, quarter them lengthways. Indians rarely remove the seeds.

Red chillies, dried:
India has many varieties of dried red chilli. The average is more like dried red Italian peperoncini, which you can use as a substitute. It is about 5 cm/2 inches long and its heat can be medium or hot. In the north, these chillies are often used whole, whereas in the south, they are generally broken into 2–3 pieces. Another dried chilli that I like very much is the byadgi, commonly used in the Indian state of Karnataka. It imparts a paprika-like red colour and has a medium heat. Sadly, it is not easily found in the West. At my insistence, some stores (such as Kalustyan in New York City) have started selling it. These chillies are long and slim, with a crinkly, uneven skin. I love them for the colour they give. As they are milder, you can use several of them. In India you can also buy a powder made with these chillies. It gives both flavour and a lovely red colour to the foods it is used with. Sometimes I combine red chilli powder and a good red paprika to get the same effect.

Cumin seeds, roasting and grinding:
My Indian grocer now sells ground, roasted cumin seeds. Who would have thought it! Here is how you can do it yourself and make a very fresh, aromatic batch:

Put 3–4 tablespoons cumin seeds into a small, cast-iron frying pan and set over a medium heat. Stir the seeds around until they emit a lovely roasted aroma and turn a shade darker. Do not let them burn. Transfer to a sheet of kitchen paper to cool. Empty into clean grinder or spice mill (I use a coffee-grinder reserved for spices) and grind them as finely as possible. Store in a tightly closed jar.

Curry leaves, fresh:
These are essential for cooking foods from southern and western India. Either buy a plant online (the botanical name is *Murraya koenigii* – I keep two in my house) or find a source that sells the leaves. They are sold as sprays, and all Indian grocers have them. They last several weeks in the refrigerator.

Ginger, to grate:
Peel as much of the ginger as you need (a 2.5 cm/1 inch piece yields about 1 teaspoonful), then grate it on a Microplane. Microplanes come in all sizes. I use the size up from the smallest one. You are aiming for a fine pulp.

Tarka:
An extra jolt of flavour given to a dish at the beginning or in the middle or at the end of making it. This technique is common throughout India and may be used on a salad, a yoghurt relish, or in a cooked dish. It has different names in different places, including chhownk, baghaar and vaghaar. You heat a small amount of oil in a small pan, then drop spices into it in quick succession until they pop, caramelize, darken or otherwise intensify in flavour. These spices and the oil are then either tipped over the food, or the food is allowed to cook in the mixture. As tarkas take just a few seconds to make, it is important to have all the ingredients required close at hand. Many Indian grocers sell little pots, sometimes shaped like small woks, specifically for preparing the tarkas that are made at the end of the cooking. If you get one of them, make sure that it has good balance and a long handle. A small frying pan will also do. In south India, small quantities of dals (split peas) are frequently used as a spice in the tarka. As they darken, they add a very pleasant nutty flavour.

Tomatoes, to peel:
I like to peel my tomatoes before chopping them as I do not like the little curls of skin that appear in cooked foods. Indians generally do not peel their tomatoes, but then Indian tomato skins are not as tough as those grown elsewhere. I peel a firm tomato just like an apple – with a paring knife. If the tomato is soft, you can drop it into boiling water for a minute and then pull off the skin.

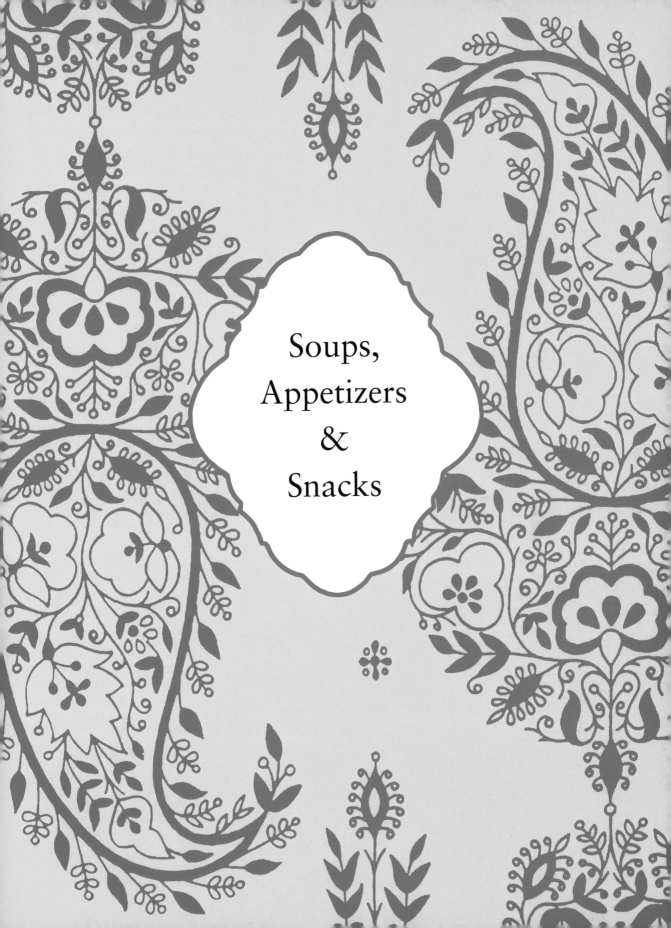

Soups, Appetizers & Snacks

Red Pepper & Tomato Soup
Lal Shimla Mirch aur Tamatar ka Soup

A very nutritious and delicious soup. If you leave out the cream, it could be completely vegan.

As stock, I use the broth from cooking a dal, a trick commonly used in south India. In that area the leftover dal is used to make a curry (sambar), but I have used it later to make a 'risotto' (see page 189).

SERVES 6

200 g/7 oz skinned moong dal
  (skinned and split mung beans)
4 tablespoons olive or peanut oil
1 onion (about 140 g/5 oz),
  peeled and chopped
2.5 cm/1 inch piece of fresh ginger,
  peeled and chopped
900 g/2 lb red peppers, seeded and
  coarsely chopped
½ teaspoon whole fennel seeds
½ teaspoon ground turmeric
1 teaspoon ground cumin
1 teaspoon ground coriander
¼ teaspoon nice red chilli powder
2 tomatoes (about 285 g/10 oz in
  all), chopped
1½ teaspoons salt
6 tablespoons double cream
  (optional)

Wash the dal in several changes of water. Drain. Put in a pan with 3 litres/5¼ pints water and bring to the boil. Cover partially, then lower the heat and simmer gently for 45 minutes. Take the pan off the heat and let it sit for 15 minutes. Scoop off and reserve 1.2 litres/2 pints of the liquid. Discard the dal solids or use them to make a 'risotto' (see page 189).

Put the oil in a large pan over a medium-high heat. When hot, add the onion, ginger, red peppers and fennel seeds. Stir and fry for 5–6 minutes, or until the vegetables just start to brown. Add the turmeric, cumin, coriander, chilli powder and tomatoes. Stir and cook for another 2 minutes. Now add 475 ml/16 fl oz of the reserved liquid and bring to a simmer. Cover and simmer gently for about 25 minutes. Set aside to cool a little, then blend the soup and strain it through a coarse strainer.

Return the soup to the empty pan. Add the salt, 475 ml/16 fl oz more of the reserved liquid and the cream (if using). Stir to mix and see if the thickness is what you want. You can thin the soup further with some of the remaining liquid. Reheat, stirring, when you are ready to eat.

Red Lentil & Courgette Soup
Masoor Dal aur Courgette ka Soup

SERVES 4–5

2 tablespoons olive or peanut oil

4 cloves

1 onion (about 180 g/6 oz), peeled
   and chopped

2 teaspoons peeled and grated
   fresh ginger

1 teaspoon peeled and crushed garlic

1 teaspoon ground coriander

1 teaspoon ground cumin

¼–¾ teaspoon nice red chilli powder

½ teaspoon ground turmeric

200 g/7 oz masoor dal (red lentils),
   picked over, washed and drained

1 potato (about 115 g/4 oz), peeled
   and diced

handful of fresh green coriander tops

10–12 fresh curry leaves, lightly
   crushed in your hand

200 g/7 oz chopped courgette or
   yellow squash

about 1¾ teaspoons salt

For the yoghurt sauce

250 ml/8 fl oz natural yoghurt

1 tablespoon lime or lemon juice

45 g/1½ oz fresh coriander, leaves
   and small stems only

2 fresh hot green chillies, chopped

¼ teaspoon salt

This delicious soup is a meal in itself as it has legumes and vegetables in it and is served with a yoghurt sauce. Slices of wholemeal bread offered on the side would make the meal nutritionally complete.

The sauce that accompanies the soup is really a chutney, which may also be used to dress simply cooked vegetables, such as boiled potatoes, carrots and peas, as well as diced and steamed courgettes.

Put the oil in a good-sized pan and set over a medium-high heat. When hot, add the cloves and let them sizzle for a few seconds. Add the onion and fry them, stirring, for about 6–7 minutes, or until they just start to brown. Lower the heat to medium and stir in the ginger and garlic. Add the ground coriander, cumin, chilli powder and turmeric and stir for a minute. Now add 1.2 litres/2 pints water, the masoor dal, potato, fresh coriander and curry leaves (take care as these will splutter). Stir, turn up the heat and bring to the boil. Turn the heat to very low, cover and cook for 40 minutes.

Add the courgette and salt. Stir and bring to a simmer. Cover, lower the heat again and cook for another 10 minutes. Set aside to cool a little.

Blend the soup finely in two batches. Return it to the pan and add 250 ml/8 fl oz water or more to thin it to your liking. Reheat as and when needed.

To make the yoghurt sauce: put all the ingredients for it in a blender in the order listed and whiz until smooth. This sauce should be refrigerated if not used soon. Serve it cold or at room temperature, drizzled generously over the very hot soup. More sauce should be offered on the side.

Tomato Rasam Soup
Tamatar Rasam ka Soup

Rasams in south India are thin, watery drinks that are very hot, sour and spicy. They are generally served with rice or just drunk on their own, but you can read more about them on page 315. For this particular recipe, I have thickened the drink so it can be served as a soup. Occasionally, I like to serve it with a little dollop of plain rice in the centre. At other times, I serve it in small coffee cups even before my guests come to the dinner table. They just drink it from the cups.

Indian grocers sell rasam powder. Get a good south Indian brand, such as MTR.

SERVES 4–5

4 tablespoons plain toovar dal, well washed in several changes of water and drained

¼ teaspoon ground turmeric

1 tablespoon chickpea flour (besan or gram flour)

¾ teaspoon tamarind concentrate (sold in bottles)

1 tablespoon rasam powder

475 ml/16 fl oz tomato passata

1½ teaspoons salt

2 teaspoons olive or peanut oil

generous pinch of ground asafoetida

¼ teaspoon urad dal

½ teaspoon whole brown mustard seeds

1 dried hot red chilli

6–8 fresh curry leaves, lightly crushed in your hand

Put the dal and 900 ml/1½ pints water in a good-sized pan and bring to the boil. Skim off the froth, then stir in the turmeric. Cover partially, lower the heat and cook for 30–40 minutes, or until the dal is soft.

Meanwhile, put the chickpea flour, tamarind concentrate and rasam powder into a large bowl. Add 1 tablespoon of water and mix to a smooth paste. Add another tablespoon of water and mix again. Add the tomato passata, salt and 350 ml/12 fl oz water and mix well.

When the dal is done, add the passata mixture to the pan. Mix and bring to the boil. Cover partially, lower the heat and simmer gently for 10 minutes. Let the soup cool a bit, then blend until smooth. Return it to the pan.

Put the oil in a small frying pan and set over medium-high heat. When hot, add the asafoetida and let it sizzle for a few seconds. Add the urad dal. As soon as it starts to pick up colour, add the mustard seeds and chilli. When the mustard seeds pop and the chilli darkens, a matter of seconds, add the curry leaves (take care as these will splutter). Stir once and pour the contents of the frying pan into the soup. Stir and cover.

Reheat the soup, removing the chilli and curry leaves before serving.

Cauliflower Soup *Gobi ka Soup*

A simple soup that I used to love as a child. It reminds me of Indian hotel soups in the waning years of the Raj.

SERVES 4–6

3 tablespoons olive or peanut oil

½ teaspoon whole cumin seeds

¼ teaspoon whole fennel seeds

1 onion (about 195 g/6½ oz), peeled and chopped

1 potato (about 195 g/6½ oz), peeled and chopped

2 teaspoons peeled and grated fresh ginger

2 cloves garlic, peeled and chopped

1 fresh hot green chilli, chopped

2 teaspoons ground coriander

1 teaspoon ground cumin

¼ teaspoon ground turmeric

¼ teaspoon nice red chilli powder

about 285 g/10 oz cauliflower florets

2 medium tomatoes, peeled and chopped

1½ teaspoons salt, or to taste

generous handful of fresh coriander, chopped

freshly ground black pepper

2 teaspoons lime juice (optional)

4–5 tablespoons double cream

Put the oil in a good-sized pan and set over a medium-high heat. When hot, add the cumin seeds, and a few seconds later the fennel seeds. Wait 2 seconds and add the onion and potato. Stir and sauté for 5 minutes. Add the ginger, garlic and green chilli. Stir for 1 minute.

Turn the heat to medium-low and add the ground coriander, cumin, turmeric and chilli powder. Stir for 1 minute. Now put in the cauliflower, tomatoes, salt and fresh coriander. Stir for 1 minute. Add 1 litre/1¾ pints water, stir and bring to the boil over a medium-high heat. Cover, lower the heat and simmer gently for 25 minutes.

Let the soup cool a bit, then blend it in two batches. Taste for seasoning, adding some black pepper, the lime juice if you want it, and the cream. You can push the soup through a sieve or food mill if you want a very smooth texture. Reheat to serve.

From the Chinmaya Mission in Delhi

Spicy Paneer Slices
Tala Masaledar Paneer

My friends Juji and Viru Dayal had told me that the food at the Chinmaya Mission in Delhi was very good and had taken me to sample some of it. I knew that the main branch was attached to the Guruvayur Temple in Kerala, so the food would be both northern and southern. The first dish I was offered was this spicy paneer from the north. It was superb.

You can make your own paneer (see Note on page 256), or buy ready-made paneer from Indian grocers. It is generally frozen in rectangles, but does not take long to defrost. I just put the whole packet in a bowl of warm water.

SERVES 4

340 g/12 oz paneer, defrosted
   if frozen
scant ½ teaspoon salt
½–1 teaspoon nice red chilli powder
scant ½ teaspoon ground turmeric
1 tablespoon rice powder
1 tablespoon chickpea flour
   (besan or gram flour)
oil, for frying
sprinkling of chaat masala (optional)

Cut the paneer into slices about 4 cm/1½ inches square and 1 cm/½ inch thick. The shape of your slab of paneer will dictate the actual shape, but make the slices no thicker than 1 cm/½ inch.

Lay the slices out in a single layer. Dust the first side with half the salt, half the chilli powder and half the turmeric. Rub these in as evenly as you can. Turn the slices over and do exactly the same on the other side with the remaining salt, chilli powder and turmeric.

Combine the rice powder and chickpea flour in a small bowl. Dip one paneer slice at a time into the bowl. Shake off the excess flour and put the slice on a board or plate. Repeat with the remaining slices. You can cover these slices and hold them for an hour.

Just before you are ready to eat, heat a 1 cm/½ inch depth of oil in a medium frying pan over a medium heat. When hot, slide in half the slices and fry them for about a minute on each side, or until golden brown. Remove with a slotted spoon and transfer to a plate lined with kitchen paper. Do a second batch the same way.

Lightly sprinkle the paneer with the chaat masala, if desired, and serve immediately.

Cabbage Fritters *Cabbage Vepadu*

I was in Rajahmundry, a town on the banks of the mighty Godavari River – the widest river I have ever seen – in Andhra Pradesh. It was lunchtime and I was desperately hungry. Someone thought that I should try a Mess. That suggested a military set-up, but it turned out to be nothing of the kind, though the name may have originated there in British times.

Andhra messes are places to eat local food very cheaply. The one I went into was in a basement, dark and sad. But the food was vegetarian, clean and excellent. For 50 rupees (65 pence) I got two types of rice, one plain and one Tomato Rice (see page 164), vegetables cooked in buttermilk, a jackfruit curry, two dals, including Sambar (see page 150) as well as Rasam (see page 315), a spicy drink, some chutneys and yoghurt relishes and this Cabbage Vepadu.

Vepadus are fried or stir-fried dishes. Crisp, fried foods are a basic part of every south Indian meal, as crunchy foods are considered an essential texture. Sometimes just a poppadom will do, but here we actually had two such dishes – these cabbage fritters and crispy, mesh-like squares made with potato.

All this was served on what looked like metal thalis (plates) that were gold on the outside and silver on the inside. They were actually made out of a thin foil that initially had to be anchored to the table with a glass of water as the fan just blew them away. At the end of the meal they were crumpled up and thrown away, just as banana leaves might have been in earlier times.

Serve these fritters as part of a meal, as a snack, or as a first course with a chutney.

Continued overleaf

MAKES 10–12

½ head of cabbage
    (about 450 g/1 lb)
1 tablespoon cornflour
3 tablespoons chickpea flour
    (besan or gram flour),
    plus more as needed
1 teaspoon salt
½–¾ teaspoon chilli powder
2 teaspoons ground coriander
¼ teaspoon ground turmeric
handful of raw peanuts, with
    or without skin (optional)
8–10 fresh curry leaves,
    shredded
handful of fresh coriander tops,
    well washed, dried and chopped
olive or peanut oil,
    for deep-frying

The fritters have a spidery look when fried, with wild strands sticking out from a more solid centre. To achieve this, the cabbage has to be cut by hand. Cut the cabbage in half lengthways, and in half again. Remove the hard core. Now set a piece down on one of its flat sides and, using a bread knife, cut its other flat side lengthways into the finest long shreds you can manage, the thinner, the better. Do the same with the other sections of the cabbage. Put all the cabbage shreds into a bowl. Add all the remaining ingredients, except the oil. Using your hands (you can wear plastic gloves if you wish), rub all the seasonings and flours into the cabbage. If you fry the fritters immediately, (this is best), you will not need more chickpea flour. If you wait, the cabbage will weep and get watery, so you might need to rub in 1–2 more tablespoons of flour (making the fritters denser).

Put the oil for frying in a wok or medium frying pan and set over a medium-low heat. When hot enough, a cabbage shred placed in the oil should sizzle immediately. Using your hand and a light touch, pick up a tablespoon or so of the cabbage mixture, keeping it flat rather than ball-like. Carefully lower it into the oil. Repeat, adding as many fritters as the pan will hold easily. Fry, turning now and then, for 5–6 minutes, or until golden red, crisp and cooked all the way through. Remove with a slotted spoon and place on a tray lined with kitchen paper.

Make all the fritters this way, adjusting the heat as needed. Serve immediately.

Onion Fritters
Kanda Bhajia or Pyaz Ki Pakori

It is Indian restaurants in the West, particularly Britain, that have popularized onion bhajias as a first course. That name comes from western India, where all varieties of fritters are called 'bhajias' and eaten at teatime or as a snack with lots of hot chutney for dipping.

In most of northern India, fritters made with potatoes, green beans, aubergine and other vegetables are known as 'pakoras' or 'pakoris', and eaten as a snack at teatime, and with drinks (both soft and alcoholic).

In Bengal, where fritters are known as 'bhaja', they can, indeed, be a first course, eaten with rice and dal, the soft and the crunchy together considered a perfect balance. They may also be offered at 'jalkhabar', the mid-morning snack. Bengalis prepare all manner of vegetable fritters, including those made with potato skins and dusted with kalonji (nigella seeds).

In the south, where the fritters have a variety of names, including 'vepadu', they are often an essential part of the meal, along with poppadoms, providing crunch and texture to the more soft and flowing rices and dals.

The flour used to bind the fritters is usually the nutritious chickpea flour, rice flour or a combination of the two.

Serve piping hot with Green Chutney (see page 268) and/or Simple Tamarind Chutney (see page 273), diluting every tablespoon of the latter with a tablespoon of water.

Put the onions, chilli powder, ginger, fresh coriander, green chilli (if using), cumin and turmeric into a bowl. Toss lightly to mix. Dust with the chickpea flour but do not mix it in yet. About 15 minutes before eating, add the salt. Now mix thoroughly with your hands, mashing the seasonings and flour into the onions. Do this for about 5 minutes, or until you draw out enough water from the onions to be able to hold the slices together in cohesive lumps.

Put a 1 cm/½ inch depth of oil in a medium frying pan and set over a medium heat.

Continued overleaf

MAKES 12 MEDIUM-SIZED FRITTERS

3 smallish onions (225 g/8 oz in all), peeled and cut into 3 mm/⅛ inch rounds (you could use a mandoline here) and the rounds cut into halves

⅛ – ¼ teaspoon nice red chilli powder

1 teaspoon peeled and finely grated fresh ginger

3 tablespoons chopped fresh coriander

1 fresh hot green chilli, cut into fine rounds (optional)

½ teaspoon ground cumin

generous pinch of ground turmeric

4 tablespoons chickpea flour (besan or gram flour)

⅓ teaspoon salt

olive or peanut oil, for deep-frying

Meanwhile, make 12 rough patties from the onion mixture, placing them in a single layer on a board or plate as you make them. Onion pieces will stick out, but that is how it should be.

When the oil is hot, turn the heat to medium-low and put in half the patties in a single layer. Fry for 1 minute on the first side. Turn the patties over and fry for another minute on the second side. Turn again and fry for another 30 seconds or so on each side. The patties should be reddish-gold and crisp. Remove with a slotted spoon and drain on kitchen paper. Make a second batch the same way.

Serve hot with chutney on the side, as suggested on the previous page.

Spinach Bhajias *Palag Ki Pakori*

These are best served piping hot with some Green Chutney (see page 268) and/or Simple Tamarind Chutney (see page 273), diluting every tablespoon of the latter with a tablespoon of water.

For more on Indian fritters in general, see the introduction to Onion Fritters (see page 25).

MAKES 12 MEDIUM-SIZED FRITTERS

115 g/4 oz chopped fresh spinach, dried thoroughly (you can use a salad spinner if you like)

6 tablespoons chickpea flour (besan or gram flour)

2 tablespoons rice flour (also called powdered rice)

1–3 generous pinches of nice red chilli powder

½ teaspoon ground roasted cumin seeds (see page 11)

1 fresh hot green chilli, finely chopped (optional)

2–3 tablespoons chopped fresh coriander

⅓ teaspoon salt

olive or peanut oil, for deep-frying

½ teaspoon kalonji (nigella seeds)

Combine the spinach, chickpea flour, rice flour, chilli powder, roasted cumin seeds, green chilli (if using), fresh coriander and salt in a bowl. Mix well, mashing the mixture with your hand. Slowly add about 6 tablespoons water, mashing and mixing until the mixture can hold together in small clumps. Do not add more water than necessary.

Put a 1 cm/½ inch depth of oil in a medium frying pan and set over a medium heat.

Meanwhile, make 12 rough patties from the spinach mixture, placing them in a single layer on a board or plate as you make them. Sprinkle the kalonji evenly over the top of the patties.

When the oil is hot, turn the heat to medium-low and put in half the patties in a single layer. Fry for 1 minute on the first side. Turn the patties over and fry for another minute on the second side. Turn again and fry for another 30 seconds or so on each side. The patties should be reddish-gold and crisp. Remove with a slotted spoon and drain on kitchen paper. Make a second batch the same way.

Serve hot with chutney on the side, as suggested above.

Spiced Potato-ball Fritters
Bonda or Batata Vada

Wherever Indian snack-sellers congregate, such as Chowpatty Beach in Bombay, you are likely to find some version of these bondas. Round in shape, with a chickpea flour skin on the outside and spicy crushed potatoes inside, they are served still hot and crisp from the karhais (woks) in which they are fried. Very popular in western and southern India, they are eaten with chutneys, such as Simple Tamarind Chutney (see page 273), Green Chutney (see page 268), Fresh Coriander, Ginger and Coconut Chutney (see page 271) and Red Chutney from the Konkan Coast (see page 280).

Peel the potatoes and crush them. You are aiming for a very coarse version of mashed potatoes.

Put the 2 tablespoons of oil in a medium, preferably non-stick frying pan and set over a medium heat. When hot, add the asafoetida. A second later, add the mustard seeds. As soon as they pop, a matter of seconds, add the onions, ginger, green chillies, cumin and fresh coriander. Stir for a minute. Add the crushed potatoes, lime juice and salt. Turn the heat to low and mix all the ingredients well. Taste for balance of flavours and make adjustments, if needed. Set aside until cool enough to handle, then make 16 balls, each about 4 cm/ 1½ inches in diameter. Transfer to a plate and set aside.

Combine all the ingredients for the batter in a bowl. Slowly add water, about 2 tablespoons less than 250 ml/8 fl oz, mixing and breaking up any lumps as you go. You should have a thick but flowing batter.

Put a 5 cm/2 inch depth of oil in a deep frying pan, wok or karhai and set over a medium-low heat. Give it time to get hot.

Dip a potato ball in the batter, making sure it is well covered. Carefully lower it into the hot oil. Do this rapidly with half the balls. Fry, turning frequently for 5–6 minutes, or until the outside batter looks crisp. It should not turn dark. Remove with a slotted spoon and drain on kitchen paper. Make a second batch the same way.

Serve while still crisp and hot.

MAKES 16 BONDAS

675 g/1½ lb unpeeled waxy potatoes (I use red ones), freshly boiled and cooled

2 tablespoons olive or peanut oil

generous pinch of ground asafoetida

¼ teaspoon whole brown or yellow mustard seeds

4 tablespoons finely chopped onions

2 teaspoons peeled and very finely chopped fresh ginger

1–2 fresh green chillies, finely chopped

1 teaspoon ground cumin

3 tablespoons chopped fresh coriander

1½–2 teaspoons lime or lemon juice

1 teaspoon salt, or to taste

olive or peanut oil, for deep-frying

For the batter

140 g/5 oz chickpea flour (besan or gram flour)

30 g/1 oz rice flour (also called powdered rice)

½ teaspoon baking powder

½ teaspoon salt

¼ teaspoon ajowan seeds

generous pinch of ground asafoetida

½ teaspoon ground turmeric

Spicy Matchstick Potatoes
Aloo ka Tala hua Laccha

This is a wonderful snack to nibble on, especially when enjoying favourite TV programmes and films at home. You could serve it with Simple South Indian Tomato Sauce (see page 303), plain old tomato ketchup or nothing at all. It is good just by itself.

SERVES 4

2 teaspoons lemon juice

1 onion (about 140 g/5 oz), peeled and chopped

2 cloves garlic, peeled and chopped

2.5 cm/1 inch piece of fresh ginger, peeled and chopped

1 hot dried red chilli, crumbled

1 teaspoon ground cumin seeds

4 medium potatoes (about 560 g/ 1¼ lb in total)

olive or peanut oil, for frying

1 tablespoon whole sesame seeds

¾–1 teaspoon salt

freshly ground black pepper

1 teaspoon sugar

Put the lemon juice, onion, garlic, ginger, red chilli and cumin into a blender or food processor. Whiz, pushing down as necessary, until you have a smooth paste.

Peel the potatoes and cut them lengthways into slices 3 mm/⅛ inch thick. (You can use a mandoline if you wish.) Stacking a few slices together at a time, cut them into strips of the same thickness. If not frying immediately, put the potatoes into a bowl of water, then drain and pat dry before the next step.

Put a 1.5 cm/½ inch depth of oil in a large frying pan and set over a medium heat. When hot, put in as many potatoes as will fit easily. Stir and fry until they are golden and crisp. Remove with a slotted spoon and spread out on kitchen paper to drain. Do all the potatoes this way.

Remove all but 4 tablespoons of oil from the frying pan. Put the sesame seeds into the hot oil. Stir and fry until they begin to pop. Pour in the onion mixture, then stir and fry slowly until it has browned and is quite dry. This is important.

Now put in the fried potatoes, salt, pepper and sugar. Mix, breaking up the spice clumps and spreading them about. Remove with a slotted spoon and serve hot or at room temperature.

Savoury Pastry Strips with Ajowan Seeds *Namakpara*

You can put a bowl of these snacks near the sofa, with another bowl of chutney to be used as a dipping sauce, and you are all set for an evening watching television. Namakparas, a great favourite in our family, are savoury nibbling food flavoured with the thyme-like seeds known as ajowan (or ajwain). Amongst the chutneys you can use as a dip are Fresh Coriander & Yoghurt Chutney and Quick Yoghurt & Pickle Chutney (see pages 270 and 278), or just plain old tomato ketchup.

Namakparas can be made ahead of time and stored in airtight tins, just like biscuits.

SERVES 4–6

130 g/4½ oz plain flour
2 tablespoons sooji (see page 176)
¾ teaspoon salt
¼ teaspoon ajowan seeds
2 tablespoons olive or peanut oil, plus more for deep-frying

Put the flour, sooji, salt and ajowan seeds in a bowl and mix well with a fork. Dribble in the 2 tablespoons of oil and rub the flours until you have a rough, breadcrumb-like texture. This must be turned into a very firm dough, so add some water a bit at a time. I used only 4½ tablespoons, but you might need a little more or a little less. Knead the dough for 2–3 minutes and shape into a ball. Set aside in the mixing bowl, covered by a damp tea towel, for 20 minutes or so. Knead the dough again for a minute or so, then divide it into two equal balls. Set one aside, covered.

Take the other ball and flatten it, then roll it out into a 23 cm/9 inch circle. You will need to push down hard as the dough will be firm. (You will not need any extra flour to help with the rolling.) Using a sharp knife, cut the circle into long strips 1 cm/½ inch wide. Now cut across the centre, dividing each strip in half. Make similar strips with the second ball of dough. Keep both lots lightly covered.

Put 4 cm/1½ inch depth of oil into a wok, karhai or frying pan and set over a medium-low heat. When the oil is hot – a piece of dough dropped in should sink to the bottom, rise very slowly and start sizzling – put in as many namakparas as will fit easily in a single layer. Fry, turning them over every minute or so, until they are golden. This should take about 5 minutes. If they are cooking too fast, adjust the heat. Lift them out of the hot oil with a slotted spoon and spread them out on a baking sheet lined with kitchen paper. Make all the namakparas this way. Allow them to cool completely, then store them in an airtight tin or a ziplock bag.

Okra Fries *Tali Bhindi*

Crisply fried okra is eaten all over India. I remember that in our family we cut the okra into thin rings, fried them until very crisp, then ate them with a sprinkling of salt, amchoor (sour green mango powder) and some chilli powder. In Tamil Nadu, where crisp foods, such as poppadoms, are a basic part of every meal, they cut the okra into chunky rounds, dip them in a thick, well-seasoned chickpea flour batter and serve this fritter-like vegetable dish with the main meal. This particular recipe comes from western India, where a mound of delicate crisp okra strands, cut on the vertical, may be eaten as a snack with drinks, or as part of a meal.

SERVES 4

225 g/8 oz fresh okra,
 wiped with a damp cloth
 and air-dried (young
 tender okra is best)
¾ teaspoon chilli powder
¼ teaspoon ground turmeric
¾ teaspoon chaat masala
3 tablespoons chickpea flour
 (besan or gram flour)
peanut or olive oil,
 for shallow-frying
about ⅓ teaspoon salt
½ teaspoon amchoor powder

Remove the very top cones on the okra pods, as well as the tips at the bottom. Cut each pod in half lengthways, then cut each half into 3 lengthways strips. Put in a bowl. Dust with ½ teaspoon chilli powder, the turmeric, ¼ teaspoon of the chaat masala and all the chickpea flour. Toss the okra gently with your hands to mix evenly. Set aside for 30–60 minutes.

Put a 1.5cm/½ inch depth of oil in a medium frying pan and set over a medium heat until hot. Meanwhile, line a large plate or tray with kitchen paper. Drop the okra rapidly, a piece at a time, into the hot oil so that you have a crowded single layer and fry, turning now and then, for about 3 minutes. The okra should become golden and crisp. Adjust the heat, if necessary. Remove with a slotted spoon and spread on the prepared tray. Do several batches until all the okra has been fried. Dust immediately with salt, the amchoor powder, ¼ teaspoon chilli powder and ½ teaspoon of chaat masala. Serve immediately.

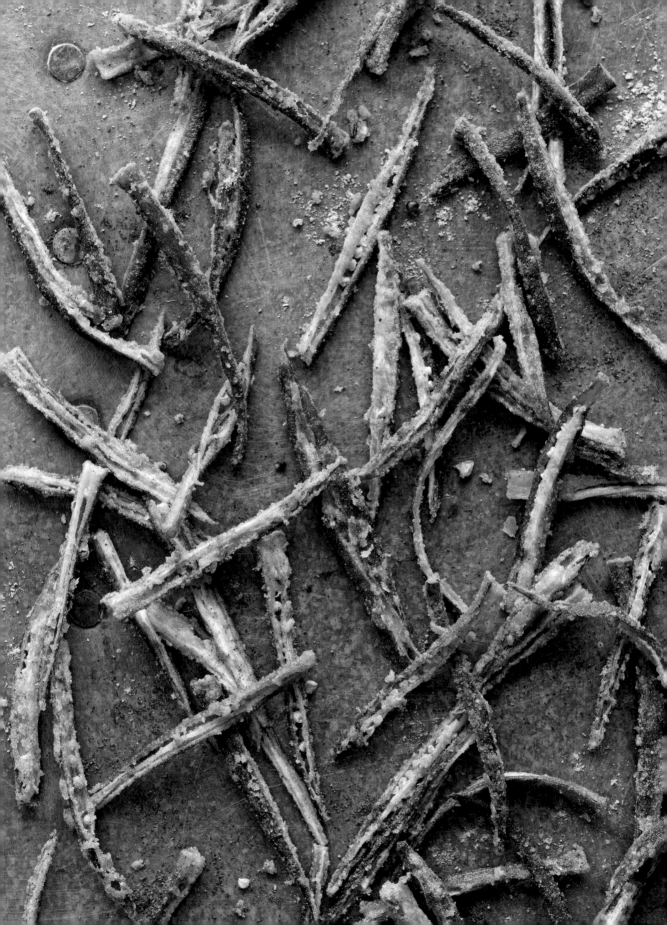

Kaveri Ponnapa's
Grilled Portobello Mushrooms in the Kodaga Style *Chutta Kumme*

During the four-month rainy season in the hills of Coorg (southern Karnataka), most people get their food by foraging in the dense forests that surround the rice fields and the massive coffee plantations. It is an age-old tradition followed by the rich and poor alike. It is at this time of year that delicacies, such as wild mushrooms, young bamboo shoots, unfurled colocasia leaves and ferns, become suddenly available.

It is also a tradition, certainly amongst the landed gentry, to take some of the larger mushrooms, such as the aalandi kumme or the plate-sized nethelé kumme, and hold them over a wood fire with tongs until they are well singed. They then dress them with crushed green chillies, lime juice and salt and serve them with drinks. Even the juice left behind in the serving plate is delicious.

Needless to say, I cannot get the mushrooms that grow in Coorg, so I buy large Portobello mushrooms. You can also use large porcinis, if available. They can be cooked on a barbecue in the summer, but I use my oven grill all year round.

I serve these snacks with drinks, cutting them into wedges and inserting a cocktail stick into each one. But I also serve them as a first course – one large mushroom per person, with a small portion of Cherry Tomato Salad with Curry Leaves (see page 42), both on the same plate.

SERVES 4

4 Portobello mushrooms (340–370 g /12–13 oz), with large caps, each about 13–15 cm/5–6 inches in diameter (use smaller mushrooms if large ones are not available)

2 tablespoons olive or peanut oil

¾ teaspoon salt, or to taste

4 teaspoons lime juice, or to taste

2 fresh hot green chillies, pounded to a paste in a mortar, or 1–2 generous pinches of nice red chilli powder (such as Kashmiri)

Preheat the grill until very hot, making sure the oven shelf is 10–13 cm/4–5 inches away from the source of the heat.

Break off and discard the mushroom stems. Wipe the caps with damp kitchen paper and leave to dry for 5 minutes. Put the caps, gill-side up, in a baking tin. Brush all the mushrooms with 1 tablespoon of the oil. Place under the grill for about 1½ minutes, or until well singed. Turn the caps over. Brush with the remaining 1 tablespoon oil and grill for another 1½ minutes.

Transfer the mushrooms to a large plate, placing them gill-side up again. Sprinkle with half the salt, half the lime juice and half the chilli paste or powder. Spread gently with your fingers. Turn the mushrooms over and sprinkle the remaining seasonings on the top in exactly the same way. Serve hot or at room temperature.

Wild Mushroom Stew
with Coconut Sauce
Khumbi ki Tarkari

This makes a lovely first course, served plain or on toast.
I make it with a mixture of the fresh mushrooms that are
available to me – hon-shimeji (also called beech mushrooms,
as they grow on beech trees), shiitake and oyster mushrooms.
Although all these mushrooms once grew wild in eastern
Asia, they are now cultivated and may be procured fairly
easily in the West as well. If you cannot get one of them, just
get more of the other two, or add some other wild mushroom
that you like. After trimming, I end up with about 450 g/1 lb
of mushrooms.

Wipe the dirt off the mushrooms with damp kitchen paper
and trim them as follows: shiitake – break off and discard
the stems; cut the caps into 4–8 wedges, depending upon size;
oyster – cut off the lower, hard part of the stems, separate
the mushrooms and cut larger caps into 4 cm/1½ inch pieces;
hon-shimeji – remove the bottom, hard part of the stems, and
divide the larger bunches into smaller bunches.

Put the oil in a medium, preferably non-stick pan and set
over a medium-high heat. When hot, add the mustard seeds.
As soon as they begin to pop, a matter of seconds, add the cumin
seeds. Let them sizzle for a few seconds, then add the curry
leaves (take care as they will splutter), followed immediately
by the shallots, green chilli and garlic.

Stir for about 3 minutes, then put in all the mushrooms and
¼ teaspoon of salt. Stir gently for about 4 minutes, or until
the mushrooms appear wet. The pan will seem overcrowded
at first, but the pile of mushrooms will soon settle down. Add
the ground coriander, chilli powder and turmeric. Stir and
cook for another 2 minutes. Check for salt and add another
¼ teaspoon or so, as needed.

Pour in the coconut milk, bring to a simmer, then simmer
gently for 2 minutes. Stir in the lime juice and taste again to
check the balance of seasonings. Adjust as necessary.

If this dish sits around, the coconut milk can thicken up.
In this case, add 1–2 tablespoons of water when reheating.

SERVES 4–5

about 675 g/1½ lb mushrooms,
   including about 6 fresh shiitake
   mushrooms with thick caps about
   7.5–9 cm/3–3½ inches in diameter
   (get more if the caps are smaller),
   oyster mushrooms and hon-
   shimeji (beech) mushrooms
3 tablespoons olive or peanut oil
½ teaspoon whole brown
   mustard seeds
½ teaspoon whole cumin seeds
6–7 fresh curry leaves, lightly
   crushed in your hand
3 medium shallots (about 70 g/2½
   oz in all), peeled and finely
   chopped
1 fresh hot green chilli,
   finely chopped
2 cloves garlic, peeled and
   finely chopped
salt
1 teaspoon ground coriander
generous pinch of nice red
   chilli powder
generous pinch of ground turmeric
180 ml/6 fl oz coconut milk,
   from a well-shaken can
2 teaspoons lime juice

Malathi Srinivasan's
Aubergine 'Gojju' on Toast
Suttid Badankai Gojju

Gojjus, beloved by the Madhwa Brahmin community of Karnataka, are hot, sweet and sour relishes, normally eaten with rice. This gojju, a kind of chutney, may be served as such with most Indian meals, but I love it as a dip with crackers or oatcakes, or, better still, spread out on lightly toasted baguette slices as a kind of Indian bruschetta.

Madhwa Brahmins worship at the Udipi Temple, famous for training the thousands of cooks who have later gone out into the world to start south Indian restaurants in distant parts. They eat mostly locally grown, traditional vegetables, such as aubergines, Indian gourds and squashes, and sweet potatoes. Their most important spice is asafoetida – pure lump asafoetida that can be crushed and put into water for kitchen use. If you go to the Udipi Temple, you can buy little bowls to do just that!

SERVES 4

1 medium aubergine (about 400 g/14 oz)

1½ teaspoons tamarind concentrate (sold in bottles)

½–¾ teaspoon salt

1½ tablespoons light or dark brown sugar

¼–½ teaspoon nice red chilli powder

2 teaspoons olive or peanut oil

generous pinch of ground asafoetida

½ teaspoon whole brown mustard seeds

1 dried hot red chilli

6–7 fresh curry leaves, lightly crushed in your hand

12 baguette slices, cut at a slight diagonal, and toasted lightly if you wish

butter, for spreading

Preheat the oven to 230°C/gas mark 8.

Prick the aubergine with a fork 12–15 times. Place in a roasting tin and bake for about 45 minutes, turning every 15 minutes. The aubergine should flatten out and get soft and pulpy inside. Set aside until cool enough to handle.

Peel the cooled aubergine, then chop the flesh and put in a bowl. Mash the pulp some more, adding and mixing in the tamarind concentrate, salt, sugar and chilli powder. Taste for balance and adjust the seasonings as necessary.

Put the oil in a small frying pan and set over a medium heat. When hot, add the asafoetida. Five seconds later, add the mustard seeds. As soon as they start to pop, a matter of seconds, add the dried red chilli. Let it turn dark. Now throw in the curry leaves (take care as they will splutter), stir once or twice, then pour the oil and seasonings over the aubergine purée. Stir to mix, then remove the red chilli and curry leaves.

Spread out all your baguette slices and butter them very lightly. Spread the gojju – warm or at room temperature – over the bread and serve immediately.

Pan-grilled Courgettes with a Spicy Tomato Sauce
Tala hua Courgette

SERVES 6 AS A FIRST COURSE
AND 4 AS A MAIN MEAL

about 2 tablespoons olive or
   peanut oil
2 medium courgettes (about
   180 g/6 oz in all), trimmed and
   cut into long diagonal slices
   7 mm/⅓ inch thick
salt and freshly ground black pepper
ground roasted cumin seeds
   (see page 11)
nice red chilli powder
about 250 ml/8 fl oz Simple
   South Indian Tomato Sauce
   (see page 303)

You can grill the courgettes outdoors in the summer, but
I usually fry them indoors in a heavy frying pan.

Set a cast-iron frying pan over a medium-high heat. When
hot, spread 1 tablespoon of the oil over the bottom. Arrange
a single layer of the courgettes in the pan and let them brown
for about 2 minutes. You might need to move the slices around
to brown them evenly. Turn the slices over and brown the
opposite side, also for about 2 minutes. Transfer to a plate.

Add another tablespoon of oil to the pan and cook the
remaining slices the same way.

Lay out all the courgettes in a single layer in a serving dish
and sprinkle lightly with salt, pepper, the ground cumin seeds
and chilli powder. Spoon the tomato sauce over their centres
and serve.

Cucumber Spears *Kheeray ki Phankay*

Whenever I am looking for a snack that is not too fattening, I turn to these cucumber spears. We used to eat a simpler version as children, cucumber halves or quarters just sprinkled with lime juice and dusted with spices, but now I have started giving the dish a final 'tarka', which makes it even better. You can serve them with drinks (hand out napkins) or with all meals, Western or south Asian.

You need to use seedless cucumbers here. I like to use the ones that are labelled Armenian or Persian. They are about 15 cm/6 inches long, about 3 cm/1¼ inches wide, and are quite free of developed seeds. You can, of course, use other similar cucumbers.

Ideally, the cucumbers should be dressed shortly before you eat them as salt makes them wilt.

SERVES 4

4 cucumbers, as described above, or the nearest substitutes
1 teaspoon lemon juice
¼ teaspoon salt, or to taste
⅛ teaspoon ground roasted cumin seeds (see page 11)
⅛ teaspoon chilli powder
2 teaspoons olive or peanut oil
⅛ teaspoon whole brown mustard seeds
⅛ teaspoon whole cumin seeds
5–6 fresh curry leaves or small basil leaves

Peel the cucumbers and halve them lengthways. Arrange them on a plate, cut-side up. Dribble the lemon juice over them as evenly as you can manage. Now sprinkle the salt, cumin seeds and chilli powder over them in the same even manner.

Put the oil in a small frying pan over a medium-high heat. When hot, add the mustard seeds. As soon as they start to pop, a matter of seconds, add the cumin seeds and let them sizzle for a few seconds. Throw in the curry leaves and turn off the heat. Now tilt the frying pan and spoon the oil and spices evenly over the cucumbers. They are ready to be served.

Cherry Tomato Salad
with Curry Leaves
Chhote Tamatar ka Salaad

Apart from being delicious, this is a very pretty salad that
I often serve as a first course, sometimes combining it with
Cucumber Spears (see page 41). It is prettiest when made
with cherry tomatoes of different sizes and colours. Placed
in a single layer on a white plate, they look like jewels.

If using small cherry tomatoes, cut them in half through
their 'equator'. Larger ones may be quartered. If using grape
tomatoes, cut them in half lengthways.

Arrange the tomatoes, cut-side up, in a single layer on
a plate. You can leave spaces between them.

Shortly before serving them, dust the tomatoes lightly
with salt and pepper.

Put the oil in a small frying pan and set over a medium-
high heat. When hot, put in the mustard seeds. As soon as
they start to pop, a matter of seconds, add the red chilli,
stirring until it darkens. Quickly add the curry leaves,
then lift up the pan and spoon the oil and spices over the
tomatoes. Serve as soon as you can, leaving the red chilli
on top as a garnish, but warn people not to eat it. It will
have already done its job by flavouring the oil.

SERVES 4

285 g/10 oz cherry or grape
  tomatoes, preferably in
  different colours and sizes
salt and freshly ground black pepper
2 tablespoons olive or peanut oil
¼ teaspoon whole brown
  mustard seeds
1 dried hot red chilli
7–8 fresh curry leaves or
  small basil leaves

Tomato Salad *Tamatar ka Salaad*

During the winter months, the tomatoes in our garden in India bore endless fruit. Some were made into juice for us to have mid-morning, some were added to vegetable dishes and dals, and some were used to make salads. My father did not grow any heirloom tomatoes in shades of green, yellow and pink, but I do, and I've had great success with them.

One day, when I was making lunch for four people, I thought we might start with our gorgeous tomatoes. I had been inspired by a tall salad I had eaten at my favourite tapas place in London, Barrafina, and by the shallot-filled dressing they used on another dish, their baby gem salad. I wanted to combine all this with the flavours of my mother's tomato salad. You can taste the result below.

This salad needs to be put together at the last moment, but the ingredients should all be gathered on the work surface before you start.

The dressing used for this salad is also very good on boiled and sliced beetroot (which you can combine with halved hard-boiled eggs for a delicious salad), boiled and diced potatoes, and parboiled or steamed green beans (which you can mix with canned, drained chickpeas).

First make the dressing: put the shallot, vinegar, mustard, ginger juice, salt, pepper and cumin into a bowl. Mix and set aside for 10 minutes or longer. Now slowly whisk in the oil, pouring in just a little at a time.

Just before you sit down to eat, slice the tomatoes about 7 mm/⅓ inch thick. Put one slice each of the same colour in the centre of each serving plate. Dust it with a pinch of salt and a little cumin. Pick up slices of a second colour and put them on top of the first. Sprinkle with salt and cumin. Proceed this way until you have 5–6 rainbow slices, one on top of the other in a 'tower'. If they slide and you end up with a mound, that is fine.

Whisk your dressing again and spoon a little over each tower, using only as much as you need. Scatter the mint around the plate and serve immediately.

SERVES 4

6 or more ripe summer tomatoes, in shades of pink, green, yellow and red, if you can get them (the number depends on size)
salt
ground roasted cumin seeds (see page 11)
a few small fresh mint leaves (optional)

For the dressing
1 medium shallot, peeled and finely chopped
1 tablespoon red wine vinegar
1 tablespoon Dijon mustard
juice from 1 teaspoon peeled and finely grated fresh ginger
¼ teaspoon salt, or to taste
freshly ground black pepper
½ teaspoon ground roasted cumin seeds (see page 11)
4 tablespoons extra virgin olive oil

Boiled Peanuts in Their Shells
Ubli Moomphali

India is the second largest producer of peanuts in the world, after China, and vegetarians make ample use of the protein-rich product by adding it to their meals, either cooked along with vegetables and legumes (peanuts are actually a legume too), or by adding it to various snack foods, such as Bombay Mix. These peanuts are, of course, fully mature and completely dried. But when peanuts are young and fresh, they are often just boiled in their shells, rather like soya beans, and people just sit around peeling and eating them.

It is only in one season that fresh peanuts are available. I buy them as soon as I lay eyes on them in any country I happen to be in, and I cook them in the following way.

SERVES 6 AS A SNACK OR
TO EAT WITH DRINKS

2 dried hot red chillies
1 teaspoon black peppercorns
1 teaspoon whole fennel seeds
1 teaspoon whole cumin seeds
1 teaspoon whole fenugreek seeds
2 teaspoons salt
285 g/10 oz fresh peanuts in
   their shells

Put 1 litre/1¾ pints water in a pan. Add all the spices and the salt and bring to a simmer. Cover and simmer gently for 10 minutes. Strain the liquid and put it back in the pan.

Add the peanuts to the flavoured water and bring to the boil. Cover, lower the heat and simmer gently for about 10 minutes (15 if the peanuts are large). Strain thoroughly and serve lukewarm or cold. Shell and eat.

Orange & Radish Salad
Narangi aur Lal Mooli ka Salaad

Here is another wonderful combination of fruit and raw vegetables that we often use to make our snack foods and salads. I find that it makes a light and delightful first course. This recipe may easily be doubled or tripled.

You can use different types of radishes here: thin white ones, known as mooli in India and the UK, and as small daikon in the US; red, pink and white Chinese radishes; and the larger versions of plain red radishes.

SERVES 2

2 navel oranges

30 g/1 oz radishes, very finely sliced (use a mandoline, if you have one)

⅛ teaspoon salt

freshly ground black pepper

⅛ teaspoon ground roasted cumin seeds (see page 11)

¹⁄₁₆ teaspoon chilli powder

2 small sprigs of fresh coriander or mint

For the radishes

½ teaspoon lemon juice

freshly ground black pepper

generous pinch of salt, or to taste

⅛ teaspoon ground roasted cumin seeds (see page 11)

a few sprinkles of chilli powder

Peel the oranges in such a way that you remove all the white pith. Slice off a good chunk of the top and bottom (I just eat these bits) and cut the remainder crossways into circles 7 mm/⅓ inch thick. Set aside in a single layer.

Put the sliced radishes into a bowl and set aside.

Half an hour before you eat, sprinkle the oranges with the salt, pepper, cumin and chilli powder as evenly as you can.

Just before you eat, sprinkle the radishes with the lemon juice, pepper, salt, cumin and chilli powder. Toss lightly.

Lay half the orange slices on a salad plate. Put half the sliced radishes to one side of them and garnish with a sprig of coriander or mint. Serve immediately.

A Note about Puffed Rice

Puffed rice – fully cooked rice grains that are puffed up and crisp – is eaten in some form or other throughout India. It is generally added to snack foods, as illustrated in the two recipes that follow, but in eastern India it is so beloved that it is eaten for breakfast as well. Rather like Rice Krispies, it is combined with creamy milk, seasonal fruit, such as mangoes and ripe jackfruit, and some liquid palm sugar.

In a mélange that is highly popular in West Bengal's countryside and in Bangladesh, puffed rice is tossed together with green chillies, chopped onion and a drizzle of pungent mustard oil. Najmul Chaudhury, the gentleman from Dhaka that I buy my spices from at Kalustyan's in New York, always keeps a stash of the basic ingredients under the counter in front of him. Whenever he feels peckish, he just tosses them together in a bowl that he also stores under the counter, and eats. If he feels like it, he adds some thin chickpea flour noodles called sev that he also sells in the store. If he wants to add a bit of sweetness to the pungency, he may, like his countrymen, suck on a piece of solid palm sugar as he nibbles.

Puffed rice has many names in India: murmura, kurmura, churmura, mumra and moori being just a few of them. When you shop at an Indian store, you would be quite safe asking for murmura.

I like to crisp up my puffed rice before I prepare any snack as this improves its texture and refreshes it. I have done this for the salad on page 50, where the puffed rice is used as is, straight from the packet without any toasting or frying. If you want to use it for your morning cereal – and why not? – you should follow this quick step first: Put a wok or medium frying pan over a medium heat and let it get hot. Add the puffed rice and stir it about for 3–4 minutes, or until it crisps up a bit. It should not change colour. (Eat a grain each of the untoasted and toasted rice to check the difference.) Empty into a bowl and set aside to cool. Store leftovers in an airtight jar or tin.

Spicy, Crisp Puffed Rice Nibbles
Masaledar Murmura

Many nations eat some sort of puffed rice. In the West it is generally used for breakfast cereal, to be eaten with milk and sugar. In India it is eaten in hundreds of different ways, some sweet, but most others savoury and spicy.

The recipe here is for a crunchy, nutty nibble, perfect with drinks. If I invite friends to watch television or a film at home, I hand them a drink and a home-made paper cone filled with this spicy murmura. That is the name for it in Delhi, and I find that most Indian stores in the West sell it by that name as well. Just ask for puffed rice or murmura and the grocer will get what you want.

This recipe cooks in 5 minutes or less, so have everything assembled before you start.

SERVES 4 AND FILLS A
1 LITRE/1¾ PINT MEASURE

3 tablespoons olive or peanut oil

generous pinch of ground asafoetida

½ teaspoon whole brown
  mustard seeds

1–2 fresh hot green chillies,
  cut into fine rings

6–7 fresh curry leaves, or Thai basil
  or small basil leaves, lightly
  crushed in your hand

45 g/1½ oz raw cashews (this is a
  good opportunity to buy cashew
  halves or broken cashews)

45 g/1½ oz raw peanuts (red skins
  on or off)

70 g/2½ oz puffed rice (murmura)

½ teaspoon salt

¼ teaspoon nice red chilli powder,
  if needed

1 teaspoon fine sugar

Put the oil in a wok, karhai or frying pan and set over a medium heat. When hot, add the asafoetida, quickly followed by the mustard seeds. As soon as the mustard seeds pop, a matter of seconds, add the green chillies and curry leaves (take care as they will splutter). Stir and fry for a minute or less, or until the last two ingredients dry out. Add the cashews and peanuts. Stir and fry briskly until they just turn golden.

Quickly add all the puffed rice. Stir and fry for a minute. Add the salt, chilli powder, if needed, and the sugar. Stir well, then turn off the heat. Let the mixture cool down completely, and transfer to an airtight jar or tin.

Salad of Puffed Rice, Cucumbers, Onions & Tomatoes *Jhal Moori*

SERVES 6

about 3 seedless baby cucumbers
(130 g/4½ oz), cut into
7 mm/⅓ inch dice

70 g/2½ oz onion, peeled and cut
into 5 mm/¼ inch dice

200 g/7 oz firm tomatoes cut into
7 mm/⅓ inch dice

1 waxy potato (about 180 g/6 oz),
freshly boiled, cooled, peeled and
cut into 5 mm/¼ inch dice

½–1 fresh hot green chilli, finely
sliced crossways (optional)

3 tablespoons chopped fresh
coriander

¼ teaspoon ground roasted cumin
seeds (see page 11)

freshly ground black pepper

¾ teaspoon salt

½ teaspoon chaat masala

1–3 generous pinches of nice red
chilli powder

½ teaspoon Simple Tamarind
Chutney (see page 273, optional)

½ teaspoon Green Chutney
(see page 268, optional)

1 teaspoon mustard oil (for a true
Bengali taste) or extra virgin
olive oil

1 tablespoon lime juice,
plus 1 teaspoon extra if not
using the chutneys

30 g/1 oz puffed rice

An inspired and variable mixture of vegetables, nuts, legumes, noodles, chutneys and, most importantly, puffed rice, jhal moori is Calcutta street food par excellence, a kind of nutritious Bengali salad. It can be picked up from a vendor and eaten as a snack while on an evening stroll, while office workers might have it in the afternoon with their tea, or even gobble some up for lunch.

I have eaten it at all these times, but now I find myself frequently making it as a first course at home when I am entertaining. I like to assemble all the parts in advance and put them together at the last minute. The salad holds well for 10–15 minutes, but gradually begins to get soggy. It still tastes excellent 2 hours later, but loses all its crispness. You could also serve this mixture on top of lightly dressed salad greens for lunch. It is very good that way.

If you do not have the chutneys mentioned, just leave them out. The salad will still taste just fine.

Put the cucumbers, onion, tomatoes, potato, chilli (if using) and fresh coriander into a large bowl.

Put the cumin seeds, pepper, salt, chaat masala and chilli powder into small bowl.

Have the chutneys (if using), mustard oil and lime juice at the ready.

Put a wok or medium frying pan over a medium heat and let it get hot. Add the puffed rice and stir it about for 3–4 minutes, or until it crisps up a bit. It should not change colour. Empty into a bowl and set aside.

Now you need just a few minutes to throw the jhal moori together. Add the dry spices and puffed rice to the cucumber mixture. Also add the chutneys (if using), the mustard oil and lime juice. Toss well to mix. Taste for balance of seasonings and serve.

Vegetables

Jayanti Rajagopalan's
Roasted Aubergine & Tomato
Baigan Chokah

Chokah is eaten all over Bihar. In the villages there, it could be the only dish of the day eaten with simple wholemeal flatbreads, such as Chapatis (see page 193) or rice. (Similar dishes, known as 'bharta', exist all across north India.) It can also be served as a part of a meal in small, individual bowls.

In India the aubergine is roasted over a simple wood fire, or sometimes buried in very hot embers. The tomatoes are simply held over a wood fire with chimta (tongs) until the skin blackens. Both vegetables are peeled, mashed together and seasoned. That is all there is to it. The mustard oil used here gives it the true flavour of eastern India, but is not essential.

In my family, we sometimes mix this chokah with yoghurt and serve it as a relish-like accompaniment.

SERVES 4

450 g/1 lb slim, tender aubergines (I used 4 of the Japanese variety, but Italians ones can be substituted)

2 medium (225 g/8 oz) plum tomatoes

⅓–½ teaspoon salt

freshly ground black pepper

1–2 fresh green chillies, finely chopped

1½ tablespoons peeled and finely chopped shallots

2 teaspoons finely chopped mint

2 tablespoons chopped fresh coriander

2–3 teaspoons lime juice

3 teaspoons mustard oil, or a fruity, good-quality extra virgin olive oil

Preheat the grill until very hot. Line a baking tray with foil.

Using a fork, prick the aubergines all over. Prick the tomatoes in just a few places. Place both vegetables on the prepared tray and put it under the grill, as close to the heat source as possible. Grill, turning the vegetables a little when one side is charred. This may not happen evenly, so keep checking. Slim, tender aubergines take 15–20 minutes, about the same as the tomatoes, but larger aubergines will take longer, up to 40 minutes. The vegetables need to get very brown or charred all over and become soft inside. Remove them as they get done and put in a sieve set over a bowl.

Set the vegetables aside until cool enough to handle, then peel them and remove their pulp.

Chop the vegetable pulp finely and put in a bowl. Add the salt, pepper, green chillies, shallots, mint, coriander, lime juice and 2 teaspoons of the mustard oil. Mix and taste for balance of seasonings, adjusting as necessary. Refrigerate until needed.

Put the choka in a serving bowl and drizzle the remaining teaspoon of mustard oil over the top. Serve cold or at room temperature.

Simple, Twice-cooked Aubergine
Baigan Bharta

When an Indian child fighting with another Indian child says, 'I am going to make a bharta out of you,' he or she means that the intention is to make a mash out of the other child. This is my way of explaining that bhartas are mashed vegetables, seasoned in a variety of ways.

We in the northern half of India (Punjab, Delhi, Uttar Pradesh) normally eat bhartas with flatbreads, while other areas (Bihar, Orissa and West Bengal) eat them with rice. Here I have cooked the bharta partly in the Delhi way and partly in the Bengali way. If you want more of the Bengali flavour, cook this bharta in mustard oil.

Note that it really helps to use a large, well-seasoned or non-stick wok, karhai or frying pan here.

Preheat the oven to 200°C/gas mark 6.

Using a fork, prick the aubergines all over. Place them in a roasting tin in the oven for 1¼ hours until tender. Peel them and chop them finely.

Put the oil in a non-stick wok, karhai or frying pan and place over a medium-high heat. When hot, add the cumin seeds. Let them sizzle for 3–4 seconds, then add the fennel and nigella seeds. After 2 seconds, add the onion, stirring and sautéing for 5–6 minutes, until just starting to brown at the edges.

Now add the ginger, garlic and green chillies. Stir and cook for 2 minutes. Add the tomatoes and keep cooking for 5–6 minutes, or until the tomatoes soften.

Add the aubergine and salt and cook for 5 minutes. Stir in the coriander and cook for another 3 minutes.

SERVES 3–4

900 g/2 lb aubergines (I used 3 medium purple ones)
4 tablespoons olive, peanut or mustard oil
½ teaspoon whole cumin seeds
½ teaspoon whole fennel seeds
¼ teaspoon nigella seeds (kalonji)
1 onion (200–225 g/7–8 oz), peeled and finely chopped
7.5 cm/3 inch piece of fresh ginger, peeled and very finely chopped
3 large cloves garlic, peeled and very finely chopped
1–2 fresh hot green chillies, finely chopped
2 good-sized tomatoes (about 340 g/12 oz in all), peeled and finely chopped
1 teaspoon salt
3 tablespoons chopped fresh coriander

A Note on Poriyals

Poriyals, although technically from Tamil Nadu, are found all over south India. They are stir-fries, generally made in the wok-like karhai. The method is simple: you put a tiny amount of oil in your pan, add mustard seeds and one or two dals (which act as spices), then some broken dried red chillies and curry leaves. All this takes a few seconds. Then you add cooked or raw vegetables and stir-fry them, adding some salt. Cooked vegetables might include beetroot, cauliflower, potatoes, broad beans and spinach, while uncooked vegetables would include cabbage and carrots. In the USA I have even eaten poriyals made with broccoli and asparagus. There are, of course, hundreds of possible variations and permutations. Coconut may be added, or onion, garlic and ginger may be stir-fried before the vegetable is put in.

The poriyals you will find in this chapter are made with aubergine (see page 58), beetroot (see page 68) or carrot (see page 71). All have different flavourings. In the south, such stir-fried, unsauced dishes are referred to as 'curries' by those speaking in English.

Poriyals serve as the vegetable that goes with the main dish, which in the south would be a combination of a rice, a dal and something with yoghurt or buttermilk.

Stir-fried Aubergines Cooked in a Tamil Nadu Style *Kathirikai Poriyal*

Here is another wonderfully delicious southern poriyal. (For more on the subject, see the Note on page 57.) This is a dry stir-fry, so it does not have a sauce. It is eaten with rather flowing dishes, such as Sambar (see South Indian Dal with Vegetables, page 150), rice and yoghurt relishes. You can also serve it with flatbreads and a mixture of northern and southern dishes, such as Potatoes with Cumin & Asafoetida (see page 99), a dal and a simple yoghurt relish. Add Stir-fried Spinach, Andhra Style (see page 106) if you have company.

In India slim green aubergines are often used for this dish, but those are hard to find in the West. Small purple ones or the lighter pinkish Japanese aubergines work very well too.

Cut off the very top of each aubergine. Whatever kind you have, cut them into 2.5 x 2 cm/1 x ¾ inch dice. (I quarter the 'baby' Italian ones lengthways, then cut them crossways into 2 cm/ ¾ inch pieces.) Put the cut pieces into a bowl of water until you are ready to start cooking. At that point, drain well and pat dry.

Place a small, cast-iron frying pan over a medium-high heat. Add the chana dal, coriander seeds and dried red chillies, stirring and roasting them until they turn a few shades darker. Empty the mixture on to a piece of kitchen paper and set aside. When cool, place in a clean coffee-grinder or spice mill and grind as finely as possible.

Pour the oil into a medium, preferably non-stick frying pan set over a medium-high heat. When hot, add the mustard seeds. As soon as they start to pop, a matter of seconds, throw the curry leaves into the frying pan (take care as these will splutter). Quickly follow with the onion. Stir for about 2 minutes, then lower the heat to medium and stir-fry for another 2 minutes.

Now add the aubergine, which you have drained and dried, and stir for a minute. Add the salt and the ground spice mixture. Stir to mix. Sprinkle with about 3 tablespoons of water, stir and cover. Cook 6–7 minutes, stirring now and then. Lift the cover, add another similar sprinkling of water and stir gently. Cover again. Keep doing this – stirring, adding sprinklings of water and covering again – every 6–7 minutes for 20–25 minutes, until the aubergines are tender, turning the heat down if necessary.

SERVES 3–4

450 g/1 lb smallish purple aubergines (I used 3 'baby' Italian aubergines, but the long Japanese variety is also fine)

1 tablespoon chana dal

1 tablespoon whole coriander seeds

2–5 dried hot red chillies

3 tablespoons olive or peanut oil

½ teaspoon whole brown mustard seeds

7–8 fresh curry leaves, lightly crushed in your hand

1 onion (about 180 g/6 oz), peeled and chopped

¾ teaspoon salt, or to taste

Aubergine in a Peanut & Sesame Sauce *Bhagara Baigan*

Baghara baigan is one of Hyderabad's most famous and most luscious sweet and sour vegetarian dishes. It calls for small aubergines that are partially quartered lengthways, stuffed, fried, and then put in a sauce filled with roasted and ground sesame seeds and nuts, and dozens of other roasted, fried, strained or grated seasonings. It is delicious but complicated to make. I wanted to make a version that was much simpler but just as delicious, and here is the result.

I have cut down its numerous steps, which may be heretical, but it works beautifully. There are still a great many ingredients involved, but the cooking itself is simple.

This is a perfect dish for parties, served with a rich pilaf and other vegetable dishes.

Cut the aubergines lengthways into quarters, then crossways into 4 cm/1½ inch pieces.

Put 6 tablespoons of the oil in a large non-stick wok, karhai or frying pan and set over a medium-high heat. When hot, add the aubergine pieces and fry until lightly browned. They should be three-quarters cooked through. Using a slotted spoon, transfer them to a bowl.

Put the peanut butter and tahini in a separate small bowl. Slowly add 250 ml/8 fl oz boiling water, stirring with a whisk as you do so, until you have a paste. Add the tomato purée, brown sugar, tamarind concentrate and another 250 ml/8 fl oz boiling water, stirring as you go. Mix well and set aside.

Most of the oil in the pan will have been absorbed by the aubergines. Add 2 tablespoons of oil to whatever is left and set over a medium-high heat. When hot, add the mustard seeds. As soon as they start to pop, a matter of seconds, add the cumin seeds and let them sizzle for a few seconds. Now add the curry leaves (take care as these will splutter) and, a second later, the onion. Stir and fry for about 3 minutes, or until the onion just starts to brown. Turn the heat to medium low and stir-fry for another 2–3 minutes.

SERVES 6

900 g/2 lb medium Italian aubergines (I used 3)

8 tablespoons olive or peanut oil

1 tablespoon peanut butter (from a healthfood store is best)

1 tablespoon tahini (roasted sesame paste, sold in many supermarkets)

1 tablespoon tomato purée

2 tablespoons dark brown sugar

1½ teaspoons tamarind concentrate (sold in bottles)

½ teaspoon whole brown mustard seeds

½ teaspoon whole cumin seeds

6–8 fresh curry leaves, lightly crushed in your hand

1 onion (225 g/8 oz), peeled and finely chopped

1 tablespoon peeled and finely grated fresh ginger

1 tablespoon peeled and finely chopped garlic

¼ teaspoon ground turmeric

1 teaspoon ground coriander

1 teaspoon ground cumin

¼–¾ teaspoon nice red chilli powder

1¼ teaspoons salt, or to taste

Add the ginger and garlic. Continue to stir and cook for 2 minutes. Add the turmeric, coriander, cumin and chilli powder. Stir for a minute, then add 250 ml/8 fl oz water. Cook on a low heat for 8–10 minutes.

Add the peanut sauce and cook gently, stirring all the time, for 5 minutes. Add the aubergine and the salt. Cook for another 10 minutes or so on a lowish heat, stirring gently now and then, until the aubergine pieces are soft but still whole. If the sauce feels too thick, feel free to add water at any time, especially when you are reheating the dish. There should always be some thick sauce in the pan.

Meera Prasad's
Steamed Green Beans with Mustard & Coconut *Hura Likaya Pallya*

Meera Prasad is a very successful doctor in Bangalore. She belongs to a community of Shivalli Brahmins whose main temple, dedicated to Lord Krishna, is in Udupi, in northern Karnataka. Hundreds of people are fed at the temple daily and it is here that young men come to study for two much admired futures – priesthood and the culinary arts.

It is there that the Udupi chefs have introduced South Indian food to the rest of India, and to much of the world, through chains with names like Udupi and Woodlands. The famous Mavalli Tiffin Rooms in Bangalore are also owned by Shivalli Brahmins.

Pallyas are dry dishes with coconut, which makes them slightly sweet, and with ground mustard seeds, which gives them a touch of bitterness. Indians not only like the bitter flavour, they consider it healing.

SERVES 4

250 g/9 oz green beans (round or flat), cut crossways into 5 mm/¼ inch pieces

1¼ teaspoons whole brown mustard seeds

1–2 hot dried red chillies, broken into small pieces

4 tablespoons fresh grated coconut, or defrosted if frozen

1 tablespoon olive or peanut oil

¼ teaspoon urad dal

about 10 fresh curry leaves, lightly crushed in your hand

½ teaspoon salt

Put the green beans into a steamer and steam them for about 12 minutes, or until they are tender.

Meanwhile, put 1 teaspoon of the mustard seeds into a small mortar and pound them until well crushed. Add the red chillies and pound until they too are well crushed. Now add the coconut and crush it as much as you can. (Alternatively, you could put the mustard seeds and red chillies in a clean coffee-grinder or spice mill and whiz until they become a coarse powder. Add the coconut and whiz again.) Set aside.

When the beans are done, take them off the steaming water. Put the oil into a medium frying pan and set over a medium-high heat. When hot, add the urad dal. As soon as it starts to change colour, add the remaining ¼ teaspoon of mustard seeds. When they pop, a matter of seconds, add the curry leaves (take care as these will splutter). About 3 seconds after that, add all the green beans. Sprinkle with the salt and stir for about 2 minutes.

Take the pan off the heat and add the crushed mixture from the mortar. Stir a few times to mix thoroughly. Serve hot, warm or, in the summer, at room temperature.

Delhi-style Green Beans with Ginger & Green Chilli
Sem ki Sabzi

SERVES 4

450 g/1 lb green beans, topped,
   tailed and cut into 2.5 cm/
   1 inch pieces
2 tablespoons olive or peanut oil
generous pinch of ground asafoetida
½ teaspoon whole cumin seeds
1–3 fresh hot green chillies,
   finely chopped
2 teaspoons peeled and finely
   chopped fresh ginger
¾ teaspoon salt, or to taste
1 teaspoon ground coriander

I love to eat this simple dish from north India with a dal, such as the Nepalese Black-eyed Peas with Potatoes & Bamboo Shoots (see page 118), rice and a yoghurt relish. It may also be served with a Western meal.

Beans in India are generally fully cooked and rarely crisp. They absorb the spices much better this way. If you wish to steam the beans instead of parboiling them, as I have done here, do so for about 12 minutes.

Plunge the beans into a saucepan of rapidly boiling water and cook them for about 5 minutes, or until crisply tender. Drain and set aside in a strainer or colander set over a bowl.

Put the oil in a medium frying pan set over a medium-high heat. When hot, add the asafoetida. A few seconds later, add the cumin seeds and let them sizzle for a few seconds. Take the pan off the heat and add the chillies and ginger. Stir a few times. Put the pan back on the heat, turning it down to medium-low.

Add the beans, salt and coriander, then stir and cook for 2–3 minutes. Add 2 tablespoons of water, cover, lower the heat and cook very gently for another 5 minutes.

Green Beans with Potatoes
Sem aur Aloo ki Sabzi

Here is a simple green bean dish that I just love. It is good with any meal, but I also have it frequently as a snack. It can be rolled inside a Plain Delhi Paratha (see page 195), along with some Tomato, Onion & Cucumber Koshambari (see page 299). If you do not have a leftover paratha, a pitta bread will do instead. Just warm it and stuff the bean mixture and salad inside.

SERVES 4–5

2 tablespoons olive or peanut oil

generous pinch of ground asafoetida

½ teaspoon whole cumin seeds

¼ teaspoon nigella seeds (kalonji)

1 tablespoon peeled and finely chopped fresh ginger

1–2 fresh hot green chillies, cut into fine rounds

2 tablespoons tomato purée

340 g/12 oz green beans (flat or round), cut into 2.5 cm/1 inch pieces

2 medium boiled, waxy potatoes (about 225 g/8 oz in all), cut into 2.5 cm/1 inch dice

1¼ teaspoons salt, or to taste

¼ teaspoon nice red chilli powder

½ teaspoon garam masala

Put the oil in a large frying pan and set over a medium-high heat. When hot, add the asafoetida. A few seconds later add the cumin and nigella seeds and let them sizzle for a few seconds. Add the ginger and green chillies, lower the heat to medium-low and stir for a minute. Add the tomato purée and stir until the paste turns thick and dark red.

Stir in 250 ml/8 fl oz water, plus the beans, potatoes, salt and chilli powder. Mix well and bring to a simmer. Cover and cook on a low heat until the beans are tender and the sauce has thickened, about 20 minutes. If there is too much sauce, raise the heat a bit and boil it off, stirring gently. Stir in the garam masala.

Punjabi-style Beetroot with Ginger
Punjabi Chukandar ki Sabzi

North Indians nearly always start beetroot dishes with the raw vegetable, and generally cut it quite small so the pieces can be picked up easily with morsels of local flatbreads or rice. Save the stems and leaves, if you have them, for another dish.

Serve this sweet, sour and hot dish with a dal of your choice and a green vegetable, such as Green Beans with Potatoes (see page 65). In the Punjab the meal would be eaten with a flatbread, but rice is fine too. At an Indian or Western meal, you could serve this dish cold, as a salad. You could also swirl some of it into beaten yoghurt to make a raita.

SERVES 4

2 tablespoons olive or peanut oil

⅛ teaspoon ground asafoetida

½ teaspoon whole cumin seeds

¼ teaspoon whole fenugreek seeds

675 g/1½ lb beetroot (I used 2 large ones), peeled and cut into 2 cm/¾ inch dice

2 teaspoons peeled and finely grated fresh ginger

1 teaspoon ground coriander

½ teaspoon ground cumin

¼ teaspoon ground turmeric

¼–½ teaspoon chilli powder

salt

2 medium tomatoes (about 285 g/ 10 oz), peeled and finely chopped

Put the oil in a medium, preferably non-stick frying pan and set over a medium-high heat. When hot, add the asafoetida, quickly followed by the cumin seeds. Let them sizzle for a few seconds. Add the fenugreek seeds and, a second later, put in all the beetroot plus the ginger, coriander and cumin. Stir for 2–3 minutes. Add the turmeric and chilli powder and stir for a few seconds.

Stir in 250 ml/8 fl oz water and ½ teaspoon of salt, then bring to the boil. Cover, lower the heat and cook gently for 20 minutes, or until the beetroot is tender. Add the tomatoes and cook, uncovered, stirring over a high heat, for another 2–3 minutes, or until the tomatoes are tender and well combined, and most of the liquid has been absorbed. Sprinkle in some more salt as needed.

From the Windflower Resort
and Spa, Chef Srinivasan's

Mysore-style Stir-fried Beetroot
Mulangi Poriyal

For more information about this dish, see the Note about poriyals on page 57.

SERVES 3–4

1 tablespoon olive or peanut oil

¼ teaspoon whole brown
mustard seeds

¼ teaspoon urad dal

¼ teaspoon chana dal (if you do not
have this, double the urad dal)

2 dried hot red chillies, broken into
2–3 pieces, depending on size

5–6 fresh curry leaves, lightly
crushed in your hand

1 onion (100 g/3½ oz), peeled
and chopped

400 g/14 oz beetroot, boiled, peeled
and cut into 1 cm/½ inch dice

½ teaspoon salt, or to taste

1–3 fresh hot green chillies,
finely chopped

3 tablespoons fresh grated coconut,
or defrosted if frozen

2 tablespoons chopped fresh
coriander

Put the oil in a wok or medium frying pan and set over a medium heat. When very hot, add the mustard seeds, urad dal and chana dal. As soon as the mustard seeds pop and the dals turn golden-red, add the red chillies. They will darken in seconds. Add the curry leaves (take care as these will splutter), quickly followed by the onion. Stir and fry until the onion has softened and just begun to brown, about 5 minutes.

Reduce the heat to medium-low and add the beetroot, salt, green chillies and coconut. Stir and toss for a minute. Add 4 tablespoons of water and cook gently on a low heat for another 10 minutes, stirring now and then. The water should have evaporated. If it has not, boil it away. Add the coriander and stir to mix.

Mehreen Khosla's
Everyday Carrots & Peas
Gajar Matar ki Sabzi

A simple meal in north India might well consist of freshly made chapatis, a dal, these carrots and peas, and perhaps a second vegetable, as well as the usual complement of pickles, chutneys and raita.

SERVES 4

1½ tablespoons olive or peanut oil

½ teaspoon whole cumin seeds

4 medium carrots (225 g/8 oz in all), peeled and cut into 1 cm/½ inch dice

250 g/9 oz peas, defrosted if frozen, and parboiled if fresh

1 teaspoon ground coriander

¼ teaspoon ground turmeric

generous pinch of nice red chilli powder, or more as desired

½ teaspoon salt

Put the oil in a medium frying pan and set over a medium heat. When hot, add the cumin seeds. Let them sizzle for a few seconds, then add the carrots and peas. Stir and fry for 2–3 minutes.

Add the ground coriander, turmeric, chilli powder and salt. Reduce the heat to medium-low and stir a few times. Add 4–5 tablespoons of water, cover and cook on a low heat for 3–4 minutes, or until the vegetables are tender.

Stir-fried Carrots *Carrot Poriyal*

This simple carrot dish can be served with most Indian meals. Leftovers may be added to salads. For more on south Indian poriyals, see the Note on page 57.

For more on south Indian poriyals, see the Note on page 57.

SERVES 3–4

5 medium carrots (about 340 g/
  12 oz)
1 tablespoon olive or peanut oil
½ teaspoon urad dal
½ teaspoon whole brown
  mustard seeds
2 dried hot red chillies,
  broken in half
1 teaspoon peeled and finely
  grated fresh ginger
½ teaspoon salt
3 tablespoons finely grated
  fresh coconut or defrosted
  frozen coconut
2 tablespoons roughly chopped
  fresh coriander

Peel the carrots and cut them into rounds 7 mm/⅓ inch thick. Larger pieces from the top of the carrots should be halved.

Put the oil in a frying pan, wok or karhai set over a medium heat. When hot, add the urad dal. As soon as it begins to change colour, add the mustard seeds and red chillies. When the mustard seeds pop and the chillies darken, a matter of seconds, add the carrots, ginger and salt. Mix well, then add 4 tablespoons of water. Cover and cook on a low heat for 3–4 minutes, or until the carrots are tender. Add the coconut and coriander and mix well.

Fatma Zakaria's
Stir-fried Cabbage
Bandh Gobi ki Sabzi

Here the cabbage is finely shredded and barely cooked. It is delightfully light, part salad and part vegetable dish. It may be served hot, warm, at room temperature or cold. You could put it on a plate with stuffed Indian pancakes or omelettes, or serve it as part of any meal.

For shredding the cabbage, I prefer to use one of the newer, lighter mandolines. Some are made in Japan, but Oxo makes an excellent one too. You could also use your food processor or just cut by hand. I like to use a bread knife for cutting cabbage.

SERVES 6

1 small green cabbage (about 675 g/1½ lb)

1–3 fresh hot green chillies, finely chopped

2½ tablespoons olive or peanut oil

¾ teaspoon whole brown mustard seeds

7–8 fresh curry leaves, lightly crushed in your hand

1–1¼ teaspoons salt

3–4 teaspoons lemon juice

Remove the damaged outer leaves of the cabbage. Quarter it lengthways and remove the hard core. Now shred it or cut it into slivers 3 mm/⅛ inch thick. You should have about 560 g/1¼ lb. Place in a bowl and add the green chillies.

Put the oil in a wok or large, wide pan and set over a medium heat. As soon as it is hot, add the mustard seeds. When they pop, a matter of seconds, add the curry leaves (take care as they will splutter), quickly followed by the cabbage mixture. Stir and fry until the cabbage has just wilted, about 2–3 minutes.

Lower the heat and add the salt and lemon juice. Stir thoroughly, then turn off the heat. The cabbage should be wilted but still crunchy. Taste for balance of flavours and adjust as necessary.

Roasted Cauliflower
with Punjabi Seasonings
Oven ki Gobi

I wanted to simplify a cauliflower dish that I love, where I fry the cauliflower until it is lightly browned, and then sauté it with spices, such as ginger, coriander and cumin. After many tries, here is the beautiful result. I marinate florets of cauliflower with all the seasonings and then just roast them in a hot oven.

Serve with a dish of chickpeas, or any other dal, a flatbread or rice, and a yoghurt relish.

SERVES 4–5

1 large head of cauliflower, broken into florets about 4 cm/1½ inches wide and 5 cm/2 inches long (about 675 g/1½ lb florets)

1½ tablespoons lemon juice

½ teaspoon ground turmeric

1 teaspoon peeled and finely grated fresh ginger

1 teaspoon salt

¼–½ teaspoon cayenne pepper

2 teaspoons ground cumin

2 teaspoons ground coriander

2 tablespoons chopped fresh coriander leaves

4 tablespoons olive or rapeseed oil

1 teaspoon whole cumin seeds

Put all the cauliflower florets in a large bowl. Combine the lemon juice, turmeric and ginger in a small bowl, then pour over the cauliflower. Add the salt, cayenne, ground spices and fresh coriander and mix well, using a plastic glove if preferred. Set aside for 2 hours, tossing now and then. Preheat the oven to 220°C/gas mark 7. Put the oil in a small frying pan and set over a medium-high heat. When hot, add the cumin seeds, let them sizzle for a few seconds, then pour the spiced oil over the cauliflower. Toss well. Spread out the cauliflower in a single layer in a large roasting tin. Place in the oven for 15 minutes, then turn the pieces and roast for another 10–15 minutes, or until lightly browned and cooked through.

Cauliflower with Potatoes
Aloo Gobi

This is an easy dish that I make frequently. A karhai or wok is ideal for cooking it, but a large frying pan will work as well. Serve with an Indian flatbread or rice, a dal, a raita, such as Yoghurt Raita with Tomato, Shallots & Cucumber (see page 293) and perhaps a green vegetable. Day-old boiled and refrigerated potatoes work beautifully for this dish, but you could cook them that day and let them cool off before you dice them.

SERVES 4

4 tablespoons olive or peanut oil

¼ teaspoon whole cumin seeds

400 g/14 oz cauliflower florets, about 2.5 cm/1 inch wide

2 medium waxy potatoes, boiled, cooled and cut into 2 cm/¾ inch dice

For the spice mixture

2 teaspoons peeled and finely grated fresh ginger

1 teaspoon ground cumin

2 teaspoons ground coriander

¼ teaspoon ground turmeric

¼ teaspoon nice red chilli powder, or to taste

½ teaspoon salt, plus more as needed

First make the spice mixture. Simply combine all the ingredients for it in a bowl, add 50 ml/2 fl oz water and mix thoroughly. Set aside.

Put the oil in a large karhai, wok or frying pan and set over a medium-high heat. When hot, add the cumin seeds, and a few seconds later add the cauliflower and potatoes. Stir and cook for about 10 minutes, or until the vegetables are well browned in spots.

Add the spice mixture and stir-fry for 1 minute. Add another 50 ml/2 fl oz water, lower the heat and cook gently, stirring now and then, for 2–5 minutes, until the vegetables are tender and the spices amalgamated. There should be no liquid left. Taste and adjust the salt. You will probably need a bit more.

Rajul Gandhi's
Cauliflower with Peas
Flower Vatana Nu Shaak

Rajul is a Jain from Palanpur in northern Gujarat, but she lives in Bombay. Under the British, Palanpur was a princely state with a Muslim nawab, but Jains prospered there, eventually becoming leaders of the diamond trade in Bombay and around the world. Jainism is about as old as Buddhism, and its adherents are not only complete vegetarians, but often refrain from eating garlic, onions and many root vegetables and bulbs that require the total destruction of plants when they are harvested.

This is a Palanpur Jain dish. It may be served with rice or Indian breads, along with a dal, a raita and relishes. You could also serve it at a Western meal. I often mix it with pasta (penne) and some grated Parmigiano Reggiano cheese.

I used fresh peas as there was a profusion of them in my garden. Frozen peas should be defrosted thoroughly in warm water, drained and put in 3–4 minutes before the cooking is finished.

SERVES 4–6

1 large head of cauliflower (about 800 g/1¾ lb), broken into 5 cm/ 2 inch florets that weigh a little over 450 g/1 lb

3 tablespoons olive or peanut oil

generous pinch of ground asafoetida

1 teaspoon whole brown mustard seeds

1–2 fresh hot green chillies, sliced crossways into thin rounds

1 tomato (about 180 g/6 oz), peeled and finely chopped

1 teaspoon salt

¼ teaspoon ground turmeric

¼ teaspoon nice red chilli powder (optional)

2 teaspoons ground coriander

1 teaspoon peeled and very finely grated fresh ginger

100 g/3½ oz shelled fresh peas, or defrosted frozen peas

2–3 tablespoons chopped fresh coriander, to serve

Wash the cauliflower and put the florets in a large bowl filled with water. Set aside for 10–30 minutes while you set out and prepare the other ingredients.

Put the oil in a large, preferably non-stick frying pan or sauté pan and set over a medium-high heat. When hot, add the asafoetida. A second later, add the mustard seeds, and as soon as they start to pop (a matter of minutes) add the green chillies and stir once. Now put in the tomato, salt, turmeric, chilli powder, ground coriander and ginger. Stir and fry for a few minutes until the tomato thickens into a paste.

Drain and add the cauliflower and the peas. Stir a few times, then lower the heat to medium-low. Add 50 ml/2 fl oz water and bring to a simmer. Cover and cook gently, stirring now and then, for about 10 minutes, or until the cauliflower is tender. Check the salt. If there is liquid left at the bottom of the pan, turn the heat up a bit and boil it away, stirring gently as you do this. Sprinkle the fresh coriander over the top before serving.

From the Aurobindo Ashram in Delhi
Cauliflower with Ajowan & Ginger
Ajwainwali Gobi

Ashrams in India cater to hundreds, if not thousands, of people at a time, so I was very interested in knowing just what they served and if they had any underlying principles to guide their chefs.

Ashram foods, as I should have expected, differ from ashram to ashram. The Aurobindo Ashram has its headquarters in Pondicherry in south India. I went to the very modern, beautifully designed branch in Delhi, which boasted a vast, all-granite, circular dining area, open to the skies in the centre. Food is served from large pots set on tables at opposite ends of the room. All who wish may eat. There are signs, kindly reminders, everywhere: 'Wasting Food is a Sin'; 'Please Take Only as Much Food as You Need'; 'Second Helpings Are Served with Pleasure'.

Stainless steel metal trays with depressions for each dish are neatly stacked, as are the metal tumblers for water. Guests have to wash them up after the meal and restack them.

The kitchen posts its all-vegetarian menus for lunch, tiffin (in this case, tea and snacks) and dinner on the walls. The foods are neither too spicy nor too oily. Red chillies are never used in the cooking. Fresh green chillies are allowed. Eggs may not be used in the baking. They have wonderful eggless coconut and chocolate cakes. The inspiration for the dishes comes from all over India. When I was there for lunch, there were chapatis, lemon rice and plain rice, as well as idlis (steamed rice cakes) for the starch; there were whole red lentils and yoghurt for protein; potatoes, radishes, peas, cauliflower and carrots were all cooked together, and there was a salad as well.

This cauliflower dish is based on an Aurobindo Ashram recipe. Ajowan seeds are rich in thymol, renowned for its medicinal properties, and impart a thyme-like flavour. All Indian grocers sell them.

SERVES 4

1 large head of cauliflower
 (about 800 g/1¾ lb), broken
 into 5 x 5 cm/2 x 2 inch florets
 (about 450 g/1 lb florets)
4 tablespoons olive or peanut oil
1 teaspoon ajowan seeds
5 cm/2 inch piece of fresh ginger,
 peeled and finely chopped
4 cloves garlic, peeled and
 finely chopped
½ teaspoon ground turmeric
½ teaspoon salt
1–3 fresh hot green chillies, cut
 crossways into very thin slices

Wash the cauliflower and put the florets in a large bowl filled with water. Set aside for 10–30 minutes while you set out and/or prepare the other ingredients.

Put the oil into a very large frying pan set over a medium heat. When hot, add the ajowan seeds. Stir a few times, then add the ginger and garlic. Stir for a minute and add the turmeric. Stir once, then quickly add all the cauliflower, scooping it up with both hands from the water with open fingers. Add the salt and green chillies, stir a few times and cover. Cook on a low heat, stirring now and then, for about 6–10 minutes, or until the cauliflower is tender enough to break with your fingers.

Quick Stir-fry of Young Courgettes & Squash
Courgette aur Squash ki Sabzi

Many vegetarians in India, especially in the central desert region of Rajasthan, where there is a dearth of wood for fuel, stir-fry their vegetables quickly in a little yoghurt. This gives them creaminess and tartness, as well as added protein. Here is one such quick-cooking and delicious dish. It is generally served with Indian flatbreads, such as chapatis, and a dal. You can also serve it with rice.

A nice, sour natural yoghurt is best here. Indian stores sell it as 'dahi', and healthfood stores sell an acidophilus yoghurt that is tart, but any natural yoghurt will do. If it is not at all sour, just leave the required amount unrefrigerated in a warmish place for 24 hours.

SERVES 4

450 g/1 lb young courgettes and young squash (I used 2 small courgettes and 2 small yellow squashes, but just one or the other could be used if you prefer)

3 tablespoons natural yoghurt

½ teaspoon ground turmeric

½ teaspoon ground coriander seeds

¾ teaspoon salt

freshly ground black pepper

¼ teaspoon or more nice red chilli powder

1 tablespoon olive or peanut oil

pinch of ground asafoetida

¼ teaspoon whole brown mustard seeds

¼ teaspoon whole cumin seeds

Cut the courgettes and squashes in half lengthways, then cut crossways into 1 cm/½ inch pieces.

Combine the yoghurt, turmeric, coriander, salt, pepper and chilli powder in a small bowl and mix well.

Heat the oil in a medium frying pan set over a medium-high heat. When hot, add the asafoetida, mustard seeds and cumin seeds. As soon as the mustard seeds pop, a matter of seconds, add all the cut vegetables. Stir and fry for 3–4 minutes, or until the vegetables just start to take on colour.

Turn the heat down to medium and add 1 tablespoon of the yoghurt mixture. Stir a few times, then add another tablespoon of the mixture. Do this again with the remaining mixture, stirring for a minute after each addition. Taste for salt. Add 1 tablespoon of water and stir a final time. Turn off the heat.

From Kaveri Kaul
Stir-fried Baby Kale Cooked in a Bengali Village Style
Kale ki Sabzi

The style that I have used to cook this kale is the one used in some Bengali villages to prepare finely chopped stems of mixed green vegetables in a dish called 'dahta'. If, indeed, you have an assortment of stems from your garden, chop them into small pieces and generally follow this recipe. If you do not, use just kale or spring greens. If the leaves are more mature, add more water and cook longer than specified, until the leaves are very tender.

Serve with any legume or dried bean dish, rice and a yoghurt relish. Chutneys and pickles can be added to the meal as desired.

SERVES 3–4

2–3 tablespoons mustard oil (use a good virgin olive oil as a substitute)

¾ teaspoon nigella seeds (kalonji)

2 fresh hot green chillies (such as bird's eye), cut into thin rounds

285 g/10 oz young kale leaves, chopped

½ teaspoon salt

¼ teaspoon sugar

Put the mustard oil in a medium pan and set over a medium heat. When hot, add the nigella seeds and allow them to sizzle for a few seconds. Add the chillies, stir once, then add the kale, salt and sugar. Stir a few times and add 120 ml/4 fl oz water. Bring to the boil. Cover, lower the heat and cook gently 5–10 minutes, or until the kale is just tender.

Lacinated Winter Kale in a Kashmiri Style
Kale ki Kashmiri Sabzi

Kale can cook quickly or slowly, depending upon its age. I picked some lacinated or black kale in December and it took about 30 minutes to cook. In Kashmir it is always cooked in mustard oil and served with rice. I like to add a whole bean dish and a salad to the meal as well.

SERVES 4

2 tablespoons mustard or olive oil
⅛ teaspoon ground asafoetida
1 dried hot red chilli
½–1 fresh green chilli, slit open
   lengthways
½ small onion, peeled and
   thinly sliced
285–310 g/10–11 oz lacinated/
   black kale, cut crossways into
   5 mm/¼ inch strips
½ teaspoon salt

Put the oil in a medium saucepan and set over a medium heat. When hot, add the asafoetida. Let it sizzle for a few seconds, then add the red and green chillies. When the red chilli darkens, add the onion and sauté until golden.

Add all the kale, 475 ml/16 fl oz water and the salt. Bring to the boil. Cover, lower the heat and simmer gently for 30 minutes, or until the kale is tender. Drain and serve.

Kaveri Ponnapa's
Kodava Mushroom Curry
with Coconut *Kumme Curry*

I cannot tell you how scrumptious – and simple – this curry is. I had never eaten it before in my life until Kaveri made it for me in her large, beautiful modern home in Bangalore, replete with vaulted ceilings and two kitchens, one for Kaveri, who is a food writer, and one for the staff. She and her husband, Naresh, are both from Coorg (the British name, but now referred to frequently as Kodagu, its original name) where they have vast holdings that include coffee plantations and tracts of the forested, mountainous wilderness that this area is famous for.

Many of the Kodavas are of the Kshatriya or warrior caste and, perhaps not so strangely, have risen in the ranks of the Indian army to gain the highest positions. Kodavas are not vegetarians, but they have such unusual vegetarian dishes that I had to travel up and down Coorg to learn more.

Traditionally, the people here are farmers (rice grows in the valleys), but they are also hunter-gatherers because their misty land in the mountainous Western Ghats of south-western India is filled with game and fish. The British called it India's Scotland. They grow cardamom, coffee and black pepper, and some shops in Madikeri, the capital city, specialize in selling just those three items. They have wonderful honey, which is also sold in the Madikeri market. The forests provide wild mangoes and bitter oranges, and in the very wet, four-month rainy season, it is the wilderness that provides the hunter-gatherers with most of their fresh produce. At this time it bursts over with bamboo shoots (which mysteriously disappear every 60 years and then slowly regenerate), wild greens such as ferns, colocasia (they cook the tender leaves while they are still uncurled), and many, many varieties of mushrooms.

The wild mushrooms, with names such nucchie kumme and aalandi kumme, range from tiny ones that carpet the forest floor to wood-ear types that grow on tree trunks and those that look like petalled flowers. The largest ones, nethelé kumme, can grow to the size of a large dinner plate, and are simply roasted over wood and seasoned with salt, lime juice and crushed green chillies (see my version, Grilled Portobello Mushrooms in the Kodaga Style, page 34.

For this dish of curried mushrooms, the white cultivated variety works just as well, and that is what Kaveri uses when she is not on her Coorg estate or when local mushrooms are out of season.

Housewives in Coorg use a tiny amount of their thick, sticky local vinegar, called kachampuli, when making this curry and many of their other dishes as well. Even though I was given a precious triple-wrapped bottle that I carried all the way back home, I did not use it when I tested this recipe as I know that it is found nowhere outside Coorg. I just used more of the lime juice. It still tasted wonderful.

Serve this creamy curry with rice. At one of my dinners I made Berry Pilaf (see page 168), Eggs in a Hyderabadi Tomato Sauce (see page 252), Toovar Dal with Spinach & Sorrel (see page 148) Cabbage Fritters (page 23) and this mushroom curry. It was a lovely combination.

This dish is also quite wonderful with rice noodles (see Note on Sevai, page 231) and superb when served on toast.

SERVES 4

1 x 400 ml/14 fl oz can coconut milk, left undisturbed for 24 hours to allow the cream to rise to the top
450 g/1 lb small button mushrooms
1 teaspoon salt, or to taste
½ teaspoon ground turmeric
4 tablespoons olive or peanut oil
6 tablespoons peeled and finely chopped shallots
2 teaspoons ground coriander
¼–½ teaspoon nice red chilli powder
2–3 fresh hot green chillies, slit in half lengthways or finely chopped
1 tablespoon lime juice

Open the can of coconut milk without disturbing it too much and spoon the thick cream at the top into a bowl. Leave the thin coconut milk in the can.

Halve the mushrooms. Any large ones may be quartered. Place them all in a bowl and sprinkle the salt and turmeric over them. Wearing plastic gloves if you wish, as the turmeric can stain, thoroughly rub these flavourings into the mushrooms. Set aside for about 10 minutes.

Put the oil in a medium frying pan and set over a medium-high heat. When hot, add the shallots and stir-fry until they just start to brown. Take the pan off the heat and add the coriander and chilli powder. Stir a few times.

Put the pan back on the hob, turning the heat to medium-low. Add the green chillies and stir a few times. Now add the mushrooms and their accumulated liquid. Stir and cook on a medium-high heat for 2 minutes. Add 175 ml/6 fl oz of the thin coconut milk and bring to a simmer. Simmer, uncovered, for 10 minutes.

Add 175 ml/6 fl oz of the coconut cream and stir to mix. Bring to a simmer over a medium-high heat, then reduce the heat to very low and simmer gently, uncovered, for about a minute, stirring now and then. Turn the heat off. Add the lime juice and stir it in.

Mynah Pemmaiah's
Simple Kodova Mushroom Curry
Kumme Curry

Another lovely mushroom curry from Coorg, this time made without coconut milk. Serve with rice, rice breads, rice noodles or a poha dish, and (if you eat eggs) also Eggs in a Hyderabadi Tomato Sauce (see page 252) and a green vegetable.

Mynah's house has fields along the front, where she keeps guinea fowl; and around the back are forests, whence come her fiddlehead ferns, her still-curled colocasia leaves, her wild mushrooms and bamboo shoots. She provides lodging to paying guests and also gives cooking classes in her simple kitchen.

This dish can be made with chanterelles, shiitake, ceps, morels and any other wild mushrooms you can access. Wipe them clean, remove the stems if they are hard and cut them so they are about 2.5 cm/1 inch at their widest. I used button mushrooms.

SERVES 4

450 g/1 lb small button mushrooms

1 teaspoon salt, or to taste

½ teaspoon ground turmeric

½–¾ teaspoon nice red
    chilli powder

2 tablespoons olive or peanut oil

¼ teaspoon whole brown
    mustard seeds

1–2 fresh hot green chillies,
    finely chopped

1 onion (200–225 g/7–8 oz),
    peeled and cut into half-rings
    5 mm/¼ inch thick

1½ teaspoons ground coriander

Halve the mushrooms. Any large ones may be quartered. Place them all in a bowl and sprinkle the salt, turmeric and chilli powder over them. Wearing plastic gloves if you wish, as the turmeric can stain, thoroughly rub these flavourings into the mushrooms. Set aside for about 10 minutes.

Put the oil in a medium frying pan and set over a medium-high heat. When hot, add the mustard seeds. As soon as the mustard seeds start to pop, a matter of seconds, add the green chillies and the onion slices. Stir and fry until the onions just start to brown, 3–4 minutes. Add the ground coriander and stir once.

Add the mushrooms and their accumulated liquid and stir over a medium-high heat for about 3 minutes. Add 175 ml/ 6 fl oz water and bring to a simmer. Cover and simmer on a low heat for 10 minutes.

My Everyday Okra
Roz ki Bhindi

When buying okra, always look for young, tender pods, which tend to be small as well.

Okra is cooked in dozens of ways throughout India. This remains one of the simplest and most delicious north Indian ways of preparing it. Here it is not at all glutinous – it turns nicely brown and can be eaten with rice or flatbreads and a selection of legumes and relishes.

SERVES 4–6

675 g/1½ lb okra

1 medium onion

4 tablespoons olive or peanut oil

1 teaspoon ground coriander

1 teaspoon ground cumin

generous pinch of nice red
   chilli powder

¾ teaspoon ground amchoor or
   1 tablespoon lemon juice

1 teaspoon salt, or to taste

1 medium tomato, peeled and diced

Wipe off each okra pod with a damp cloth and leave it briefly to air-dry. Cut off the tops and tails. Slice the pod crossways into 7 mm/⅓ inch pieces.

Peel and cut the onion into dice about the same size as the okra.

Pour the oil into a large frying pan and set over a medium-high heat. When hot, add the okra and onion. Stir and fry until the okra starts to brown, turning down the heat little by little and stirring gently now and then. In about 15 minutes, the okra should be almost done and the pan should be over a very low heat.

Add the ground coriander and cumin, along with the chilli powder, amchoor and salt. Stir for 2–3 minutes more, then add the tomato and stir gently for another 3–4 minutes.

Okra Dry-cooked with Yoghurt
Sookhi Dahi Wali Bhindi

Here the okra is cooked until it is quite dry, oozing none of the viscous juices normally associated with it. It can be served with most Indian meals, and goes particularly well with any black-eyed peas dish, a potato dish and some flatbread.

SERVES 4

450 g/1 lb okra (small tender pods are best)

2 tablespoons olive or peanut oil

generous pinch of ground asafoetida

¼ teaspoon whole brown mustard seeds

¼ teaspoon whole cumin seeds

1 dried hot red chilli

1 medium onion, peeled and chopped

¼ teaspoon garam masala

½–¾ teaspoon salt

½ teaspoon ground coriander

¼ teaspoon ground turmeric

3 tablespoons natural yoghurt

Wipe off each okra pod with a damp cloth. Spread out the pods to let them air-dry. Cut off and discard the very tops and tails of the pods, then cut them crossways into 1 cm/½ inch pieces.

Put the oil into a large frying pan or sauté pan and set over a medium-high heat. When hot, add the asafoetida, then, a second later, the mustard seeds. As soon as the mustard seeds start to pop, a matter of seconds, add the cumin seeds and the red chilli. Let them sizzle for a few seconds, then add the onion and okra. Stir and fry until they just start to brown. Cook, stirring, over a medium heat for about 10 minutes, lowering the heat gradually until the okra is almost cooked. By then it should be on a medium-low heat.

Add the garam masala, salt, coriander and turmeric. Stir for a minute, then add 1 tablespoon of the yoghurt. Stir until it seems to vanish. Add a second and third tablespoon of yoghurt the same way. Turn the heat to low and cook the okra, stirring, until it is cooked through. Check the salt and adjust as necessary.

Punjabi-style Okra Masala
Punjabi Bhindi

The day starts early in the villages of the Punjab, one of India's 'granary' states. Cows have to be milked, breakfasts prepared (very often stuffed parathas served with buttermilk or tea) and lunches made for those who work in far-away wheat fields. These lunches could consist of simple wholemeal tandoori breads and a vegetable, perhaps this okra. There may be a small raw onion or a pickle to add an extra fillip. A majority of the villagers in the Punjab are vegetarian and basically wheat-eaters, so no meal is really complete without the flatbreads of the area.

Okra ripens mostly in the summer or the monsoon season here, and it is a beloved vegetable that comes at a time when mostly squashes hold sway. It is prepared the way many Punjabi vegetables are prepared – with onion, garlic ginger, tomatoes and some basic spices, such as cumin and coriander. Very often dried fenugreek leaves are added as well for that special umami flavour.

SERVES 4

400 g/14 oz okra (small tender pods are best)

5 tablespoons peanut or olive oil

salt and freshly ground black pepper

1 medium onion, peeled and very finely chopped

1 teaspoon peeled and very finely grated fresh ginger

1 teaspoon peeled and finely crushed garlic

2 tomatoes (about 285 g/10 oz in all), peeled and finely chopped

½ teaspoon ground coriander

½ teaspoon ground cumin

¼ teaspoon ground turmeric

¼–¾ teaspoon nice red chilli powder

2 tablespoons dried fenugreek leaves (kasuri methi)

Wipe each okra pod with a damp cloth, then spread them out to air-dry. Remove the very top cones on the pods as well as the tips at the bottom, then slice the pods crossways into 1 cm/½ inch pieces.

Put 3 tablespoons of the oil in a medium, preferably non-stick frying pan and set over a medium-high heat. When hot, add all the okra. Stir and fry for about 5 minutes, or until the okra begins to take on a little colour. Turn the heat down to medium. Keep frying and lowering the heat as you go for about 15 minutes, or until the okra is cooked through and lightly browned all over. Sprinkle in about ¼ teaspoon of salt and some pepper and mix well. Remove the okra with a slotted spoon and transfer to a bowl.

Add enough of the remaining oil to the pan to make 3 tablespoons. Turn the heat to medium-high and add the onion. Stir and fry for about 5 minutes, or until lightly browned. Add the ginger and garlic, lower the heat to medium and stir-fry for a minute. Add the tomatoes, coriander, cumin, turmeric, chilli powder and fenugreek leaves. Stir and cook, breaking up the tomato pieces, until you have a thick sauce.

Fold in the cooked okra, adding ½ teaspoon of salt as you do so. Mix gently and cook on low heat for a minute. Check the salt.

Okra Cooked in a Konkan Style
Bhendi Bhaji

The Konkan region runs along the central west coast of India. Here is one of its simple everyday okra dishes that I just love.

Serve the okra with other vegetables and perhaps Whole Moong & Masoor Cooked with Meat Seasonings (see page 137), a rice dish or a flatbread, and a yoghurt relish.

SERVES 3

340 g/12 oz okra (small tender pods are best)

3 tablespoons olive or peanut oil

1 teaspoon urad dal

½ teaspoon whole brown mustard seeds

½ teaspoon whole cumin seeds

1 small hot green chilli, slit in half lengthways, or ¼ teaspoon nice red chilli powder

10–15 fresh curry leaves, lightly crushed in your hand

1 onion (about 195 g/6½ oz), peeled and chopped

¼ teaspoon ground turmeric

½ teaspoon salt, or to taste

1 tablespoon lemon juice

Wipe each okra pod with a damp cloth, then spread them out to air-dry. Cut off and discard the very tops and tails of the okra, then cut the pods crossways into 1 cm/½ inch pieces.

Put the oil in large frying pan or sauté pan and set over a medium-high heat. When hot, add the urad dal. As soon as the dal begins to colour, add the mustard and cumin seeds. When the mustard seeds begin to pop, a matter of seconds, add the chilli, curry leaves and onion (take care as the curry leaves will splutter). Stir and fry until the onion just begins to brown at the edges, about 6 minutes.

Add the turmeric, stir once and add the okra. Lower the heat to medium-low and stir gently for 5–6 minutes. Add the salt and lemon juice and stir gently. Lower the heat again, then sprinkle in some water. Cover and cook on a low heat for 5–6 minutes, or until the okra is just tender, sprinkling in more water if it seems to be catching. Taste and add a little more salt if needed.

Okra with Onions & Green Chilli
Pyaz kay Saath Bhuni hui Bhindi

Another dish from northern India, where okra, to prevent it from releasing its viscous innards, is never covered as it cooks. The cooking starts on a medium-high heat, which is slowly lowered as the ingredients start to brown. The process takes 15–20 minutes and produces an unctuous dish, where the onions brown perfectly and meld with the now much darker, okra.

I like to eat this with an Indian flatbread or a wholemeal pitta bread, a potato dish, a dal and a yoghurt relish.

SERVES 3–4

340 g/12 oz okra (small tender pods are best)

3 tablespoons olive or peanut oil

1 onion (180–200 g/6–7 oz), peeled and chopped

1–2 fresh hot green chillies, chopped

1 teaspoon ground coriander

½ teaspoon salt

¼ teaspoon ground turmeric

¼ teaspoon nice red chilli powder

Wipe the okra pods with a damp cloth, then spread them out to air-dry. Cut off their tops and tails, then cut the pods crossways into 7 mm/⅓ inch pieces.

Put the oil into a medium, preferably non-stick frying pan and set over a medium-high heat. When hot, add the onion, chillies and okra. Stir and cook for about 10 minutes, or until the onions are lightly browned. Lower the heat to medium-low and add the coriander, salt, turmeric and chilli powder. Mix gently, then cook, stirring, for another 4–5 minutes.

Lower the heat to low and continue to stir gently and cook for another 2–4 minutes, or until the okra is tender.

Vinita Pittie's
Simple Marwari-style Peas
Matar ka Sisua

Sometimes it is hard to fathom how a few carefully chosen seasonings can make a vegetable shine. In the case of peas, ginger, cumin and green chillies will do just that – every time. This is Vinita Pittie's recipe. For more about her and her community, and her life in Hyderabad, see page 102.

The peas can be served with Potatoes in a Marwari Style (see page 102) a yoghurt relish, a dal and perhaps some Marwari Layered Griddle Breads (see page 204) or rice.

SERVES 4

2 tablespoons ghee (clarified butter), olive oil or peanut oil, or a mixture of any oil and ghee

¼ teaspoon whole cumin seeds

1 tablespoon peeled and finely grated fresh ginger

1–2 fresh hot green chillies, finely chopped

285 g/10 oz peas, parboiled and drained, if fresh; defrosted under running water if frozen

¾ teaspoon salt

freshly ground black pepper

Put the ghee or oil in a medium, preferably non-stick pan and set over a medium heat. When hot, add the cumin seeds. Let them sizzle for 10 seconds, then add the ginger and green chillies. Stir for a minute.

Add the peas, salt and pepper and stir for 2–3 minutes, sprinkling with a little water if the peas get too dry.

Peas & Potatoes Cooked in a Bihari Style *Matar ki Ghugni*

This recipe is very similar to the previous one, but has a few additions and comes from Bihar. Ghugnis, made out of small red chickpeas, regular beige chickpeas, fresh green chickpeas and fresh green peas, are breakfast food for many vegetarians in Uttar Pradesh and Bihar. They are eaten with flatbreads, such as Chapatis, Parathas or Fried Puffed Breads (see pages 193–209). They can also be eaten as a snack. In Bihar they are sometimes served with crisped flattened rice.

If you have a boiled potato sitting in your refrigerator, this is the time to use it up. Otherwise boil one and let it cool off before peeling and cutting it.

SERVES 4

2 tablespoons olive oil, peanut oil or mustard oil

½ teaspoon whole cumin seeds

1 medium onion, peeled and chopped

1 tablespoon peeled and finely grated fresh ginger

1–3 fresh hot green chillies, finely chopped

¼ teaspoon ground turmeric

285 g/10 oz peas, parboiled and drained if fresh; defrosted under running water if frozen

1 medium waxy potato (about 115–140 g/4–5 oz), boiled, peeled and cut into 2 cm/¾ inch dice

1 teaspoon salt, or to taste

freshly ground black pepper

Put the oil in a medium, preferably non-stick pan and set over a medium heat. When hot, add the cumin seeds and let them sizzle for 10 seconds. Add the onion, then stir and fry for about 5–6 minutes, or until the onion is soft.

Add the ginger, green chillies and turmeric and stir for a minute. Add the peas, potato, salt and pepper and stir for 2–3 minutes, sprinkling with a little water if the peas get too dry.

Potato & Onion Mélange
Dosa Walay Aloo

This is the very traditional stuffing for south Indian dosas (savoury pancakes). It may also be served as a vegetable with any meal. It goes particularly well with Indian breads.

560 g/1¼ lb waxy potatoes, peeled and cut into 1 cm/½ inch dice

2 tablespoons olive or peanut oil

½ teaspoon chana dal

½ teaspoon urad dal

½ teaspoon whole brown mustard seeds

6–7 fresh curry leaves, lightly crushed in your hand

1 onion (about 180 g/6 oz), peeled and cut into 7 mm/⅓ inch dice

1 teaspoon peeled and finely chopped fresh ginger

1 fresh hot green chilli, finely chopped

1¼ teaspoons salt

½ teaspoon ground turmeric

2 tablespoons chopped fresh coriander

Boil the potatoes until tender, then drain, reserving about 250 ml/8 fl oz of the cooking water in a jug. Crush the potatoes very coarsely.

Put the oil in a medium non-stick frying pan and set over a medium heat. When hot, add the chana dal. Wait 15 seconds, then add the urad dal. As soon as the dals begin to take on any colour, add the mustard seeds. Stir until the mustard seeds start to pop, then quickly add the curry leaves (take care as these will splutter), followed a few seconds later by the onion, ginger and green chilli. Stir for 3–4 minutes and then add 5 tablespoons of the potato water. Cover and cook on a low heat for about 3 minutes, or until the onion is soft.

Add the potatoes, salt and turmeric. Stir and mix on a low heat for 2–3 minutes. Add another 6 tablespoons of the potato water and stir for 2 more minutes. Finally, stir in the coriander.

Potatoes with Cumin & Asafoetida
Heeng Zeeray ke Aloo

This is a simplified version of the very first dish I learnt to cook. I was in London, a student at the Royal Academy of Dramatic Art and desperate for family foods. I could not cook at all. I begged my mother in India to teach me and she answered with three-line recipes written on flimsy air-letters. That was the cheapest way to communicate then. I devoured those letters with my eyes first, and then rushed off to the Indian shop near the college to buy the ingredients. My landlords, a kind young couple in north London, let me use their kitchen and I was off and away.

I cook this potato dish in 15 minutes, starting with boiled potatoes, which speeds up the process. Here I used fingerlings (long, thin potatoes, such as Anya), but if you do not have access to them, any waxy potatoes will do. I like to eat this dish with flatbreads – Chapatis or Fried Puffed Breads are best (see pages 193 and 206) – but you can choose any flatbread. You could also use wholemeal pitta breads and heat them, one at a time, in the microwave for 20–30 seconds each. You should serve a dal, a green vegetable, such as spinach, and a yoghurt relish with it as well.

SERVES 3–4

340 g/12 oz waxy potatoes, boiled and cooled (leftover potatoes are fine)

1 tablespoon olive or peanut oil

generous pinch of ground asafoetida

¼ teaspoon whole cumin seeds

1 dried hot red chilli

1 fresh hot green chilli, cut crossways into fine slices

1 tomato (140 g/5 oz), chopped

½ teaspoon salt

Peel the potatoes and cut them into 1cm/½ inch dice. If they are fingerlings, just cut them crossways into 1 cm/ ½ inch rounds.

Pour the oil into a medium non-stick frying pan and set over a medium-high heat. When hot, add the asafoetida and, a second later, the cumin seeds. Allow to sizzle for a few seconds, then add the red chilli. When it darkens, add the potatoes and green chilli. Stir for a minute or two, until the potatoes brown a little. Then add the tomato, salt and 120 ml/4 fl oz water. Bring to the boil, mashing up the tomatoes as you do so. Cover and simmer gently for 10 minutes.

Potatoes Cooked in a Banarasi Style
Banarasi Aloo

A very typical dish from the bazaars of the old city of Banaras (yes, I and many others still use the old name for Varanasi). Serve with Fried Puffed Breads (see page 206) or any other Indian flatbreads, as well as other vegetables, chutneys and raita.

SERVES 4

4 tablespoons olive or peanut oil

generous pinch of ground asafoetida

1 teaspoon whole brown
    mustard seeds

½ teaspoon whole cumin seeds

5 mm/½ inch piece of fresh ginger,
    peeled and cut into minute dice

1–2 fresh hot green chillies,
    very finely chopped

1½ teaspoons ground coriander

¼ teaspoon ground turmeric

½ teaspoon nice red chilli powder

675 g/1½ lb waxy potatoes, boiled,
    peeled and cut or broken into
    small pieces, none larger on
    any side than 7 mm/⅓ inch

1–1½ teaspoons ground amchoor
    or lemon juice

1–1½ teaspoons salt

¾ teaspoon garam masala

Put the oil in a large non-stick frying pan or wok and set over a medium heat. When hot, add the asafoetida and, a second later, the mustard seeds. As soon as the seeds start to pop, a matter of seconds, add the cumin seeds. Two seconds later add the ginger and green chillies. Stir for a few seconds. Add the coriander, turmeric and chilli powder. Stir once, then quickly add all the broken potatoes. Stir and fry for a minute.

Add 120 ml/4 fl oz of water, lower the heat and mix until well incorporated. Add the amchoor, salt and garam masala. Stir gently and cook for another minute.

Vinita Pittie's
Potatoes in a Marwari Style
Aloo Sabzi

Marwaris are a highly successful business community that originated in Marwar, in the deserts of Rajasthan. Many left their home-towns to create large businesses elsewhere in India. They are completely vegetarian, with a distinct and much-admired cuisine.

Vinita has married into a family long settled in Hyderabad. They still live in the 230-year-old haveli (mansion) that fills an entire block in the heart of the city. The inner city is crumbling and so is the mansion, but Vinita, with her great sense of style, has taken up a corner of it and filled it with antique furniture and family paintings that match the half-lost frescoes on some of the walls.

Vinita is a very popular dress designer. She has given part of the mansion over to the tailors and embroiderers she works with. She also cooks, the kitchen being right next to the room with the disappearing frescoes. She made these delicious potatoes for me as part of a dinner that included Simple Marwari-style Peas, Mixed Dal in a Marwari Style, Marwari Layered Griddle Breads and a yoghurt dish (see pages 95, 141 and 204).

SERVES 4

5–6 medium waxy potatoes (about 450 g/1 lb), boiled, cooled and peeled

¾ teaspoon salt, or to taste

¼ teaspoon ground turmeric

⅛–½ teaspoon nice red chilli powder

1 teaspoon ground coriander

2 tablespoons olive or peanut oil

generous pinch of ground asafoetida

½ teaspoon whole cumin seeds

1 dried hot red chilli, broken in half

½ medium onion, peeled and thinly sliced

1½ teaspoons peeled fresh ginger, grated to a pulp

1 fresh hot green chilli, thinly sliced

2 tablespoons chopped fresh coriander

Cut the potatoes lengthways into fat chips and put them in a bowl. Add the salt, turmeric, chilli powder and ground coriander, then (wearing plastic gloves if you wish, as turmeric can stain) mix gently so that the spices cling to the potatoes.

Put the oil in a well-seasoned wok, karhai or non-stick frying pan and set over a medium-high heat. When hot, add the asafoetida. Two seconds later add the cumin seeds and let them sizzle for a few seconds. Throw in the broken red chilli and stir for a second or two. Now add the onion and stir for a minute. Stir in the ginger and green chilli. Still on medium-high heat, add the potatoes and stir gently, lifting them from the bottom, for 4–5 minutes. The potatoes should get lightly browned. Check the salt, toss in the fresh coriander and mix.

Vinita Pittie's
Stir-fried Potatoes with Chaat Masala
Chaat Masalay Walay Aloo

Here is another of Vinita's inspired dishes. Although it uses potatoes and might seem very similar to the previous recipe, it is actually very different. This is a 'chaat', a spicy, hot and sour snack food, which in India could be eaten by itself with a cup of tea. However, I often serve it as part of a lunch or dinner, along with Cauliflower with Ajowan & Ginger (see page 78), Chana Dal with Spinach & Tomato (see page 120), any Indian bread and a yoghurt relish.

SERVES 4

5–6 medium waxy potatoes
   (about 450 g/1 lb in all),
   boiled, cooled and peeled
1 teaspoon ground coriander
½–1 teaspoon nice red chilli powder
1 teaspoon chaat masala
¾–1 teaspoon salt (start with
   the smaller amount)
¼ teaspoon ground black pepper
¼ teaspoon garam masala
1½ teaspoons whole cumin seeds
2 tablespoons chopped fresh
   coriander
1 tablespoon lime juice
2 tablespoons olive or peanut oil

Cut the potatoes lengthways into fat sticks and put them in a bowl.

Put the ground coriander in a small bowl with the lower amount of chilli powder, the chaat masala, the lower amount of salt, the black pepper and garam masala.

Put a small, heavy-based frying pan over a medium heat. When hot, add the cumin seeds and stir them around until you get a roasted aroma and they turn a shade darker. Add all the ground spices in the small bowl. Stir for 5 seconds, then tip on to a piece of kitchen paper. Once cool, put the spice mixture into a clean grinder or spice mill and grind as finely as you can.

Sprinkle the spice mixture, fresh coriander and lime juice over the potatoes and mix well with a gentle hand.

Put the oil in a well-seasoned wok, karhai or non-stick frying pan and set over a medium heat. When hot, add the potatoes and stir for a minute. Taste for salt and chilli powder, adding more if you wish.

Goan Potatoes *Batata Bhaji*

This dish, from a Hindu Goan restaurant in Bombay, tastes best if made with waxy potatoes. It is generally eaten with rice or rice breads, but can also be rolled up in a chapati, along with some chopped tomatoes and cucumber, and eaten as a snack or for lunch.

Urad dal is a split legume, often used as a seasoning as well. All Indian grocers sell it.

SERVES 4

560 g/1¼ lb waxy potatoes, boiled, peeled and cut into 1 cm/½ inch dice

½ teaspoon salt, plus a little extra

5 tablespoons olive or peanut oil

generous pinch of ground asafoetida

¼ teaspoon urad dal

¼ teaspoon whole brown mustard seeds

¼ teaspoon whole cumin seeds

generous pinch of whole fenugreek seeds

15 fresh curry leaves, lightly crushed in your hand

2 fresh hot green chillies (such as bird's eye), sliced into thin half-rings

1 onion (140–180 g/5–6 oz), peeled and cut in half lengthways and then into fine half-rings

¼ teaspoon sugar

2 tablespoons chopped fresh coriander

Put the potatoes in a bowl. Add the ½ teaspoon of salt and mix well, separating the pieces. Set out and/or prepare all the remaining ingredients as the dish will cook quite fast.

Put the oil into a medium, non-stick frying pan and set over a medium-high heat. When hot, add the asafoetida and, a second later, the urad dal. As soon as the dal starts to colour, add the mustard seeds and cumin seeds. As soon as the mustard seeds start to pop, a matter of seconds, add the fenugreek seeds and, a second later, the curry leaves and green chillies (take care as the curry leaves will splutter). Stir once or twice and add the onion. As soon as you see a hint of browning in the onion, add a tablespoon of water. Do this three times, cooking the onion for about 7–8 minutes.

Add a dash of salt and the sugar to the pan. Tip in all the potatoes and add about 120 ml/4 fl oz water. Stir and cook on a very low heat for 10 minutes, mixing every now and then. Some of the potatoes should melt into the water. Scatter the fresh coriander over the top.

Spinach with Dill *Dakhini Saag*

A simple but very flavourful spinach dish from the royal palaces of Hyderabad. Serve it at meals with either breads or pilafs, along with a dal, such as Hyderabadi 'Sour Dal' (see page 149). At the Falaknuma Palace Hotel where I first ate this, the spinach had been blended into a smooth purée. I just chop mine, as I like the texture.

SERVES 3–4

530 g/1 lb 3 oz spinach, well washed and drained

2 tablespoons olive oil

2 tablespoons unsalted butter

¼ teaspoon whole cumin seeds

1 medium onion, peeled and cut into fine half-rings

3 good-sized cloves garlic, peeled and finely chopped

2 tablespoons very finely chopped fresh dill

¾ teaspoon salt

¼ teaspoon ground turmeric

¼–½ teaspoon nice red chilli powder

2 tablespoons finely sliced spring onions (white parts only)

4 tablespoons peeled and finely diced tomatoes

Bring a large pan of water to a rolling boil. Drop all the spinach into it. As soon as the leaves have wilted, drain them in a colander and run cold water over them until cool enough to handle. Squeeze out most, but not all of, the water, then chop finely and set aside.

Put the oil and butter into a medium, preferably non-stick frying pan and set over a medium heat. When hot, add the cumin seeds and let them sizzle for 10 seconds. Add the onion and sauté for 3–4 minutes. Add the garlic and sauté for another 2 minutes. Lower the heat to medium-low, then add the chopped spinach, dill, salt, turmeric and chilli powder. Mix well, then stir and cook on a low heat for 2 minutes. Add the spring onions and diced tomatoes. Stir and cook for another 2 minutes.

Stir-fried Spinach Andhra Style
Palakoora Vepadu

In Andhra, 'vepadu' refers to dishes that are either stir-fried or deep-fried until they are crisp (see page 23 for vepadus and more on Andhra meals). In the south this delicious, spicy spinach is generally served on the side, along with rice, thin dals and yoghurt dishes. I love it that way. I also love to eat it with north Indian chapatis, a potato dish and a dal, such as those on pages 99 and 116.

SERVES 3–4

500 g/1 lb 2 oz spinach, well washed

2 tablespoons olive or peanut oil

¼ teaspoon whole cumin seeds

3 cloves garlic, peeled, 1 halved lengthways and 2 finely chopped

4–5 whole fenugreek seeds

6–7 fresh curry leaves, lightly crushed in your hand

1 onion (130 g/4½ oz), peeled and finely chopped

1 teaspoon peeled and very finely grated fresh ginger

generous pinch of ground turmeric

½ teaspoon ground coriander

¼–1 teaspoon nice red chilli powder

½ teaspoon salt

Bring a large pan of water to a rolling boil. Drop all the spinach into it. As soon as the leaves have wilted, drain them in a colander and run cold water over them until cool enough to handle. Squeeze out most, but not all, of the water by picking up balls of spinach and gently pressing them between your palms. Chop the spinach coarsely and place in a bowl.

Put the oil in a medium, preferably non-stick pan and set over a medium-high heat. When hot, add the cumin seeds. Let them sizzle for 3–4 seconds, then add the halved garlic clove. Stir once or twice. Add the fenugreek seeds and, a second later, the curry leaves (take care as these will splutter). Quickly add the onion and reduce the heat to medium-low. Stir and sauté for 5–6 minutes, or until the onion becomes soft and begins to pick up a little colour at the edges.

Add the ginger and chopped garlic. Sauté for another minute, then add the turmeric, coriander and chilli powder. Stir for a minute. Now add the chopped spinach, any accumulated liquid in the bowl, and the salt. Stir and sauté gently for another 8–10 minutes to allow all flavours to meld.

Stir-fried Orange Pumpkin or Butternut Squash
Lal Kaddu ki Sabzi

I have combined northern and southern Indian seasonings to make this dish, a great favourite in our household. Indians often add jaggery, a raw brown sugar, to pumpkin dishes, which, when combined with hot spices, makes the dish most addictive. I have used dark brown sugar instead.

India does not really have butternut squashes, but they are so similar to orange pumpkins that they make perfect substitutes. These days they can be found everywhere, all peeled, cut and ready to cook, making our lives much easier. Whether you use the orange pumpkin or butternut squash, the net weight after peeling and removing the seeds should be about 450 g/1 lb.

Serve in a meal that also has a spinach dish, a dal and a yoghurt relish or a salad of some sort. Eat with Indian breads or rice.

SERVES 4

2 tablespoons olive or peanut oil

¼ teaspoon urad dal

¼ teaspoon whole brown mustard seeds

1–2 dried hot red chillies

1 onion (about 85 g/3 oz), peeled and chopped

450 g/1 lb orange pumpkin or butternut squash (see note above), cut into 1 cm/½ inch dice

¾–1 teaspoon salt

1 tablespoon dark brown sugar

1 teaspoon ground cumin

freshly ground black pepper

Put the oil into a medium, non-stick frying pan and set over a medium heat. When hot, add the urad dal. As soon as it starts to change colour, add the mustard seeds and the red chillies. When the mustard seeds start to pop and the chillies darken, a matter of seconds, add the onion. Stir and fry for 2 minutes. Add the pumpkin or squash, then stir and fry for about 4 minutes, or until the pumpkin and the onion starts to brown.

Add 175 ml/6 fl oz water, the salt, brown sugar, cumin and black pepper. Mix well and bring to the boil. Cover, lower the heat and simmer gently for about 10 minutes, or until the pumpkin is soft enough to pierce easily with a knife. Taste for seasoning and make adjustments if needed.

When you are getting ready to serve, boil away any water that may remain, stirring as you do so.

Yasmin Tayebbhoy's
Turnip Bharta *Shaljum Bharta*

For more on bhartas (mashed vegetables) see page 56. The seasonings here are very north Indian.

Serve with any Indian bread or warmed wholemeal pitta, perhaps a paneer dish and a cauliflower dish.

SERVES 5–6

6 medium turnips (about 725 g/ 1 lb 10 oz in all)

4 tablespoons olive or peanut oil

½ teaspoon whole cumin seeds

1 onion (200 g/7 oz), peeled and chopped

1 tablespoon peeled and finely grated fresh ginger

3–4 cloves garlic, peeled and finely chopped

1–3 fresh hot green chillies, finely chopped

2 tomatoes (285 g/10 oz in all), peeled and finely chopped

¾–1 teaspoon salt

freshly ground black pepper

4 tablespoons chopped fresh coriander

Peel the turnips and cut them into 8 pieces. Put them in a pan, cover generously with water and bring to the boil. Cover, lower the heat and cook gently until tender. Drain thoroughly and mash well.

Put the oil in a medium, non-stick frying pan and set over a medium-high heat. When hot, add the cumin seeds and let them sizzle for 10 seconds. Add the onion and fry for 2 minutes. Stir and sauté over a medium heat for another 3–4 minutes.

Add the ginger, garlic and green chillies and stir for a minute. Add the tomatoes and cook over a medium heat for 5–6 minutes, or until they are paste-like and the oil begins to show at the edges.

Add the mashed turnips and salt, then cook for 20–25 minutes, turning the heat down as needed, until the turnips are well sautéed. Check the salt, then add the pepper and 3 tablespoons of the fresh coriander. Stir well.

Sprinkle the remaining chopped fresh coriander over the top when serving.

Kerala Vegetable Stew
Kerala Eshtew

SERVES 3–4

1 teaspoon black peppercorns

seeds from 5 cardamom pods

4 cloves

2.5 cm/1 inch piece of cinnamon stick

1 bay leaf

2 tablespoons olive or peanut oil

½ teaspoon whole brown
   mustard seeds

1 dried hot red chilli

15 or so fresh curry leaves,
   lightly crushed in your hand

2 medium shallots, peeled and
   chopped

2 fresh hot green chillies, slit in
   half lengthways

2 cloves garlic, peeled and cut
   into fine slivers

1 teaspoon fresh ginger, peeled
   and finely grated

1 medium potato, cut into
   2 cm/¾ inch dice

1 teaspoon salt, or to taste

130 g/4½ oz cauliflower florets
   of medium size

130 g/4½ oz green beans (round or
   flat), cut into 2 cm/¾ inch pieces

1 medium carrot, peeled and cut
   into 2 cm/¾ inch dice or rounds

115 g/4 oz peas, defrosted if frozen

1 x 400 ml/14 oz can coconut milk,
   well shaken

1 teaspoon vinegar (rice vinegar is
   ideal, but white wine or red wine
   vinegar is fine)

There are probably as many recipes for this in Kerala as there are families. Locally called 'eshtew', a charming mispronunciation of the English word, it is generally eaten with appam (rice pancakes) or idi appam (rice noodles) or plain rice. There are many ingredients involved, but the dish cooks quite fast.

Put the peppercorns, cardamom seeds, cloves, cinnamon stick and bay leaf into a grinder and grind to a powder.

Put the oil in a wok or frying pan and set over a medium-high heat. When hot, add the mustard seeds. As soon as they start to pop, a matter of seconds, add the dried red chilli, then, a few seconds later, the curry leaves (take care as these will splutter). Stir once and add the shallots, green chillies and garlic. Stir for about 2 minutes, then add the ginger. Stir once or twice and add the potato. Stir a few times and add 250 ml/8 fl oz water and ¼ teaspoon salt. Bring to the boil. Cover, lower the heat and cook gently for about 10 minutes, or until the potato is almost done.

Add the cauliflower, green beans, carrot and peas followed by the ground spices and ¾ teaspoon of salt. Pour in just enough water to cover the vegetables, then stir and bring to the boil. Cover, lower the heat and cook for about 6–8 minutes, or until the vegetables are tender.

Add the coconut milk and bring to a simmer. Stir in the vinegar and turn off the heat. Taste for salt, adding more if needed.

Dals:
Dried Beans
&
Legumes

A Note on Dals

Pronounced 'daal' (with a soft Spanish 'd'), the word 'dal' in India stands for the whole family of dried beans, pulses, legumes and split peas. Indian grocers generally have a large section devoted just to dals. This includes various versions of the same dal – whole with skin, whole without skin, split with skin, split without skin, as well as dal flours and combinations of dal flours for specific dishes.

In China and much of the Far East, only the soya bean and, to a much lesser extent, the mung bean, have been explored to reveal the bounty they can offer. It is only India that has taken almost every legume it grows (other than the soya bean), and that it has received in the past from other continents, and revealed all their potential.

Dals are a very important part of every Indian's food world. For Indian vegetarians this is doubly true, as all legumes are a major source of protein. Each dal has its own taste and texture. For variety, not only can different dals be cooked every day, but the seasonings can be varied, as can the vegetables the dal is cooked with. Dals may also be combined in various ways not only for the somewhat soupy or porridge-like dishes we eat with our rice and breads, but to make savoury cakes, pancakes, pastas, snacks, starters, dry chutneys and sweet desserts. Chickpea flour alone can account for foods in all these categories.

Indians are hard put to understand why the Americas, which grow so many wonderful varieties of legumes, do so little with them, other than boiling them up whole.

There are further minute distinctions in the dal dishes cooked in various parts of India. For example, in south India an 'usali' is a somewhat dry combination of a dal and a vegetable, a 'kootu' is a slightly wetter combination, and a 'sambar' a very soupy one. In the north you could have a very rich creamy dish of the black whole urad dal one day, the very light moong dal with crisply browned onions the next, and a dish of sprouted mung beans on the third day. (If you want to learn how to sprout your own mung beans the easy Indian way, see page 132.) Eating dal every day is never boring for an Indian, any more than eating meat every day is boring for meat-eaters. It is a matter of what meat you eat and how it is cooked. In both cases, the variety is endless.

Whole beans need to be soaked overnight before they are cooked. If the split dals are going to be made into savoury pancakes, they too need to be soaked and blended into a batter. Recipes for pancakes are in chapter 5 (see page 190).

The dals used in this book are discussed opposite in alphabetical order, but the list does not, by any means, cover all the dals cooked in India.

Black-eyed peas: I have seen the fresh version of this bean only in India, but I am sure it is available in that form wherever it is grown. Most of the time it is sold in its dried form, or cooked and canned. I have used only the dried peas in my recipes. They need to be soaked overnight.

Chana dal: This is really the split, skinned version of a smaller yellow chickpea. It makes for a meaty dal. It is also used as a spice in south India.

Chickpeas: In India, chickpeas come in many sizes and colours. In the spring, markets sell fresh green ones on the bush in large bunches. The only kind of chickpeas I have used in this book are canned because they are so easy to prepare. Try to get organic ones, as they not only taste better, but so does the liquid they are in.

Chickpea flour: Also called 'besan' or 'gram' flour, this is used to make fritters, to thicken soupy dishes and to make pancakes.

Green lentils: These are just the ordinary lentils that are sold in most supermarkets.

Masoor: Sabut masoor is whole red lentils, unsplit and with skin. Masoor dal is split red lentils, generally hulled.

Mung: Sabut moong or mung beans are whole and dark green, often used for sprouting. Indian sprouts have very short tails and the sprouting process takes just 24 hours. They are also soaked and ground into a rough batter to make delicious pancakes. Moong dal is the split version of mung beans, and can be bought with or without skin. Anything with skin has much more fibre, but takes longer to cook.

Soya granules: Very popular with Indian vegetarians, these are used to make meat-like dishes.

Toovar: Also called 'arhar' and 'toor', this dal is nearly always used in its hulled and split form in India. It is very popular in south and western India, though northerners love it as well. Apart from what I call 'plain' toovar, there is also an oily form, which just means that it has been rubbed with castor oil to protect it from insects. This oil needs to be washed off before the dal is cooked.

Urad dal: This pulse has a dark skin and is used in both whole and split forms. It has a slightly glutinous texture, which has always endeared it to me. It is frequently used as a spice in south India, and for this purpose it is always hulled and split.

Black-eyed Peas with Coriander & Green Chillies

Lobhia aur Hari Chutney

A simple, everyday dish from the north that goes well with both rice and flatbreads.

SERVES 4

180 g/6 oz dried black-eyed peas, washed and soaked overnight

¾ teaspoon salt, or to taste

45 g/1½ oz fresh coriander tops, chopped

2–4 fresh hot green chillies, chopped

1 tablespoon tomato purée

2 teaspoons olive or peanut oil

generous pinch of ground asafoetida

½ teaspoon whole cumin seeds

1 dried hot red chilli

½ medium onion, peeled and cut into fine half-rings

Drain the peas, place in a pan with 1 litre/1¾ pints water and bring to the boil. Skim off the froth, lower the heat and simmer very gently, partially covered, for 1¼ hours. Mash a few tablespoons of the beans against the sides of the pan, then mix in the salt.

Put 4 tablespoons of water in a blender. Add the coriander, green chillies and tomato purée. Blend thoroughly. You might need to push the ingredients down with a rubber spatula or add a tiny bit more water.

Put the oil in a small frying pan set over a medium heat. When hot, add the asafoetida and, a few seconds later, the cumin seeds. Let the cumin sizzle for a few seconds, then add the red chilli and let it darken all over. Add the onion and fry until reddish-brown.

Tip in the paste from the blender and fry until it is thick. Pour the contents of the pan into the beans and mix thoroughly. You can make the dal as thin or as thick as you like.

Nepalese Black-eyed Peas with Potatoes & Bamboo Shoots *Aloo Tama Bodi*

A simple and very nutritious dish from Nepal, where it is made with the bamboo shoots that grow in the southern Himalayan forests. (I use canned, thinly sliced bamboo shoots instead.) While it is sometimes described as a soup, it is really a main dish, eaten with rice. You can also serve it with crusty bread and a salad.

SERVES 4

180 g/6 oz dried black-eyed peas, washed and soaked overnight

1 x 225 g/8 oz can thinly sliced bamboo shoots (140 g/5 oz drained weight), cut into 2 cm/¾ inch pieces

2 medium waxy potatoes (about 250 g/9 oz in all), peeled and cut into 2 cm/¾ inch dice

2 tablespoons olive or peanut oil

1 onion (140 g/5 oz), peeled and chopped

1½ teaspoons peeled and finely grated fresh ginger

2 cloves garlic, peeled and finely chopped

1 tomato (140g/5 oz), finely chopped

1 teaspoon ground cumin

¼ teaspoon ground turmeric

¼–1 teaspoon nice red chilli powder

1 teaspoon salt

Drain the peas and place in a pan with the bamboo shoots, potatoes and 1 litre/1¾ pints water. Bring to the boil. Skim off the froth, lower the heat and simmer very gently for 40 minutes.

Meanwhile, heat the oil in a medium frying pan set over a medium-high heat. When hot, add the onion and fry for about 5 minutes, or until it just starts to brown. Add the ginger and garlic and stir for a minute. Add the tomato and lower the heat to medium. Stir in the cumin, turmeric and chilli powder and cook on a medium heat until the sauce is thick.

When the peas are done, mix in the salt. Add the tomato mixture and mix well. Continue to cook the beans for another 20 minutes, or until all the seasonings and beans have unified.

Goan Black-eyed Peas with Coconut
Chawli Usal

Shashikala Potnis, the wife of the owner and head chef, together with her main assistant and daughter-in-law Sanjali, were extremely kind and generous when I visited. They patiently taught me many of the exquisite Hindu Goan-style dishes they cook and serve in their rather rough and ready, though highly successful restaurant, Highway Gomatak. This was one of them. It is generally served with rice or rice breads and other vegetable and fish dishes (yes, they eat fish).

SERVES 6

400 g/14 oz dried black-eyed peas, washed and soaked overnight

3 medium onions, peeled

180 g/6 oz fresh grated coconut, or defrosted if frozen

5 tablespoons olive or peanut oil

4–5 tomatoes (about 675 g/1½ lb), peeled and finely chopped

¾–1 teaspoon nice red chilli powder

2 tablespoons ground coriander

¾ teaspoon ground turmeric

2 teaspoons salt, or to taste

2 teaspoons garam masala

Drain the peas, put them into a pan with 1 litre/1¾ pints water and bring to the boil. Skim off the froth, then partially cover, lower the heat and simmer gently for 45–60 minutes, until the peas are tender. Transfer them to a bowl and wash the pan.

While the peas are cooking, chop 1 onion and place in a blender with the coconut and 175 ml/6 fl oz water. Blend until you have as fine a paste as your blender can manage, pushing down with a rubber spatula if needed. Set aside.

Finely chop the 2 remaining onions. Put the oil in the clean pan and set over a medium-high heat. When hot, add the onions and fry until they brown at the edges. Add the tomatoes and fry until they soften and turn into a dark mush. The oil should show at the edges.

Tip in the paste from the blender and stir a few times, scraping up all the good bits stuck at the bottom. Add the chilli powder, coriander and turmeric and fry over a medium heat for 7–8 minutes, or until the mixture browns lightly. Add all the cooked beans and their liquid, plus another 4–8 tablespoons of water, depending on how thick you want the beans to be. Stir in the salt and garam masala and bring to a simmer. Cook, uncovered, for 15–20 minutes, or until the beans are very tender, stirring now and then.

Chana Dal with Spinach & Tomato
Saag-Tamatar wali Chana Dal

This dish, from no specific region of India, but with a lovely mixture of northern and southern seasonings, could also be made with moong dal or toovar dal. I often make it for dinner for my husband and me, accompanying it with rice, a dish of green beans or cauliflower and natural yoghurt. I also love to make it for large groups. Just recently, I was going to have a dozen people come back with us after one of my husband's concerts. I had prepared everything beforehand for a grand meal. The spread included this dal (I doubled the recipe), the Berry Pilaf (see page 168) and the Aubergines in a Peanut & Sesame Sauce (see page 60). A yoghurt relish, Quick Yoghurt & Pickle Chutney (see page 278), was already in the refrigerator. All I had to do was heat up the food.

I like to use fresh spinach for this dish. You do not need very much. Cut the stems crossways into tiny dice and chop the leaves into small pieces.

SERVES 6

285 g/10 oz chana dal, washed in several changes of water and drained

½ teaspoon ground turmeric

1½ teaspoons salt

3 tablespoons ghee (clarified butter) or olive oil or peanut oil, or a mixture of ghee and any oil

⅛ teaspoon ground asafoetida

½ teaspoon whole brown mustard seeds

½ teaspoon whole cumin seeds

1–2 dried hot red chillies

7–8 fresh curry leaves

1 large onion (225 g/8 oz), peeled and chopped

2 cloves garlic, peeled and finely chopped

1½ teaspoons peeled and finely grated fresh ginger

2 good-sized tomatoes (about 285 g/10 oz in all), peeled and chopped

140–180 g/5–6 oz well-washed spinach, chopped (see introduction above)

¼–½ teaspoon nice red chilli powder (optional)

freshly ground black pepper

Put the dal in a medium pan along with 1.2 litres/2 pints water. Bring to the boil, skimming off the froth as it rises to the top. Do not let it boil over. Stir in the turmeric, cover partially, lower the heat and cook for 1¼ hours. When done, mix in the salt.

While the dal cooks, heat the ghee and/or oil in a small, preferably non-stick frying pan and set over a medium-high heat. When hot, add the asafoetida and, a second later, the mustard seeds. As soon as the seeds start to pop, a matter of seconds, add the cumin seeds. Stir for 5–6 seconds, then add the red chillies and fry until they darken. Throw in the curry leaves, stir once and add the onion. Sauté for about 7–10 minutes, or until the onion starts to brown.

Add the garlic and ginger and stir for another 1–2 minutes. Now add the tomatoes and stir for 5–6 minutes, until they soften, mashing them down with the back of a wooden spoon as you do so. Add the spinach and 120 ml/4 fl oz water. Stir and bring to a simmer. Cover and cook gently for 10–12 minutes, or until the spinach wilts and is very soft.

When the dal has finished cooking, add the spinach mixture and stir well. Check the seasoning and add the chilli powder if you need it. Grind black pepper over the top. If the dal feels too thick, you can stir in a little water.

Chana Dal with Yellow Squash, Chayote or Doodhi
Doodhi aur Chana Dal

This is a Gujarati dish normally made with the very long, pale green Indian squash known as 'doodhi' or 'ghiya'. Many Indian grocers sell it, but I find that chayote or sayote, the South American pear-shaped vegetable (also known as 'cho cho', 'chow chow' and 'christophene'), or yellow squash make good substitutes. Gujaratis like their dal slightly sweet, which is how I have cooked it here. This may be a no-no in the north, but it is quite delicious! I love the Gujarati combination of sweet and hot. Gujaratis also like to use ghee to finish off their dals. All Indian stores sell it.

Serve this with Chapatis (see page 193) or wholemeal pitta bread, or plain rice and a vegetable and yoghurt dish.

SERVES 6

285 g/10 oz chana dal, washed in several changes of water and drained

450 g/1 lb piece of doodhi (ghiya) or 1 chayote or 1 medium yellow squash

½ teaspoon ground turmeric

1 teaspoon salt, or to taste

2 or more teaspoons jaggery or brown sugar, according to taste

3 tablespoons ghee (clarified butter) or olive or peanut oil

generous pinch of ground asafoetida

½ teaspoon whole brown mustard seeds

½ teaspoon whole cumin seeds

3 cloves

1 teaspoon peeled and finely grated fresh ginger

¼–¾ teaspoon nice red chilli powder

Put the dal in a medium pan along with 1.2 litres/2 pints water. Bring to the boil, skimming off the froth as it rises to the top. Do not let it boil over.

Meanwhile, prepare your chosen vegetable. If using doodhi or chayote, peel and quarter it lengthways, remove the seeds, and cut the flesh into 2.5 x 1 cm/1 x ½ inch pieces. If using squash, cut it in half lengthways, then cut crossways into 1 cm/½ inch pieces.

Stir the turmeric into the boiling dal, then partially cover and cook for 1 hour. Add the salt, jaggery and your chosen vegetable. Stir and bring to a gentle simmer, then cover fully. Cook the doodhi and chayote for another 20 minutes, but the squash for just 15 minutes. Uncover the pan while you complete the final step.

Heat the ghee or oil in a small, preferably non-stick frying pan and set over a medium-high heat. When hot, add the asafoetida and, a second later, the mustard seeds. As soon as the seeds start to pop, a matter of seconds, add the cumin seeds and cloves. Three seconds later add the grated ginger, stir for 10–15 seconds, then mix in the chilli powder. Tip the mixture immediately over the dal and cover quickly to trap the aromas. Stir and remove the cloves before serving.

Chickpeas in a Simple Northern Style
Roz kay Chaney

For this recipe I used two cans of organic, low-salt chickpeas only because that is what I was able to find. I prefer to use organic chickpeas because I can use all the liquid in the can. If your chickpeas are not organic, throw away the liquid in the can and use fresh water instead. The salt is a matter of preference. I add salt later in the recipe anyway, so if you start out with a can of ready-salted chickpeas, just taste and add less salt.

I love to eat this dish with Indian flatbreads. It is particularly good with Bhaturas (see page 208), but any other Indian bread would do. The chickpeas also combine well with tortillas. Just roll them inside with some raw onion slivers, chopped radishes and cucumbers, or Tomato, Onion & Cucumber Koshambari or Green Chutney (see pages 268 and 299), and eat!

SERVES 4–6

2 x 425 g/15 oz cans chickpeas,
    preferably organic

3 tablespoons olive or peanut oil

1 medium onion (155 g/5½ oz),
    peeled and finely chopped

1 tablespoon peeled and very
    finely grated fresh ginger

3 cloves garlic, peeled and crushed

1–3 fresh hot green chillies,
    finely chopped

2 teaspoons ground coriander

1 teaspoon ground cumin

¼ teaspoon ground turmeric

3 tablespoons tomato passata

1 teaspoon salt, or to taste

Drain the chickpeas, saving the liquid (only if organic). Set both aside.

Pour the oil into a medium, non-stick frying pan and set over a medium heat. When hot, add the onion and fry for 7–8 minutes, until soft and golden. Add the ginger, garlic and green chillies. Continue to stir and fry for another 2–3 minutes, until the onions have picked up a little colour. Add the coriander, cumin and turmeric. Stir a few times, then add the tomato passata and stir again.

Add the drained chickpeas, the salt and 500 ml/18 fl oz of the chickpea liquid, or water, or a combination of the two. Bring to a simmer, then cover and simmer very gently for 30 minutes. Check the salt, adding a bit more if needed.

Chickpeas in a Fresh Coriander Sauce
Hari Chutney walay Chanay

Everything said in the introduction to the preceding recipe applies here as well, so please read that before you begin.

If you want this dish to be hot and pungent, sprinkle the chaat masala over the top just before serving and stir it in.

SERVES 4–6

1 tablespoon lime or lemon juice

½ medium tomato, chopped

50 g/1¾ oz fresh coriander leaves and tender stems

1–2 fresh hot green chillies, chopped

2.5 cm/1 inch piece of fresh ginger, peeled and very finely chopped

salt

2 x 425 g/15 oz cans chickpeas, preferably organic

3 tablespoons olive or peanut oil

generous pinch of ground asafoetida

¼ teaspoon whole cumin seeds

1 onion (155 g/5½ oz), peeled and chopped

1 teaspoon ground coriander

¼–1 teaspoon chaat masala (optional)

Put the lime juice, tomato, fresh coriander, green chillies, ginger and ¼ teaspoon of salt in a blender in this order. Add 4–6 tablespoons water (as needed) and blend until smooth.

Drain the chickpeas, saving the liquid (only if organic). Set both aside.

Pour the oil into a medium, non-stick frying pan and set over a medium heat. When hot, add the asafoetida and, a few seconds later, the cumin seeds. Let them sizzle for a few seconds, then add the onion. Stir and fry for 7–8 minutes, until it is slightly browned at the edges. Add the ground coriander and stir for 30 seconds. Add the drained chickpeas, ½ teaspoon of salt and 350 ml/12 fl oz (organic) chickpea liquid or water or a combination of the two. Stir and bring to a simmer. Cover and simmer very gently for 20 minutes.

Stir in the paste from the blender and bring to a simmer again. Cover and cook gently for another 20 minutes. Check the salt, adding a bit more if needed, and stir in the chaat masala (if using).

Hot Yoghurt Sauce from the Konkan Coast *Takka Karhi*

A 'karhi' is just heated and flavoured yoghurt. As yoghurt curdles when it is boiled, it has to be stabilized with a starch. That starch in India is usually chickpea flour (though it could be rice flour), which adds its own nutrients to the dish. All Indians eat karhis, but they vary considerably from region to region. Delhi's karhis are very thick, yellow with turmeric and filled with bobbing dumplings. Gujarati karhis can be sweet and clove-flavoured, while this takka karhi, from the Saraswat Brahmins of the western Indian Konkan Coast, is thin, unsweetened and almost white. It is generally eaten with rice, but it can also be served in individual bowls and either just drunk with the meal, or eaten with flatbreads, along with other vegetables and dals.

It is best to make this dish with sour yoghurt. Simply leave it out of the refrigerator in a warm spot for 24 hours or longer, until it has soured a bit, or else use an acidophilus yoghurt, which is already sour.

This recipe may easily be doubled.

SERVES 2–3

475 ml/16 fl oz natural yoghurt
  (do not use Greek yoghurt here)
2 teaspoons chickpea flour
  (besan or gram flour)
⅓–½ teaspoon salt, or to taste
1 teaspoon olive or peanut oil
generous pinch of ground asafoetida
¼ teaspoon whole cumin seeds
1 dried red chilli or 1 fresh hot green
  chilli, split in half lengthways
2 cloves garlic, peeled and crushed

Put the yoghurt in a bowl and whisk until smooth. Slowly add 475 ml/16 fl oz water, whisking as you go.

In a separate bowl, mix the chickpea flour with a tablespoon or so of water to make a smooth paste. Add to the yoghurt along with the salt and whisk again.

Put the oil in a small pan and set over a medium heat. When hot, add the asafoetida and the cumin seeds. Let the seeds sizzle for a few seconds, then add the chilli. Stir once, add the garlic and stir a few more times.

Pour in the yoghurt sauce, stirring constantly while it comes to a gentle simmer. Allow to simmer on a low heat for 2–3 minutes, stirring all the time.

Hot Yoghurt Sauce from Southern India *Mor Kozhambu*

In India, rice is always served with something wet and flowing because it is considered too dry on its own. The exception is a rich biryani, but even that is offered with a raita and salads. The wetness deemed necessary could come from a curry with a sauce, a dal, or maybe just some melted ghee. Of course, it could also come from this thin yoghurt sauce, known in the south as 'mor kozhambu'. The thickening, slight as it is, is provided by either chickpea flour or rice flour. Quite often in the south it is eaten last, with rice and pickles. (This always reminds me of how the Japanese like to end their meals – with rice, pickles and tea!)

There are hundreds of variations to this recipe. I find this one delicious and easy to make. I like to serve it with Stir-fried Aubergines Cooked in a Tamil Nadu Style (see page 58), Plain Rice (see page 156) and a dal. It is best to pour it into small individual bowls.

As with the preceding recipe, the yoghurt here needs to be fairly sour. You can leave it in a warm spot for 24 hours or longer until it has soured a bit, or use an acidophilus yoghurt, which is already sour.

This recipe may easily be doubled.

SERVES 2–3

475 ml/16 fl oz natural yoghurt (do not use Greek yoghurt here)
2 teaspoons rice flour (also called powdered rice) or chickpea flour (besan or gram flour)
¼ teaspoon ground turmeric
¾ teaspoon sambar powder (get a good south Indian brand)
⅓–½ teaspoon salt, or to taste
1 teaspoon olive or peanut oil
generous pinch of ground asafoetida
½ teaspoon whole brown mustard seeds
¼ teaspoon whole fenugreek seeds
1 tablespoon chopped fresh coriander
1 fresh hot green chilli, finely chopped (optional)

Put the yoghurt in a bowl and whisk until smooth. Slowly add 475 ml/16 fl oz water, whisking as you go.

In a separate bowl, mix the rice flour with a tablespoon or so of water to make a smooth paste. Add to the yoghurt, along with the turmeric, sambar powder and salt and whisk again.

Put the oil in a small pan and set over a medium heat. When hot, add the asafoetida and then the mustard seeds. When the seeds pop, a matter of seconds, add the fenugreek seeds. Stir once, then pour in the yoghurt sauce. Keep stirring and bring the mixture to a gentle simmer. Let the sauce simmer on a low heat for 2–3 minutes, stirring all the time.

Add the fresh coriander and green chilli (if using) and stir once.

Okra in a Yoghurt & Chickpea Flour Sauce *Vendekaya Majjiga Pulusu*

You will find this Andhra dish only in south Indian homes and local restaurants. I have yet to come across it in any Indian eatery in the West. It is a simple dish, very much like the karhis of northern India. It is soupy, the yoghurt in it held together with a little binding of chickpea flour. This one has sautéed okra floating around in it. It is normally eaten with rice and generally served in individual bowls. It may also be poured directly over the rice. Other vegetables can be served on the side.

If you do not have chana dal, double the urad dal.

SERVES 4

340 g/12 oz fresh okra

3 tablespoons olive or peanut oil

salt

2 tablespoons chickpea flour (besan)

350 ml/12 fl oz natural yoghurt

¼ teaspoon urad dal

¼ teaspoon chana dal

¼ teaspoon whole brown
  mustard seeds

2 dried hot red chillies

2 tablespoons peeled and
  chopped onion

1 fresh hot green chilli, partially
  split in half lengthways

¼ teaspoon ground turmeric

Wipe the okra pods with a damp cloth, then allow to air-dry. Trim off the tops and tails, then cut the pods crossways into 2.5 cm/1 inch pieces.

Put 2 tablespoons of the oil in a medium frying pan and set over a medium-high heat. When hot, add the okra and fry for 5–6 minutes, until just starting to brown. Reduce the heat to medium and fry for another 3–4 minutes, until the okra is almost cooked. Using a slotted spoon, transfer it to a plate lined with kitchen paper. Sprinkle a generous pinch of salt over the top and toss.

Put the chickpea flour in a bowl. Slowly add 2 tablespoons of water, mixing with a wooden spoon as you go. Once you have a smooth paste, whisk it into the yoghurt along with another 120 ml/4 fl oz water.

Put the remaining 1 tablespoon of oil in a medium pan and set over a medium heat. When hot, add the urad and chana dal. As soon as they start to pick up some colour, add the mustard seeds and red chillies. As soon as the seeds start to pop, a matter of seconds, add the onion, green chilli and turmeric and sauté for a minute. Stir the yoghurt mixture and pour it into the pan. Stir and bring to a simmer, and keep stirring until the mixture thickens. Add ½ teaspoon of salt and the okra and stir until you are back at a simmer. Lower the heat and simmer gently for 2–3 minutes.

As this dish sits, it can thicken up, so add a little water to thin it as you wish.

Green Lentil Curry with Kale
Haray Lentils aur Kale

This is almost a meal in itself, nutritionally complete if you add some wholemeal pitta bread (or rice) and yoghurt on the side. You could also convert it into a soup by adding a mugful of water or stock towards the end of the cooking time.

SERVES 4–6

250 g/9 oz green lentils

¼ teaspoon ground turmeric

½ teaspoon cayenne pepper

115 g/4 oz green beans cut into
  2 cm/¾ inch segments

85 g/3 oz kale, thick stems and
  veins discarded, finely chopped

3 tablespoons finely chopped
  fresh coriander

1 medium carrot, peeled and
  cut into 5 mm/¼ inch rounds

1¼ teaspoons salt

For the curry paste

1 teaspoon peeled and finely
  grated ginger

1 clove garlic, peeled and crushed

1 teaspoon ground cumin seeds

2 teaspoons ground coriander seeds

3 tablespoons olive or rapeseed oil

¼ teaspoon whole cumin seeds

1 tablespoon peeled and finely
  chopped shallot

2 tablespoons tomato passata

Put the lentils, turmeric and 1.2 litres/2 pints water into a medium pan and bring to the boil. Cover partially and simmer gently for 20 minutes. Add the cayenne, beans, kale, coriander, carrot and salt. Stir and bring to the boil again. Cover partially and cook gently for another 20 minutes.

Meanwhile, make the curry paste: combine the ginger, garlic, ground cumin and coriander in a small bowl. Mix in 50 ml/2 fl oz water.

Pour the oil into a medium frying pan and set over a medium-high heat. When hot, add the whole cumin seeds. Let them sizzle for 5 seconds, then add the shallot. Stir and fry until lightly browned. Add the spice paste and fry until you can see the oil along the edges, about 1½ minutes. Add the tomato passata and fry for about another minute, until you see the oil along the edges.

When the lentils have finished cooking, add the contents of the frying pan. Stir and cook gently for another 5 minutes.

A Note on Indian-style Mung Beansprouts *Phuti Moong*

Mung beans, or whole moong as Indians call them, are native to India. The country has been eating them in hundreds of ways, including sprouting them, as far back as can be remembered. The sprouts are not like Chinese beansprouts; they are smaller, less watery and much more delicate, yet with ample body. Chinese sprouts take 3–4 days to develop their long 'tails', while Indian sprouts develop their short, thin tails within 24 hours.

Mung sprouts are very popular in India, especially among vegetarians, as breakfast foods and snack foods because they have all the nutrients of dried beans but are easier to digest. They may be strewn raw into salads (see page 300), cooked in breakfast dishes (see page 182) or cooked as main dishes (see page 135).

Ideally, you should get your mung beans from a reliable Indian or Chinese source, where the beans are sold rapidly and replaced constantly with fresh supplies.

How to make Indian-style mung beansprouts

200 g/7 oz mung beans will yield about 450 g/1 lb beansprouts.

Pick over and wash 200 g/7 oz whole mung beans. (Throw away any broken ones.) Put them in a large bowl, cover with 9–10 cm/ 3½–4 inches tepid water and leave to soak for 12 hours. Drain the beans in a colander and let some fresh, tepid water flow over them. Leave them to drain.

Wash out your soaking bowl and line it with a triple layer of thick kitchen paper in such a way that there will be some left to fold over the beans. (You could use J-cloths or tea towels if you wish, but they will discolour.) Dampen the kitchen paper or cloths and put all the beans in the bowl. Cover with the overhanging paper, or use extra dampened kitchen paper if you need to.

Put the bowl in a dark, warm place (I use my oven) for 12 hours. The beans should sprout. Rinse them in cool water, then cover and store in the refrigerator, making sure to rinse them in cool water every day. They should keep for 3–4 days.

Mung Beansprouts with Swiss Chard
Phuti Moong aur Swiss Chard

We do not really have Swiss chard in India, but this recipe serves to illustrate that Indian sprouts can be combined with most vegetables. Serve with a yoghurt relish and a flatbread.

SERVES 4

2 large stalks of Swiss chard
  (180 g/6 oz in all)
1 tablespoon olive or peanut oil
generous pinch of ground asafoetida
1 teaspoon whole brown
  mustard seeds
3 cloves garlic, peeled and
  finely chopped
1–2 fresh hot green chillies,
  finely chopped
½ teaspoon ground turmeric
340 g/12 oz Indian-style mung
  beansprouts (see page 132)
3 tablespoons chopped fresh
  coriander
¾–1 teaspoon salt
2 tablespoons lime juice
1 teaspoon sugar

Cut the chard stems into 5 mm/¼ inch dice and the leaves into 1 cm/½ inch dice.

Put the oil in a medium frying pan and set over a medium-high heat. When hot, add the asafoetida and, a second later, the mustard seeds. As soon as the seeds start to pop, a matter of seconds, take the pan off the heat and stir in the garlic and chillies. Put the pan back on a medium heat, add the chopped chard stems and stir for 2 minutes. Mix in the turmeric, then add the beansprouts, fresh coriander, chard leaves, 6 tablespoons of water and the salt. Stir and bring to a simmer on a medium-high heat. Cover and cook very gently for 20 minutes.

Finally, stir in the lime juice and sugar, then taste to check for balance of seasonings.

Mung Beansprouts, Potato & Mushroom Curry *Phuti Moong, Aloo aur Khumbi ki Sabzi*

Full of nutrients and flavour, this dish can be served with any type of Indian bread and a yoghurt relish. For a more Western-style meal, serve it with a simple green salad.

SERVES 4–5

3 tablespoons olive or peanut oil

½ teaspoon whole cumin seeds

1 medium onion, peeled and chopped

1 teaspoon peeled and finely grated fresh ginger

3 cloves garlic, peeled and crushed

2 tablespoons tomato purée

¼ teaspoon ground turmeric

340 g/12 oz Indian-style mung beansprouts (see page 132)

2 potatoes (225 g/8 oz in all), peeled and chopped into 1 cm/ ½ inch dice

2 large mushrooms (I like cremini here), cut lengthways into 5 mm/ ¼ inch slices

1 teaspoon salt

¼–¾ teaspoon nice red chilli powder

1½–2 tablespoons lime or lemon juice

Put the oil into a large frying pan and set over a medium-high heat. When hot, add the cumin seeds and let them sizzle for 5 seconds. Add the onion and fry for 6–7 minutes, or until just starting to brown at the edges. Add the ginger and garlic and stir for a minute. Now add the tomato purée and turmeric and stir for another minute.

Pour 475 ml/16 fl oz water into the pan and mix well. Add the sprouts, potatoes, mushrooms, salt and chilli powder, stir and bring to the boil. Cover and cook very gently for 25 minutes. Stir in the lime or lemon juice.

From the home of Anita Lal

Indian-style Beansprouts with Onion, Ginger & Garlic *Matki*

Anita is a successful businesswoman, who owns 10 branches of a very popular store named Good Earth. It specializes in hand-crafted goods. On the day we met, she, with her daughter Simran and grandson, were entertaining on the landscaped terrace of their stylish Bombay flat. They are from the Punjab, but their food has taken on a few hints of Bombay as well. Nothing is too hot or too spicy or too oily, which is typical of north Indian home cooking.

The menu for lunch consisted of the beansprout dish below, which is eaten all over India, some fried fish, toovar dal, stir-fried cabbage with mustard seeds, green beans, a yoghurt with spinach raita, a turnip dish and some custard apple ice cream. It was a perfect meal for a lovely sunny, winter afternoon.

In Bombay, a common method for cooking vegetables is to put very little water in the pan. Instead, the vegetable is covered with a flat lid that has an indentation in it. Water is put in that indentation and condensation from it keeps the vegetable moist. That was the method used to cook these beansprouts.

I find that most of my flat lids have indentations so I use those. If you cannot find anything but a domed lid, put 5–6 tablespoons of water in the pan, cover tightly and cook on a very low heat for 20 minutes. Take a peek inside once or twice and sprinkle in some more water if needed.

SERVES 3

2 tablespoons olive or peanut oil

1 onion (about 180 g/6 oz), peeled and chopped

4 cloves garlic, peeled and very finely chopped

4 cm/1½ inch piece of fresh ginger, peeled and very finely chopped

½–1 fresh hot green chilli, finely chopped

1½ teaspoons ground coriander

¼ teaspoon ground turmeric

⅛–¼ teaspoon nice red chilli powder

340 g/12 oz Indian-style mung beansprouts (see page 132)

1 teaspoon salt

3–4 cherry tomatoes, cut into 1 cm/½ inch dice

1 tablespoon chopped fresh coriander

Put the oil into a medium pan and set over a medium-high heat. When hot, add the onion and fry for 6–7 minutes, or until it browns a bit. Now add the garlic, ginger and green chilli. Stir for 2–3 minutes. Take the pan off the heat and add the ground coriander, turmeric and chilli powder. Put the pan back on the heat and stir for a minute. Add the sprouts, 4 tablespoons water and the salt. Stir a few times, going all the way to the bottom, then cover and reduce the heat to very low. If you have a flat lid with an indentation in it, pour water into the indentation, replacing the water as needed. If you do not have such a lid, keep an eye on the sprouts, sprinkling in a little water when the bottom seems to have dried out. Cook, covered, for about 20 minutes, or until the beansprouts are tender.

Transfer to a serving dish when ready to eat, and garnish with the tomato and fresh coriander.

Simple Moong & Masoor Dal Cooked in the Style of Uttar Pradesh Muslims *Saadi Mussalmani Moong aur Masoor Dal*

Muslims in India rarely use asafoetida in their cooking. They use garlic instead. Here is a simple, everyday dal that I cook frequently. All that is needed with it is rice or a flatbread, some yoghurt raita and a vegetable dish made with okra, cauliflower or aubergine.

200 g/7 oz mung beans

50 g/1¾ oz masoor dal (red lentils)

½ teaspoon ground turmeric

1–2 fresh hot green chillies, finely chopped

1 clove garlic, peeled and lightly crushed

1–1½ teaspoons salt, or to taste

2 tablespoons olive or peanut oil

½ teaspoon whole cumin seeds

1 dried hot red chilli

½ medium shallot, peeled and cut into very fine slivers

Combine the dals in a bowl and wash in several changes of water. Drain, then place in a heavy-based pan with 1 litre/ 1¾ pints water. Bring to the boil, skimming off the froth that rises to the top. Stir in the turmeric, green chillies and garlic. Cover partially and simmer very gently for 45 minutes, or until the dal is tender. Mash down with a potato masher, then mix in the salt.

Put the oil in a small frying pan set over a medium-high heat. When hot, add the cumin seeds and let them sizzle for 3 seconds. Add the red chilli and stir until it darkens. Add the shallot and fry until they turn a reddish-brown.

Tip the contents of the pan over the dal. Cover to entrap the aromas, and stir before serving.

Whole Moong & Masoor Cooked with Meat Seasonings *Sabut Moong aur Masoor*

Here is a combination of two old and beloved legumes – whole mung beans, which originated in India, and whole red lentils, which came to India from the Arab world in ancient times – cooked together with seasonings used in north India today for meat dishes. Strangely enough, I came across this dish on an Indian airline. Who would have thought!

For a festive dinner, serve the 'dal', as we would call it, with a vegetable or two of your choice and rice or a flatbread, and any salad or chutney you desire. A yoghurt relish is definitely required. For a family meal just one other vegetable, rice or bread and natural yoghurt would be fine.

Remember that a dal may be as thick or thin as you like. Generally, when we are eating them with breads, they tend to be thicker than when eating them with rice. We tend to thin the latter a bit more by adding extra water at the end.

SERVES 6–8

140 g/5 oz mung beans

140 g/5 oz whole red lentils (sabut masoor)

1 teaspoon salt, or more to taste

5 tablespoons olive or peanut oil

5 cm/2 inch cinnamon stick

2 bay leaves

5 cardamom pods (you can put these in a small muslin bag for easy removal)

1 onion (200 g/7 oz), peeled and finely chopped

7.5 cm/3 inches peeled and very finely grated fresh ginger

5 cloves garlic, peeled and crushed

3 tablespoons tomato purée

1 tablespoon ground coriander

2 teaspoons ground cumin

1 teaspoon ground turmeric

½–1 teaspoon nice red chilli powder, according to taste

1 teaspoon garam masala

dollop of ghee (clarified butter) or ordinary butter (optional)

Combine the beans and lentils in a sieve, then pick over and wash them. Place them in a heavy-based pan, add 1.6 litres/2¾ pints water and bring to the boil. Boil for 2 minutes, then cover and set aside off the heat for 1 hour. Bring to the boil again, lower the heat, cover and simmer gently (there should always be a few bubbles rising) for 1½ hours. The beans will be very, very tender. Mix in the salt and set aside.

Put the oil in a medium, preferably non-stick frying pan and set over a medium-high heat. When hot, add the cinnamon, bay leaves and cardamom pods. Stir once or twice, then quickly add the onion and fry for 7–8 minutes, or until it begins to brown at the edges. Add the ginger and garlic and stir for another 2 minutes. Stir in the tomato purée a tablespoon at a time, then add the coriander, cumin, turmeric and chilli powder. Stir for 2 minutes. Now add 250 ml/8 fl oz water, stir well and simmer gently for 5 minutes. Pick out all the whole spices – the cinnamon, bay leaves and cardamom – and discard them. Mix in the garam masala.

When the beans have finished cooking, stir the spice paste into the dal. Taste and add more salt if you wish. The dal should be as thick as you like, so add more hot water if you want it thinner. Just before eating, ladle it into a serving dish and drop in a knob of ghee or butter (if using).

Mixed Dal, Delhi Style
Dilli ki Mili Jhuli Dal

As dals are eaten every day by most Indians, not just vegetarians, they are varied and sometimes mixed in different combinations. This is a simple northern combination, found in Delhi, Uttar Pradesh, Madhya Pradesh and Bihar. The north has its own variety of toovar dal called arhar dal. Either will suffice for this recipe.

SERVES 4

100 g/3½ oz mung beans
50 g/1¾ oz masoor dal (red lentils)
50 g/1¾ oz plain toovar dal
½ teaspoon ground turmeric
1 teaspoon salt
1 tablespoon olive or peanut oil
generous pinch of asafoetida
½ teaspoon whole cumin seeds
1–2 dried hot red chillies

Pictured on pages 138–139

Put the three dals in a bowl and wash in several changes of water. Drain thoroughly, then place in a heavy-based pan. Add 1 litre/1¾ pints water and bring to the boil. Skim off the froth, reduce the heat to low and stir in the turmeric. Cover partially and cook for 45–60 minutes, or until the dals are very soft. Mash coarsely with a potato masher. Mix in the salt.

Put the oil in a small frying pan set over a medium-high heat. When hot, add the asafoetida and, a few seconds later, the cumin seeds. Let the seeds sizzle for a few seconds, then add the chillies and fry until darkened on all sides.

Quickly tip the contents of the frying pan over the cooked dal and cover to entrap the aromas. Stir before serving.

Vinita Pittie's

Mixed Dal, Marwari Style
Marwari Mili Jhuli Dal

For information about the Marwari community, see the introduction on page 102. I will add here that Marwaris love their ghee. To do a final tarka (see page 11) for the dal without using ghee is to invite a look of astonishment in the eyes of a Marwari, and pity too.

This dal dish combines four dals, two with skin and two without, so it is nutritious and full of natural fibre. Generally, it is cooked to a thickish consistency, all the better to eat it with flatbreads, such as Chapatis or Puffed Fried Breads (see pages 193 and 206). You can also eat it with rice, in which case it should be thinned with about 120 ml/4 fl oz boiling water. A yoghurt relish and a vegetable dish added to the meal would make it just perfect. This is amongst my favourite dal dishes.

SERVES 4

50 g/1¾ oz chana dal

50 g/1¾ oz plain toovar dal

50 g/1¾ oz split urad with skin (sold as chilkewali urad dal)

50 g/1¾ oz split mung beans with skin (sold as chilkewali moong dal)

2 bay leaves

2 cloves

4 cardamom pods

¼ teaspoon ground turmeric

¾ teaspoon salt, or to taste

2 tablespoons ghee (clarified butter) or olive or peanut oil

generous pinch of ground asafoetida

¼ teaspoon whole cumin seeds

1 dried hot red chilli, broken in half

¼ teaspoon nice red chilli powder

1 teaspoon ground coriander

1 teaspoon peeled and grated fresh ginger

1–2 fresh hot green chillies, finely sliced crossways

2 tablespoons chopped fresh coriander

Combine all the dals in a bowl and wash them thoroughly in several changes of water. Drain, then leave to soak in a generous covering of water for 2 hours.

Drain the dals and place in a heavy-based pan with 1 litre/ 1¾ pints water. Bring to the boil, skimming off the froth that rises to the surface. Add the bay leaves, cloves, cardamom and turmeric, tied in a small muslin bag if you like. Stir and cover partially, then cook very gently for 1¼ hours, or until the dal is tender. (Remove the muslin bag now, if using.) Add the salt, then mash the dal with a potato masher.

Put the ghee in a small frying pan and set it over a medium-high heat. When hot, add the asafoetida and, a few seconds later, the cumin seeds and red chilli. After 2 seconds, add the chilli powder and ground coriander. Stir once and quickly add the ginger and green chillies. Stir once, then quickly tip the contents of the frying pan over the dal. Cover immediately to entrap the aromas.

Stir before serving and sprinkle the fresh coriander over the top.

Whole Red Lentils with Cumin & Shallots *Sabut Masoor*

A lovely, nutritious dish, full of fibre and protein. I love it with Tomato Rice (see page 164), a yoghurt relish and some leafy vegetable. You could also serve it with Indian flatbread, pickles, relishes and a potato dish.

Indian grocers sell this dal as whole masoor or sabut masoor. The red lentil is whole, not split, and still has its brownish skin.

SERVES 4

200 g/7 oz whole red lentils
   (sabut masoor)
¼ teaspoon ground turmeric
1 teaspoon salt
1½ tablespoons olive or peanut oil
generous pinch of ground asafoetida
¼ teaspoon whole cumin seeds
2–3 dried hot red chillies
1 good-sized shallot, peeled and
   cut into fine slivers
butter (optional)
lime or lemon wedges (optional)

Wash and drain the lentils. Place them in a medium saucepan, add 600 ml/1 pint water and bring to the boil. Skim off the froth from the surface and add the turmeric. Stir, cover partially and simmer gently for 1 hour. Mix in the salt.

Put the oil in a small frying pan and set over a medium heat. When hot, add the asafoetida. After a few seconds, add the cumin seeds and let them sizzle for a few seconds. Add the red chillies and fry until they darken, then quickly stir in the shallot. Fry until the slivers turn a rich reddish colour and become crisp.

Tip the contents of the frying pan over the lentils and cover immediately to entrap the aromas. Stir before serving, adding about 2 pats of butter if you wish. Serve with the lime wedges on the side (if using).

Simple Toovar Dal *Saadi Toovar Dal*

The Taj Mahal Hotel in Bombay, built at the start of the twentieth century, is a jewel, a beautifully carved, rock-like structure that sits guard by the Indian Ocean. Attacked by terrorists a few years ago for being exactly that, a symbol of beauty and power, it has several elegant shops within it. I know several of them intimately as I have been visiting them since the 1940s, when my father took me and my siblings to the hotel. One of them is the jewellery shop Gazdar, which opened its doors in the 1980s. I stare in its windows every time I am there. I have even bought a few small things.

When collecting material for this book, I wanted to go into the homes of people I meet in life casually and briefly – shopkeepers, farmers, doctors, lawyers, weavers – to see what they actually eat and how they eat it. I approached the owner of Gazdar, Ravi Gandhi, and he very kindly and generously opened up the doors to his seaside flat for me.

Ravi is a Marwari (of the merchant class whose origins lie in Rajasthan) from a Varanasi family and a vegetarian. He consciously eats healthy meals, and starts his day with raw fruit and vegetables, plus some cooked food that could take the form of light, steamed, savoury cakes called 'dhoklas'.

Lunch is at 12.30pm, and he always goes home for it. His father replaces him at the shop. This is the main meal of the day. Dinner is usually a light vegetable soup.

Perhaps because I was there, as was the whole family, there was a large spread that appeared in two courses. It was served on individual thalis (silver platters). The first course has two sweetmeats bought from a Ben gali halvai or sweet-maker: the milk-based sandesh and the crispy, thready sohan papri. You are meant to start with them.

There was also a simple toovar dal that I just loved and give the recipe for opposite, potatoes with cumin, some chickpeas, paneer, some long beans with green chilli, and a salad with cucumbers, water chestnuts, tomatoes and courgettes. Other than the sweets, everything is eaten with rice.

For the second course, the rice disappeared and warm, fresh phulkas (flatbreads like delicate, small chapatis) were offered, fresh and hot from the kitchen. There were also steamed sooji cakes and a glorious green chutney with coriander and mint. The toovar dal was served again, this time with squeezes of lime, and more of the vegetables were offered.

We ended the meal with chaas, a kind of lassi with curry leaves (see page 313).

The dal that was used in this Gandhi family recipe is sold as oily toovar dal – most of western India prefers that version – and the oil needs to be washed off.

SERVES 4

200 g/7 oz oily or plain toovar dal, picked over

¾–1 teaspoon salt

½ teaspoon ground turmeric

½–2 fresh hot green chillies, cut crossways into thin slices

10–12 fresh curry leaves, lightly crushed in your hand

1 tablespoon ghee (clarified butter) or oil

¼ teaspoon whole brown mustard seeds

¼ teaspoon whole cumin seeds

generous pinch of ground asafoetida

¼–½ teaspoon nice red chilli powder

lime wedges, to serve

Put the dal in a bowl, cover generously with water and rub with your hands to remove the oil. Drain, then repeat this step 5 or 6 times. When clean, cover generously with water again and leave to soak for 30 minutes.

Drain the dal and place in a heavy-based pan. Add 600 ml/ 1 pint water and bring to the boil, skimming off the froth that rises to the surface. Add the salt, turmeric and green chillies, cover partially, lower the heat and cook very gently for 30–45 minutes, or until soft. Mash the dal coarsely with a potato masher. Taste for salt and adjust as necessary. If the dal is too thick, which it probably will be, add 4–5 tablespoons of water. Stir in the curry leaves.

Just before you sit down to eat, heat the dal, stirring as you do so, then empty it into a serving bowl. Put the ghee in a very small pan and set over a medium-high heat. When hot, add the mustard seeds. As soon as they pop, a matter of seconds, add the cumin seeds and asafoetida. After 3–4 seconds, add the chilli powder, then immediately tip the contents of the pan over as much of the surface of the dal as you can. Serve immediately, with lime wedges if you wish.

Santha Gersappe's

Simple Toovar Dal from the Chitrapur Saraswat Brahmins of Coastal Kannada
Dali Saar

Dali Saar is comfort food for the Saraswat Brahmins of Chitrapur, who are mainly professionals from the Konkan coast. Some are academics, others lawyers. I ate with one family where every member was some kind of doctor. Most of their women are educated. Their food, which includes fish, is unique and utterly delicious.

Why these Brahmins eat fish is part legend now. Between 3000 and 2000 BC, there was a tectonic shift, and the mighty Saraswat river flowing down from the Himalaya mountains started drying up. The vegetarian Brahmins living along its shores had to flee. They were starving when a holy man they met got fish from the drying river and fed it to them. Since then, they have eaten fish. They continued their journey south and ended up in Goa, where they built their temples. After the Portuguese invasion in the 16th century, they fled further south into what is now Karnataka.

As saar is juice or juice-like, this dal tends to be very thin, meant to be eaten with rice. Those who are lucky get to eat it with the very nutritious red rice that is local to the area. The cooking talents of brides used to be judged by their ability to make a simple dali saar. I have had many dali saars that are highly flavoured with garlic, and I like them very much. Santha does not use any garlic in hers, but you can add some in your tarka (see page 11) if you wish. I do.

200 g/7 oz plain or oily toovar dal,
  picked over

½ teaspoon ground turmeric

¾ teaspoon salt, or to taste

2 tablespoons olive or peanut oil

generous pinch of ground asafoetida

1 teaspoon whole mustard seeds

1–3 fresh hot green chillies, cut
  in half lengthways

1 dried hot red chilli

3–4 cloves garlic, peeled and
  cut in half lengthways

10–12 fresh curry leaves, lightly
  crushed in your hand

Put the dal in a bowl and cover generously with water. If using oily dal, rub it with your hands to remove the oil; if using plain dal, just wash it. Pour out the water. Do this 5 or 6 times. Now cover generously with water again and leave to soak for 30 minutes.

Drain the dal, place it in a heavy-based pan and add 750 ml/ 1¼ pints water. Bring to the boil, skimming off the froth that rises to the surface. Stir in the turmeric, then partially cover the pan and cook for 35–40 minutes, or until the dal is tender. Mash the dal coarsely with a potato masher. Mix in the salt, then slowly add about 250 ml/8 fl oz water, stirring as you go, until the dal reaches the thinness you desire. Cook it over a medium-low heat for another 5 minutes.

Put the oil in a very small pan and set over a medium-high heat. When hot, add the asafoetida. A few seconds later, add the mustard seeds. As soon as they pop, a matter of seconds, add all the chillies and the garlic. Stir until the garlic pieces turn a light brown on both sides. Throw in the curry leaves (take care as they will splutter), stir once, then immediately tip the contents of the pan over the dal. Cover to entrap the aromas. Stir before serving.

S. Sampoorna's

Toovar Dal with Spinach & Sorrel
Palakooora Chukkakoora Pappu

Sour greens, both red-leafed and green-leafed, are used throughout India's south and west. If you cannot get sorrel, double the spinach and increase the amount of tamarind. The dish should taste slightly sour.

S. Sampoorna is a housewife who cooks with great efficiency and joy. She belongs to the business-orientated Chowdhary community, lives in Vijaywada (Andhra Pradesh) and specializes in Telengana foods. Her family eats meat, but she always includes a selection from her vast repertoire of local vegetarian dishes. For all her meals, she likes to include a savoury and a sweet as well.

Serve this dal with a rice dish, a vegetable dish and perhaps S. Sampoorna's Simple Seasoned Yoghurt, Telengana Style (see page 288).

SERVES 4

200 g/7 oz plain toovar dal, picked over and washed in several changes of water
60 g/2 oz spinach, finely chopped
60 g/2 oz sorrel, finely chopped
1 medium tomato, peeled and chopped
1 tablespoon peeled and finely chopped onion
½ teaspoon ground turmeric
1–3 fresh hot green chillies, each slit in half lengthways
1 teaspoon salt
½ teaspoon tamarind concentrate (sold in bottles)
½ teaspoon nice red chilli powder

For the tarka
3 tablespoons olive or peanut oil
generous pinch of ground asafoetida
½ teaspoon whole brown mustard seeds
1–2 dried hot red chillies
3 cloves garlic, peeled and lightly crushed
8–10 fresh curry leaves, lightly crushed in your hand

Soak the toovar dal in a generous covering of water for about 1 hour. Drain.

Put the dal in a heavy-based pan, add 900 ml/1½ pints water and bring to the boil on a medium-high heat. Skim the froth off the surface, then add the spinach, sorrel, tomato, onion, turmeric and green chillies. Stir, then cover partially and cook gently for 40 minutes. Add the salt, the tamarind concentrate and chilli powder. Stir and taste to check the balance of flavours. Keep cooking, partially covered on a low heat, for another 15 minutes, stirring now and again.

Put the oil in a small frying pan and set over a medium-high heat. When hot, add the asafoetida, then the mustard seeds. As soon as the seeds start to pop, a matter of seconds, throw in the red chillies. They will darken quickly. Add the garlic and brown lightly on both sides. Quickly stir in the curry leaves (take care as they will splutter), then tip the contents of the pan over the top of the dal. Cover to entrap the aromas. Stir before serving.

Sanjeeda Shareef's
Hyderabadi 'Sour' Dal *Khatti Dal*

Southern Indian dals tend to be hot and sour. When Muslim Moghul governors were sent south from Delhi to conquer and eventually rule the Hyderabad area in the 17th and 18th centuries, they succumbed to the local flavours and seasonings they found there, and slowly incorporated them into their own foods. (One thing that Muslims never took to in all of India, from Kashmir in the north to Kerala in the south, was asafoetida. They used garlic instead!) Sour foods stimulate the appetite in hot climates, as do very spicy ones. That may well be the explanation. Perhaps these northerners just liked the taste. At any rate, what is now called Hyderabadi cuisine includes many sour and fiery dishes like this dal, which is always served, southern-style, with rice. You can serve a yoghurt relish and perhaps the Spinach with Dill (see page 105) on the side.

In the India of today, this entire dish is made in a pressure-cooker and, when done, given a final tarka (see page 11). I am assuming that most people in the West do not have a pressure-cooker, so I have used an ordinary saucepan.

SERVES 4–5

200g/7 oz plain toovar dal, picked over and washed in several changes of water

¼ teaspoon ground turmeric

1 teaspoon salt

1–2 fresh hot green chillies, cut crossways into thin slices

10–12 fresh curry leaves, lightly crushed in your hand

2–3 tablespoons chopped fresh coriander

¼ teaspoon nice red chilli powder

1 teaspoon peeled and finely grated fresh ginger

7 cloves garlic, peeled, 1 crushed, 6 small ones left whole

2 good-sized tomatoes, peeled and finely chopped

¾–1 teaspoon tamarind concentrate (sold in bottles)

2 tablespoons olive or peanut oil

¼ teaspoon whole brown mustard seeds

½ teaspoon whole cumin seeds

3 dried hot red chillies

Put the dal in a bowl with a generous covering of water and leave to soak for 30 minutes. Drain.

Tip the dal into a heavy-based pan, add 750 ml/1¼ pints water and bring to the boil. Skim off the froth that rises to the surface, then stir in the turmeric. Cover partially and cook for 30–40 minutes, or until tender. Mash the dal coarsely with a potato masher. Add the salt, green chillies, curry leaves, fresh coriander, chilli powder, ginger, the crushed garlic, tomatoes, tamarind concentrate and 120 ml/4 fl oz water. Stir and bring to the boil, then cover and simmer gently for 15–20 minutes.

Put the oil in a very small pan and set over a medium-high heat. When hot, add the mustard seeds. As soon as they pop, a matter of seconds, add the cumin seeds and, 5 seconds later, the 6 whole garlic cloves and the red chillies. As soon as the garlic browns lightly, tip the contents of the pan over as much of the surface of the dal as you can. Cover to entrap the aromas. Stir before serving.

South Indian Dal with Vegetables
Sambar

A well-made sambar is one of the glories of South India. It is actually just a humble dal that is eaten daily with all manner of dosas (pancakes), idlis (steamed cakes) and plain rice. Generally, it has a fairly thin, soupy texture, though you can make it thicker if you prefer. Its daily variation comes from the addition of different vegetables, which changes its taste. Gourds and squashes are particularly popular, but whole small shallots, the New World chayote (sayote or chow chow), green beans, okra, peas, aubergine and radishes can also be used. Many of these vegetables will need to be pre-boiled first in lightly salted water with the addition of a tiny bit of tamarind concentrate. Okra is better if it is lightly sautéed and then pre-boiled.

A good sambar needs a good sambar spice mix or sambar masala. You do not need to make it yourself because many good brands are available in the market. Look for a good south Indian one, such as the MTR brand, in an Indian grocery.

Think of the sambar as a vegetable stew. I often serve it in soup plates and pass around plain rice, chutneys and a yoghurt relish (a south Indian pachadi would be ideal) to round off this main course. Sambar is always served with south Indian pancakes, such as plain dosas (see page 224). You can also serve it with the other pancakes in this book, or with plain rice or any of the upmas.

SERVES 4

130 g/4½ oz plain toovar dal, picked
    over and washed in several
    changes of water
¼ teaspoon ground turmeric
scant 3 tablespoons olive or
    peanut oil
½ medium onion, peeled and
    chopped into 1 cm/½ inch dice
salt
1 medium tomato, peeled and
    finely chopped
1 teaspoon tamarind concentrate
½ small yellow squash, cut into
    1 cm/½ inch dice
15 green beans, cut crossways into
    1 cm/½ inch pieces
1 teaspoon rice flour (also called
    powdered rice) mixed with
    1 tablespoon water
2 teaspoons sambar powder,
    or to taste
¼ teaspoon ground asafoetida
¼ teaspoon whole brown
    mustard seeds
¼ teaspoon whole fenugreek seeds
1–2 dried hot red chillies, broken in
    half, or 1–2 fresh hot green
    chillies, slit in half lengthways
10–15 fresh curry leaves, lightly
    crushed in your hand
2 tablespoons chopped fresh
    coriander

Put the dal in a bowl with a generous covering of water and leave to soak for 30 minutes. Drain.

Tip the dal into a heavy-based pan, add 750 ml/1¼ pints water and bring to the boil. Skim off the froth that rises to the surface, then stir in the turmeric. Cover partially, lower the heat and cook very gently for 50 minutes, or until tender.

Meanwhile, put 1 teaspoon of oil in a smallish pan and set over a medium heat. When hot, add the diced onion and cook for about 3 minutes, or until almost translucent. Do not let it brown.

Add 250 ml/8 fl oz water, ¼ teaspoon salt, the tomato and the tamarind concentrate. Stir, cover and cook over a low heat for 20 minutes.

Add the squash and beans and bring to a simmer again. Cover and cook over a low heat for 6–7 minutes, or until the vegetables are tender.

Once the dal is cooked, mash it well, using a potato masher. Stir in ½ teaspoon salt, the rice flour mixture and the sambar powder (start with 1 teaspoon, adding more as needed). Mix well. Add the vegetable mixture, stir and check for salt. Thin out the sambar with about 120 ml/4 fl oz hot water. You can add more if you wish.

Put 2 tablespoons of the oil in a small frying pan and set over a medium-high heat. When hot, add the asafoetida and, a second later, the mustard seeds. As soon as the seeds pop, a matter of seconds, add the fenugreek seeds and the chillies. Stir once, then throw in the curry leaves (take care as they will splutter). Pour the spices and oil over the sambar. Stir to mix, then scatter fresh coriander over the top.

From Dell' Arte Inde

Soya Bean Granules with Potatoes
Mock Keema Aloo

First of all, what kind of a name is Dell' Arte Inde? Well, it is a Frenchified and made-up name for a jewellery shop in my favourite hotel, the Taj Mahal Palace in Bombay. The Dell' stands for Delhi, where the family started its jewellery business many decades ago. When I embarked on this cookery book, I was very curious to know what various groups of people in India ate and to learn more about their eating habits. India is not a homogeneous country at all. The Taj hotel's many shops were a good place to start.

There are three brothers who run the Dell' Arte jewellery business today: Rohit, Kapil and Yogesh. They are Punjabi Hindus and all live together as a joint family. They are strict vegetarians.

The brothers arrive at the shop at different times: Kapil and Yogesh, the younger two, arrive at 8.30 and 9am, while Rohit comes at 11am for a long day of work. Lunch is anywhere between 1.30 and 4pm, depending upon work. Lunch for 30, the brothers and all the employees, comes from home. It is cooked by the wives, with the help of a Maharashtrian maid, who helps skew the seasonings in a westerly direction.

The lunch for the brothers is packed in dabbas, lunch boxes with compartments. The boxes are then put inside a checkered and very large, insulated plastic carrying case. Lunchtime is declared at around 2pm. A display case, the one with a mirror for viewing how glittering jewels look on delicate ears and necks, is cleared and a tablecloth spread on top. There is already a banquette near it. More chairs are added. The checkered plastic case is emptied. Plates, cutlery and then all the food comes dribbling out. Normally, there is one dal (we have chickpeas), one vegetable (okra), one paneer dish (scrambled paneer), and a big stack of chapatis. Today, because I am there, we have an extra dish, this keema (mock minced meat) made with soya bean granules. This recipe comes from Sarita, Rohit's wife.

All Indian grocers sell small soya bean granules. They are sometimes labelled 'soy vadis'. This dish may be served with rice or chapatis or naans, a vegetable such as okra or cauliflower, some yoghurt dish and a chutney or salad. You could also have it with just rice and a green salad.

SERVES 4

115 g/4 oz soya bean granules

4 tablespoons olive or peanut oil

2 potatoes (340 g/12 oz in all), peeled and cut into 2.5 cm/ 1 inch chunks

salt and freshly ground black pepper

generous pinch of ground asafoetida

1 onion (200 g/7 oz), peeled and chopped

2 tomatoes (about 340 g/12 oz in all), peeled and finely chopped

2.5 cm/1 inch piece of fresh ginger, peeled and very finely grated

3 cloves garlic, peeled and crushed

¼ teaspoon ground turmeric

¼–1 teaspoon nice red chilli powder

1 teaspoon ground coriander

1 teaspoon garam masala

3 tablespoons chopped fresh coriander

Soak the soya granules in 250 ml/8 fl oz hot water for 5 minutes. Drain, saving the soaking water.

Put the oil into a 25 cm/10 inch, preferably non-stick frying pan and set over a medium-high heat. When hot, add the potatoes and fry until golden brown on all sides. They do not have to cook through. Lift them out with a slotted spoon and spread them on a plate lined with kitchen paper. Sprinkle lightly with salt and pepper.

Remove all but 2 tablespoons of the oil from the pan. Still over a medium-high heat, add the asafoetida and then the onion. Stir and fry the onion for 7–8 minutes, or until it browns at the edges. Add the tomatoes and ½ teaspoon salt. Stir rapidly for 5–6 minutes, or until the tomatoes are dark and soft.

Add the ginger and garlic, stirring for 2–3 minutes. Reduce the heat to medium-low and stir in the turmeric, chilli powder and coriander. Now add the soaked soya granules, the soaking liquid plus enough water to make 300 ml/10 fl oz, the potatoes, and another ½ teaspoon salt. Bring to a simmer. Cover and cook over a low heat for about 15 minutes, stirring now and then.

Before serving, sprinkle the garam masala and fresh coriander over the top and stir to mix.

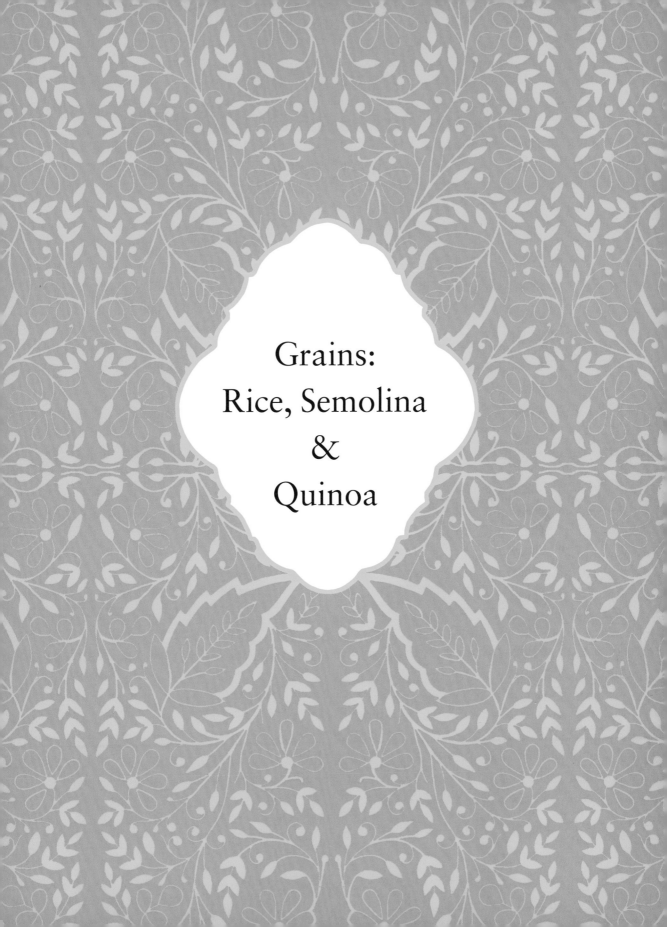

Grains:
Rice, Semolina
&
Quinoa

Plain Basmati Rice
Saaday Basmati Chawal

SERVES 4

a 475 ml/16 fl oz measure
of basmati rice

Here is the easiest way for you to cook basmati rice. Salt is generally not added as the rice is meant to be eaten with well-seasoned food.

Wash the rice in several changes of water. Drain and put in a bowl. Cover generously with water and leave to soak for 30 minutes. Drain thoroughly.

Preheat the oven to 160°C/gas mark 3.

Bring 650 ml/22 fl oz water to the boil in a heavy, ovenproof pan with a tight-fitting lid. Add the rice, stir and bring back to the boil. Cover tightly (using a layer of foil between the lid and the pan and crinkling the edges, if needed to get a tight seal) and place in the oven for 30 minutes. Remove and let the rice sit, undisturbed, for 10 minutes. Fluff up the grains with a fork and serve.

Plain Jasmine Rice
Saadi Jasmine Rice

SERVES 4–5

a 350 ml/12 fl oz measure
of jasmine rice

Put 500 ml/18 fl oz water in a pan and bring to the boil. Add the rice, stir and bring back to the boil. Cover tightly and cook over a very low heat for 25 minutes. Leave covered until you are ready to eat.

Rice with Dill & Peas
Sooa aur Matar ki Tahiri

I make this rice dish quite frequently when I have guests for dinner (and I so enjoy eating it the next day if any is left). It is aromatic and satisfyingly delicious. I like to serve it with Chana Dal with Spinach & Tomato and Carrot Raita (see pages 120 and 293). For a party, I add Green Beans with Potatoes (see page 65).

SERVES 4–6

a 475 ml/16 fl oz measure
   of basmati rice
3 tablespoons olive or peanut oil
1 medium onion, peeled and cut
   into fine half-rings
1 teaspoon garam masala
30 g/1 oz fresh dill, feathery leaves
   and fine stems only, finely chopped
1 teaspoon salt
130 g/4½ oz fresh or frozen peas,
   cooked and drained

Wash the rice in several changes of water. Drain and put in a bowl. Cover generously with water and leave to soak for 30 minutes. Drain and leave in a strainer set over a bowl.

Preheat the oven to 160°C/gas mark 3.

Put the oil in a heavy ovenproof pan and set over a medium-high heat. When hot, add the onion and cook for 7–8 minutes, until reddish-brown. Add the rice, garam masala, dill and salt and reduce the heat to medium. Stir very gently to mix, lifting the rice from the bottom and turning it over as you would if mixing a soufflé. The tender rice grains break easily at this stage. When well mixed, pour in 650 ml/22 fl oz water and bring to the boil.

Cover tightly with foil and a lid and put in the oven for 25 minutes. Quickly tip the drained peas on top of the rice, re-cover with the foil and the lid and return the pan to the oven for another 5 minutes.

Set the pan of rice aside and leave undisturbed for 10 minutes. Fluff up the grains with a fork and serve. If you wish to hold the rice for an hour, cover the pan with heavy towels.

Sanjeeda Shareef's

Spiced Hyderabadi Rice
Baghare Chaval

A lovely, well-flavoured rice dish, this is what is served with Hyderabad's famous 'dalcha', a dish of toovar dal, squash and meat. The vegetarian version, Chana Dal with Yellow Squash, Chayote or Doodhi, is on page 122. For more on Hyderabadi Muslim food, see the introduction to Tomato Kut on page 252.

This dish is usually made with basmati rice for special occasions, but with the more ordinary sona masoori, a smaller grained rice, for everyday meals. Here I have made it with basmati rice. If you wish to use the sona masoori rice, follow this recipe but increase the cooking water to 750 ml/1¼ pints.

SERVES 4–6

a 475 ml/16 fl oz measure of
   basmati rice
3 tablespoons olive or peanut oil
4 tablespoons peeled and finely
   sliced shallots
5 cm/2 inch cinnamon stick
4 cloves
4 cardamom pods
¼ teaspoon black cumin seeds
   (use ordinary cumin as a substitute)
1 large clove garlic, peeled
   and crushed
1 teaspoon peeled and finely
   grated fresh ginger
1 teaspoon salt
1–2 fresh hot green chillies,
   slit in half lengthways

Wash the rice in several changes of water. Drain and put in a bowl. Cover generously with water and leave to soak for 30 minutes. Drain and leave in a strainer set over a bowl.

Preheat the oven to 160°C/gas mark 3.

Put the oil in a heavy ovenproof pan and set over a medium-high heat. When hot, add the shallots, cinnamon, cloves, cardamom and cumin seeds. Stir as you let the shallots turn slightly brown. Add the garlic and ginger and stir for about a minute, or until golden. Pour in 650 ml/22 fl oz water and bring to the boil. Add the rice, salt and green chillies. Stir and bring to the boil, then cover tightly with foil and a lid.

Put the pan in the oven for 30 minutes. Remove and let the rice sit undisturbed for 10 minutes. Fluff up the grains with a fork and serve.

Lemon Rice
Nimmakaya Pulihora

A light, summery rice dish that can be served with vegetables, dal and relishes, and also by itself as a snack. This one most resembles Chinese stir-fried rice, except that all the ingredients are Indian.

SERVES 4

1½ tablespoons olive or peanut oil
¼ teaspoon whole brown
   mustard seeds
¼ teaspoon whole cumin seeds
2 tablespoons raw skinless peanuts
1 teaspoon chana dal
7–8 fresh curry leaves (use basil
   leaves as an alternative)
1 teaspoon peeled and very finely
   chopped fresh ginger
1–2 fresh hot green chillies,
   finely chopped
½ teaspoon ground turmeric
1 teaspoon salt
1 quantity freshly made Plain
   Jasmine Rice (see page 156)
finely grated rind from 1 lemon
1 tablespoon lemon juice

Put the oil in a non-stick, medium frying pan and set over a medium heat. When hot, add the mustard seeds. As soon as they pop, a matter of seconds, add the cumin seeds and let them sizzle for a few seconds. Stir in the peanuts and chana dal, and as soon as the nuts begin to take on a golden colour, add the curry leaves (take care as these will splutter), ginger and green chillies. Stir a few times and turn the heat to low. Add the turmeric and salt, stir once, then add all the cooked rice, the lemon rind and juice. Break up all the rice lumps with the back of a wooden spoon and mix gently but thoroughly as you reheat the mixture. Serve hot.

Tomato Rice
Thakkali Sadam or *Tomato Annam*

Rice with lime or lemon, rice with tamarind, rice with yoghurt and rice with tomatoes are all very popular throughout south India. These dishes have some things in common. Plain, unseasoned rice is cooked ahead of the meal. It is then spread out in a thali (metal platter) and seasoned, sauced and well mixed. The sauce is generally sour and spicy. Because the temperature in the south is generally balmy, there is little danger of the rice getting icy cold as there is in northern India. These mixed rices are always served at room temperature.

So what do we, who live in the West, do in our colder climes? I have worked out my own way of serving them. I make my rice so it is ready just before we eat. I make my sauce ahead of time too, if that is possible. As we are getting ready to eat, I heat up the sauce, pour it over the rice in its pan and mix it in. This way the rice may not be hot but it is still warm.

Serve at mealtimes with a dal, vegetables and relishes. See the introduction to Cabbage Fritters (page 23) to get a sense of a meal it could be served with.

SERVES 4

1½ tablespoons olive or peanut oil

8 raw cashews, split lengthways into their natural halves

1 tablespoon raw peanuts

generous pinch of ground asafoetida

1 teaspoon urad dal

½ teaspoon whole brown mustard seeds

1 teaspoon peeled and very finely chopped fresh ginger

6–7 fresh curry leaves, lightly crushed in your hand

175 ml/6 fl oz tomato passata

2 or more fresh hot green chillies, finely chopped

¼ teaspoon ground turmeric

¾ teaspoon salt, or more as needed

1 quantity Plain Jasmine Rice (see page 156)

Pictured on pages 162–163

Put the oil in a small pan and set over a medium heat. When hot, add the cashews and peanuts. Stir and fry them until they are golden. Remove with a slotted spoon and spread them out on kitchen paper to drain.

Add the asafoetida to the empty pan, and a second later, add the dal. As soon as the dal starts to take on colour, add the mustard seeds. As soon as the seeds pop, a matter of seconds, add the ginger and then the curry leaves (take care as they will splutter). Stir once, then pour in the tomato passata and 120 ml/4 fl oz water. Add the chillies, turmeric, salt and nuts. Stir and bring to a simmer, then cover and simmer gently for 10 minutes.

Your rice should be ready around the same time as you are getting ready to eat. Heat up the sauce and pour it over the rice, which should still be in its pan. Mix gently but thoroughly, then serve.

Rice with Moong Dal & Potato
Khili Khichri

I make this dish often, as it is both comforting and delicious. Sometimes I add tiny onions, browned slowly in a little oil, to the rice at about the same time as I add the water. This dish can be served with aubergine, greens, dals and all manner of relishes. You could also have it by itself with a salad.

SERVES 4–6

50 g/1¾ oz moong dal
   (skinned and split mung beans)
a 475 ml/16 fl oz measure
   of basmati rice
3 tablespoons olive or peanut oil
   or ghee (clarified butter)
½ teaspoon whole cumin seeds
1 medium waxy potato, peeled
   and cut into 1 cm/½ inch dice
   (red potatoes work well)
1 teaspoon peeled and very finely
   diced fresh ginger
1 teaspoon garam masala
2 teaspoons ground coriander
1 teaspoon salt
¼ teaspoon nice red chilli powder
½ teaspoon ground turmeric

Wash the dal in several changes of water, then leave to soak for 3 hours. Drain.

Wash the rice in several changes of water and leave to soak for 30 minutes. Drain.

Put the oil or ghee in a heavy pan with a tight-fitting lid and set over a medium-high heat. When hot, add the cumin seeds and, 10 seconds later, the potato. Stir and fry until the potato is lightly browned. Add the ginger and stir a few times, then reduce the heat to medium. Now add the rice, dal, garam masala, coriander, salt, chilli powder and turmeric. Sauté gently for 2–3 minutes, always lifting the rice from the bottom to avoid breaking the grains.

Add 650 ml/22 fl oz water and bring to the boil. Cover tightly and cook over a very low heat for 25 minutes.

From the Britannia & Company
Restaurant in Bombay
Berry Pilaf *Berry Pulav*

The restaurant where this pilaf is served has been in existence
since 1923. It is a Bombay (Mumbai) landmark. The original
owner, a Zoroastrian called Rashid Kohinoor, came from Iran
and started out serving Iranian dishes. His son, Boman, married
a Parsi, an Indian Zoroastrian, and she added many local Parsi
dishes to the menu. A third generation heads the kitchen today.

It was Boman, 90 years old, who took us to our seats and
offered us a fresh lime soda on a very hot day. 'As they say, it
will "bit the hit" [beat the heat]' – one Indian with an accent
mocking other Indians with worse accents. Indians do that all
the time. He laughs boisterously. He jokes around and is full
of stories. I ask him for the berry pilaf recipe. He laughs again
and tells us that the British Ambassador (he probably meant
the American Ambassador) once asked him for the same recipe
and he answered, 'If you give me the recipe for Coca-Cola,
I will hand over the recipe for berry pilaf.' I never did get the
Persian–Indian recipe from him, so I have created my own
version, and without the chicken meatballs they add to it. At
the restaurant this pilaf, called Chicken Berry Pulav, is served
with meats, but I have left those out. I do not recommend this
restaurant to vegetarians. Just use this recipe to make my
aromatic, yellow and white vegetarian version of their great,
signature dish.

The berry used here is the tiny Iranian barberry or zareshk,
sold by Indian and Persian grocers. If you cannot find it, use
dried cranberries. The final flavours are sweet and sour. As
there is expensive saffron in it as well, I often make this pilaf
for a dinner party. I find that it goes very well with aubergine,
spinach and paneer dishes.

SERVES 4–6

a 475 ml/16 fl oz measure of best-
quality basmati rice from India
1 teaspoon saffron threads
3 tablespoons sugar
3 tablespoons very hot milk
about 30 g/1 oz barberries or
dried cranberries
3 tablespoons olive or peanut oil
1 large onion, peeled and cut
in half lengthways, then
into fine half-rings
1½ tablespoons salt
5 cardamom pods
4 cm/2 ½ inch cinnamon stick
1 bay leaf
3 cloves
3 tablespoons melted butter

Pictured on pages 166–167

Wash the rice in several changes of water. Put in a bowl, cover generously with water and set aside to soak for 3 hours.

Combine the saffron and 1 tablespoon of the sugar in a mortar and pound together so you have a powder. Put in a small bowl. Add the hot milk, stir, then set aside for 3 hours.

Rinse the berries a few times and leave to soak for 20 minutes. Drain and pat dry.

Put the oil in a medium frying pan and set over a medium-high heat. When hot, add the onion and cook for 5 minutes, or until it starts to brown. Reduce the heat to medium-low and continue cooking until it is reddish-brown. Add the drained berries and the remaining 2 tablespoons sugar. Stir once or twice, then remove from the heat.

Preheat the oven to 160°C/gas mark 3.

Bring about 2.5 litres/4½ pints water to a rolling boil. Add the salt, cardamom, cinnamon, bay leaf and cloves. Stir once and add the rice. Let it cook in the boiling water for about 5½ minutes, or until it is three-quarters cooked but still has a thin, hard core. Drain in a colander.

Working quickly now, spread 1 tablespoon of the melted butter in a medium ovenproof pan. Spread half the rice over it. Spread another tablespoon of the butter, plus half the saffron mixture and half the onion-berry mixture and some of its oil on top of the rice. Spread the remaining rice on top of the first layer. Pour the remaining tablespoon of butter over it, followed by the remaining saffron mixture and onion-berry mixture. Cover tightly with foil and a lid and bake in the oven for 30 minutes.

Remove and let the pan sit undisturbed for 10 minutes. Toss the rice gently to mix before serving.

Rice with Aubergine
Vangi Bhaat

This is a great dish for entertaining. The recipe can easily be doubled, if needed. Add a dal, a green vegetable, chutneys and a yoghurt relish. When this dish is made in western India, the aubergines tend to be quite spicy. They mellow a bit when mixed with the plain rice. You can make your own decision about the spiciness, adding as much chilli powder as you like.

If you cannot find an aubergine of the weight you want, use two smaller or narrower ones, or use part of a large one. The usable pieces should weigh about 340 g/12 oz.

SERVES 4

1 quantity Plain Jasmine Rice (see page 156), but add 1 teaspoon salt to the cooking water

1 medium aubergine (340 g/12 oz), cut into 4 x 5 cm/1½ x 2 inch chunks

3 tablespoons olive or peanut oil

½ teaspoon urad dal

5 cm/2 inch cinnamon stick

½ teaspoon whole brown mustard seeds

2 dried hot red chillies

6–8 fresh curry leaves, lightly crushed in your hand

1 onion (155 g/5½ oz), cut into 1 cm/½ inch dice

¾–1 teaspoon salt (start with the smaller amount)

2 teaspoons ground coriander

1 teaspoon ground cumin

½ teaspoon ground turmeric

¼ teaspoon nice red chilli powder, or to taste

1 tablespoon lemon juice

4 tablespoons tomato passata

2–3 tablespoons chopped fresh coriander

While the rice is cooking, soak the aubergine chunks in a large bowl of water.

Put the oil in a medium, non-stick frying pan and set over a medium heat. When hot, add the urad dal and cinnamon stick. Stir until the dal starts to take on colour, a few seconds. Add the mustard seeds and red chillies. Stir until the seeds pop and the chillies darken, a few seconds. Quickly add the curry leaves (take care as they will splutter), followed immediately by the diced onion. Stir and fry for 1 minute.

Drain the aubergine and add the chunks to the pan along with the salt. Stir and fry for about 10 minutes, or until the pieces look slightly glazed. Turn the heat to low and sprinkle in the ground coriander, cumin, turmeric and chilli powder. Cook, stirring, for 2 minutes.

Add the lemon juice, tomato passata and about 120 ml/ 4 fl oz water. Stir and bring to a simmer, then cover and cook on a very low heat for 20 minutes, stirring gently from the bottom now and then. Check the salt, adding more if needed.

Just before serving, spread the hot rice on a large, warmed platter, breaking up any lumps with the back of a spoon. Empty the aubergine and its juices over the top and mix gently, being careful not to break the aubergine chunks. Sprinkle the fresh coriander over the top.

Vegetable Biryani with Cauliflower, Carrot & Peas

Gobi, Gajar aur Matar ki Biryani

Biryanis are generally complicated affairs: you partially cook the rice, you partially cook the vegetables, you brown onions by themselves, and then you layer the three in a pan and let them bake together. In my effort to simplify the dish for this book, what I have done is to cook the rice by itself, then quickly stir-fry the vegetables with onions, and then put everything together in a large, warmed platter or serving bowl. Biryanis are generally served with a yoghurt relish and a salad, but you could add a dal, such as the Black-eyed Peas with Fresh Coriander & Green Chillies (see page 116).

I like to remove the large spices, such as the bay leaf, cardamom pods, cloves and cinnamon, from the rice before mixing it with the vegetables. (No one does this in India as we know they are not meant for eating. We just gently push them aside on the plate.)

Here is my timetable for making the dish: I first wash the rice and set it to soak. While it is soaking, I chop up everything needed to make the vegetables. Then I cook the rice. While it is in the oven, I cook the vegetables. If I am eating immediately, I warm up a large serving bowl and empty the rice into it, gently breaking up any lumps. I empty the vegetables on top of it and mix gently but thoroughly. If I am eating much later, I wrap the pan of rice in a heavy towel and set it aside. It will stay hot for 2 hours. If it has cooled off too much, I reheat it in the oven for 20 minutes or so. The vegetables are left in the pan and they warm up easily over a low heat. Then I mix the two together.

Continued overleaf

SERVES 4–6

a 475 ml/16 fl oz measure of
  basmati rice
2 tablespoons olive or peanut
  oil or ghee (clarified butter),
  or a combination of the two
5 cm/2 inch cinnamon stick
1–2 bay leaves
4–5 cloves
4–5 cardamom pods
¼ teaspoon whole black cumin
  seeds (use ordinary cumin seeds
  if you do not have them)
12 cashews, split in half lengthways
2 tablespoons sultanas
½ medium onion, peeled and
  cut into fine half-rings
1½ teaspoons salt

For the vegetables
2 tablespoons olive or peanut oil
  or ghee (clarified butter),
  or a combination of the two
¼ teaspoon whole cumin seeds
½ medium onion, peeled and cut
  into fine half-rings
2 teaspoons peeled and finely
  grated fresh ginger
180 g/6 oz small cauliflower florets,
  about 1 cm/½ inch wide and
  2.5 cm/1 inch long, well washed
  and drained
1 medium carrot, peeled and diced
  to the size of peas
¼ teaspoon ground turmeric
¼–½ teaspoon nice red chilli powder
180 g/6 oz cooked fresh peas,
  or defrosted frozen peas
2–4 fresh hot green chillies,
  finely chopped
¾ teaspoon salt
freshly ground black pepper
½ teaspoon garam masala
1 tablespoon lime or lemon juice

Wash the rice in several changes of water. Place the rice in a bowl, cover generously with water and leave to soak for 30 minutes. Drain.

Preheat the oven to 160°C/gas mark 3.

Put the oil for the rice in a heavy, ovenproof pan with a well-fitting lid and set over a medium heat. When hot, add the cinnamon stick, bay leaves, cloves, cardamom pods and cumin seeds. Stir for a few seconds, then add the cashews. As soon as they are golden, add the sultanas. They will plump up immediately. Quickly add the onion and fry until reddish. Add 650 ml/22 fl oz water and the salt. Stir and bring to the boil, then cover tightly with foil and a lid. Place in the oven for 25 minutes.

Meanwhile, make the vegetables. Put the oil into a medium, preferably non-stick frying pan and set over a medium-high heat. When hot, add the cumin seeds and let them sizzle for a few seconds. Add the onion, ginger, cauliflower, carrot, turmeric and chilli powder. Stir gently for about 3–4 minutes, still over a medium-high heat, until the onion and cauliflower are lightly browned.

Reduce the heat to medium-low and add the peas, green chillies, salt, black pepper, garam masala and lime juice. Stir gently and cook for another 3–5 minutes, or until the vegetables are just done.

Take the rice out of the oven when it is ready and let it sit for 10 minutes. After that, empty it into a warmed bowl and break up any lumps without breaking the grains. Add all the ingredients from the frying pan and mix gently but thoroughly. Serve immediately.

A Note on Upma, Poha & Sooji

Upma

The Western world has no real equivalent to upma. It is somewhat like a risotto, except that it is not as dense and heavy, and not so wet and molten either. It is perhaps more like Chinese fried rice, except that it is a little wet and tends to collect in small clumps. Upma is, in the last analysis, deliciously itself. It is light and easy to prepare and often thrown together quickly as breakfast, a light lunch or a snack. It tends to be spicy – very spicy if you like it that way. The basic ingredient is always a grain. Vegetables and spices are added to it for nutrition and flavouring.

The grains that are most commonly used to make upma are sooji and poha, discussed below. Both are ingredients worth having in your pantry on a continuous basis as they can help you to turn out extraordinarily tasty, nutritious meals very quickly. Upmas can also be made with bread (I have one made with wholemeal bread in this book) and quinoa (you will find that here as well).

Flattened Rice (Poha)

A friend of mine in Bombay, Vikram Doctor, who has a vast knowledge of Indian food, was wondering with me why it was that other countries with ancient histories of rice culture do not have any version of flattened rice. Some have puffed rice, another 'instant' version suitable for a quick meal, but no one, to my knowledge, has the much-loved Indian poha.

Also called phov, cheewra, chivra, chuda and aval, it is used with great frequency in the rice-growing regions of eastern, western and southern India as a breakfast and snack food. Travellers in ancient times carried a bag of it, reconstituting it with water whenever they were hungry, and perhaps accompanying it with a chutney or pickle, or soaking it in milk, like a cereal.

Today large quantities of poha are made in factories, but if you go to Indian villages with rice fields, you can still see poha being made the old-fashioned way. Actually, villages seem to have their own individual techniques. In one tribal village in Jharkhand (south of Bihar) the rice grains are put into vats with a little water for steaming/parboiling. This ancient process pushes the goodness of the hull and husk right into the heart of each grain. Then the grains are roasted rather casually, in a broken section of a rounded terracotta pot set on top of a small wood fire. The grains then go into a large mortar, and two women holding a long, pole-like pestle pound rhythmically to flatten it. After the rice is flattened and the husk and hull winnowed away, what you have is poha. Here it is not cooked any further, but eaten as it is with milk and sweetened with jaggery, a form of raw lump sugar. Further north it is eaten with sweetened yoghurt, or crisped up and eaten at breakfast with Peas & Potatoes Cooked in a Bihari Style (see page 97).

The coastal Konkan region of western India produces a very nutritious red rice that is partially milled and also made into poha. It is put into hot milky tea in the mornings to give extra energy to workers going to the fields and to children going to school.

Poha is used in many religious ceremonies as well. One requirement in Baroda (Gujarat) is that it be made fresh just before it can be put into poha kheer, a pudding served as holy food at the Ram Temple after the Ram Navami prayers to celebrate Ram's birthday. In Baroda the rice grains are soaked for three days, drained thoroughly, roasted in a large cast-iron karhai (wok), pounded to the desired thickness in a mortar, then winnowed and dried.

But the poha dishes that I like best and crave constantly are the western and southern Indian ones that require the poha to be partly reconstituted and stir-fried quickly with spices and vegetables to make the wonderful risotto-like dish called upma. It cooks very easily and everyone loves it. Friendly ingredients for mixing with it include onions, potatoes, corn, tomatoes, cauliflower, peas and mung beansprouts. Poha may be also added to puddings and yoghurt dishes. It is always added to that wonderful mélange of spicy nuts and seeds sold as Bombay Mix. It is light, nutritious and very digestible, a good

version of rice to know about and to have in your pantry.

In India, three thicknesses of poha are generally available, but I have used only what is sold as 'thick' poha. It needs to be rinsed and soaked (each recipe in this book gives the necessary instructions).

For reheating the poha upmas in this section, sprinkle generously with water and place over a very low heat. Toss gently, using a flat spatula to fold the poha over from the bottom, rather like you might mix a soufflé, so the delicate grains do not get broken.

I had quite a revelatory experience recently. My husband and I were going to stay with a friend on an island off the coast of Maine. And since I seem to cook wherever I go and not much is available in the small island market, I was taking with me, among other things, all the ingredients to make a poha dish. It would be quick and easy. As I unpacked the mustard seeds, cumin seeds, chillies, potatoes, limes and onions, I realized that I had left the poha behind. It had taken us nine hours to drive up there, plus a boat ride, so there was no going back. I thought of substitutes – semolina, bulgar, farina – nothing was available. My friends did have quinoa, though, and it worked so well that I have developed a recipe for it – cooked in the poha upma style!

Sooji (Indian semolina)

Sooji is not really a true semolina. Real semolina, the kind used for Italian pasta, is a granular flour made from hard durum wheat. Indian sooji is made from soft wheat, using the same method that is used for making true semolina. However, many Indian stores call it semolina, so do not let yourself get confused.

Buy from an Indian grocer and ask for 'sooji/farina'. Don't get the fine grind, if that is what the label says. Also, do not get roasted semolina, as you should roast it yourself (the process takes just a few minutes). A packet simply labelled 'sooji' will be fine. You can tell your grocer that you want it to make upma (the 'u' being pronounced like the 'ou' in 'could'). In south India, sooji is called 'rava', which just means any granular flour. If you find yourself with a southern grocer, first try asking for 'sooji/farina'. If he does not respond (I am sure he will), try asking for 'wheat rava'.

Indian semolina behaves rather like polenta, but cooks much faster and ends up with a much lighter, fluffier texture.

A simple dish of it can be prepared in less than 15 minutes, which makes it a very popular breakfast food and makes sooji a wonderful ingredient to have on hand. For breakfast, many Indians much prefer to eat their sooji/farina in a fluffy and savoury form, not a sweet one. As one south Indian friend said to me, 'We don't like our breakfasts to be sweet. We like them hot and spicy.' Indeed, in India many Western breakfast companies have been selling instant cooking cereals filled with Indian spices and no sugar!

Sooji upmas can be served as breakfast, lunch and dinner as well. In some north Indian cities, sooji is made into rich halvas, with lots of ghee and sugar (see Sooji Halva, page 329). These are eaten for breakfast on special occasions with Fried Puffed Breads (see page 206).

A little sooji is often added to Indian foods, such as the Savoury Pastry Strips with Ajowan Seeds (see page 31), in order to make them extra crisp.

Flattened Rice with Potatoes
Phova Usli, an Upma

This is a absolutely delicious and simple breakfast or snack dish from the coastal Konkan region of western India. The texture is rice-like, but soft and much airier, and can collect in delicate lumps. I often make it for lunch and serve it with a large salad filled with lettuce, cucumbers and tomatoes. You can use one whole dried red chilli if you want the dish mild, and two (snapped in half) if you want the dish hotter. Many Indians prefer to add fiery fresh green chillies instead, one, two or three, either split in half lengthways or sliced into thin rings. Lime or lemon wedges should be served on the side.

To reheat, sprinkle with a tablespoon or two of water, put over a very low heat and cover. Toss gently now and then.

SERVES 3–4

2 medium waxy potatoes, boiled, cooled and peeled

140 g/5 oz thick poha (flattened rice)

3 tablespoons olive or peanut oil

generous pinch of ground asafoetida

½ teaspoon urad dal

½ teaspoon whole brown mustard seeds

½ teaspoon whole cumin seeds

1 dried hot red chilli (see introduction above for other options)

10–15 fresh curry leaves, lightly crushed in your hand

½ medium onion, peeled and chopped

salt

1 teaspoon sugar

2–3 tablespoons chopped fresh coriander, to garnish

4 lime or lemon wedges, to serve

Cut the potatoes into 1 cm/½ inch dice.

Put the poha into a sieve and wash gently but thoroughly under cold running water. Empty it into a bowl, cover generously with water and leave to soak for 2 minutes. Drain and leave in the sieve set over a bowl.

Put the oil into a large, non-stick frying pan and set it over a medium-high heat. When hot, add the asafoetida and the urad dal. As soon as the dal starts to pick up a little colour, add the mustard seeds, cumin seeds and the chilli (whatever type you are using). As soon as the mustard seeds start to pop, a matter of seconds, add the curry leaves (take care as they will splutter), then the onion and potatoes. Lower the heat to medium and fry, stirring now and again, until the onion and potatoes are slightly browned, 3–4 minutes. Sprinkle ¼ teaspoon salt over the top and stir.

Add the poha, gently breaking up any lumps, and sprinkle ½ teaspoon salt and the sugar over the top. Cook over a low heat for 3–4 minutes, tossing frequently by lifting all the ingredients from the bottom with a flat spatula and folding them over, until the poha is heated through. Cover and set aside until you are ready to eat.

To reheat, sprinkle with a tablespoon or two of water and warm over a very low heat. Toss gently now and then. Garnish with the fresh coriander and serve with lime or lemon wedges.

Flattened Rice with Cauliflower & Peas
Poha Upma with Cauliflower & Peas

A grand dish that looks splendid and tastes as good as it looks. Sometimes I eat this all by itself. Other dishes, such as Mixed Dal, Marwari Style (see page 141), could be added to the meal, as well as a raita, poppadoms and chutneys. For me, this is also a perfect brunch dish.

In India most people like their poha upmas to be fairly spicy, but you can use as many or as few green chillies as you like.

SERVES 4

210 g/7½ oz thick poha
(flattened rice)
3 tablespoons olive or peanut oil
generous pinch of ground asafoetida
¾ teaspoon urad dal
½ teaspoon whole brown
mustard seeds
½ teaspoon whole cumin seeds
10–15 fresh curry leaves, lightly
crushed in your hand
1 onion (about 115 g/4 oz),
peeled and chopped
2 teaspoons peeled and very
finely grated fresh ginger
180 g/6 oz very small cauliflower
florets, 1 cm/½ inch wide and
2.5 cm/1 inch long, well washed
and drained
¼ teaspoon ground turmeric
180 g/6 oz fresh cooked peas or
defrosted frozen peas
1–3 fresh hot green chillies,
finely chopped
salt
1 tablespoon lime juice

Put the poha into a sieve and wash gently but thoroughly under running water. Place in a bowl, cover generously with water and leave to soak for 2 minutes. Drain and leave in a sieve set over a bowl.

Put the oil into a large, non-stick frying pan and set it over a medium-high heat. When hot, add the asafoetida and the urad dal. As soon as the dal starts to pick up a little colour, add the mustard seeds and cumin seeds. When the mustard seeds start to pop, a matter of seconds, add the curry leaves (take care as they will splutter), then the onion, ginger, cauliflower and turmeric. Stir gently for about 3–4 minutes, still over a medium-high heat, until the onion and cauliflower are lightly browned.

Reduce the heat to medium-low and add the peas, green chillies, ½ teaspoon of salt and the lime juice. Stir gently for 1–2 minutes, always lifting the ingredients from the bottom, so the peas heat/cook through.

Add all the poha, gently breaking up any lumps. Sprinkle another ½ teaspoon of salt over it and mix gently over a very low heat for 3–4 minutes, using a flat spatula and lifting the mixture from the bottom and folding it over the rest. When the ingredients are well blended and the poha has heated through, cover and set aside until you are ready to eat.

Flattened Rice with Indian Beansprouts
Poha Upma with Indian Beansprouts

A very nutritious dish often eaten for breakfast in western India, it can also be eaten as a snack. Serve it with a yoghurt lassi or a yoghurt relish, or just plain old tea or coffee.

To reheat, sprinkle with a tablespoon or two of water, put over a very low heat and cover, tossing gently now and then.

SERVES 3–4

100 g/3½ oz thick poha
  (flattened rice)
2 tablespoons olive or peanut oil
generous pinch of ground asafoetida
½ teaspoon urad dal
1 teaspoon whole brown
  mustard seeds
10–15 fresh curry leaves, lightly
  crushed in your hand
1 medium onion, peeled
  and chopped
¼ teaspoon ground turmeric
1 teaspoon peeled and finely
  grated fresh ginger
1–3 fresh hot green chillies,
  finely chopped
115 g/4 oz Indian-style mung
  beansprouts (see page 132)
1 teaspoon salt, or to taste
lime wedges, to serve

Put the poha into a sieve and wash gently but thoroughly under running water. Empty it into a bowl, cover generously with water and leave to soak for 2 minutes. Drain and leave in a sieve set over a bowl.

Put the oil into a large, non-stick frying pan and set it over a medium-high heat. When hot, add the asafoetida and urad dal. As soon as the dal starts to pick up a little colour, add the mustard seeds. When the seeds start to pop, a matter of seconds, add the curry leaves (take care as they will splutter) and then the onion. Stir and fry for 6–7 minutes, until the onion just starts to brown. Add the turmeric, ginger and green chillies. Stir for a minute, then add the beansprouts and 70 ml/2½ fl oz water. Bring to a simmer. Cover and simmer very gently for 10 minutes, adding a little water if the pan starts to dry out.

Add the poha and salt and cook over a low heat for 3–4 minutes, tossing frequently by lifting all the ingredients from the bottom and folding them over, until the poha is heated through. Cover and set aside until you are ready to eat. Serve with the lime wedges.

Vikram Doctor's
Flattened Rice with Tomatoes
Poha Upma with Tomatoes

A lovely poha recipe sent to me by my friend and brilliant Indian food writer Vikram Doctor.

I have served this on summer days outdoors with a beetroot and hard-boiled egg salad, for which I use the same dressing as Tomato Salad (see page 44), plus Green Beans with Potatoes (see page 65) and a green salad. It is a perfect lunch. In the winter it can be paired with an aubergine dish and a paneer dish, or just have it with a cup of hot tea.

To reheat, sprinkle with a tablespoon or two of water, put over a very low heat and cover, tossing gently now and then.

SERVES 4

140 g/5 oz thick poha (flattened rice)

2 tablespoons peanut or olive oil

½ teaspoon urad dal

generous pinch of ground asafoetida

1 teaspoon whole mustard seeds

½ teaspoon whole cumin seeds

10–15 fresh curry leaves, lightly crushed in your hand

1 medium onion, peeled and chopped

1–3 fresh hot green chillies, finely chopped

¼ teaspoon ground turmeric

1 teaspoon peeled and very finely grated fresh ginger

2 tomatoes (about 340 g/12 oz in all), peeled and chopped

about ¾ teaspoon salt, or to taste

½ teaspoon sugar

Wash the poha gently but thoroughly under running water. Empty it into a bowl, cover generously with water and leave to soak for 2 minutes. Drain and leave in a sieve set over a bowl.

Pour the oil into a medium, preferably non-stick pan and set over a medium-high heat. When hot, add the urad dal and the asafoetida. As soon as the dal begins to change colour, add the mustard seeds. When they start to pop, a matter of seconds, add the cumin seeds and, a second later, the curry leaves (take care as they will splutter). Quickly add the onion, green chillies and turmeric. Reduce the heat to medium and fry for 3–4 minutes, or until the onion is translucent.

Add the ginger and stir for a minute. Now add all the tomatoes, ½ teaspoon of the salt and the sugar. Increase the heat to medium-high and fry for 3–4 minutes, or until the tomatoes have softened.

Add all the poha and sprinkle another ¼ teaspoon of salt over the top. Cook over a low heat for 3–4 minutes, gently breaking up any lumps and tossing the mixture with a flat spatula, lifting the ingredients from the bottom and turning them over. Add a sprinkling of water now and then. When heated through, cover and set aside until you are ready to eat.

Flattened Rice with Green Beans & Ginger *Poha Upma with Green Beans & Ginger*

Here is yet another variation of the poha upma, this time with ginger-flavoured green beans. By now you will know how to put flattened rice together with almost any vegetable and any flavouring of your choice.

SERVES 4

2 medium waxy potatoes, boiled, cooled and peeled

salt

140 g/5 oz green beans (rounded or flat), cut widthways into pieces 5 mm/¼ inch thick

210 g/7½ oz thick poha (flattened rice)

3 tablespoons olive or peanut oil

generous pinch of ground asafoetida

¾ teaspoon urad dal

¾ teaspoon whole brown mustard seeds

¾ teaspoon whole cumin seeds

2 dried hot red chillies, or 2 fresh hot green chillies, finely chopped

10–15 fresh curry leaves, lightly crushed in your hand

1 onion (85 g/3 oz), peeled and chopped

1 teaspoon peeled and very finely grated fresh ginger

¼ teaspoon ground turmeric

1 teaspoon sugar

1 tablespoon lime juice

2–3 tablespoons chopped fresh coriander, to serve

Cut the potatoes into 1 cm/½ inch dice.

Bring 1 litre/1¾ pints water to the boil in a medium pan. Stir in 2 teaspoons salt, then add the beans and boil for 4 minutes. Drain and refresh under cold water. Set aside.

Wash the poha gently but thoroughly under running water. Empty it into a bowl, cover generously with water and leave to soak for 2 minutes. Drain and leave in a sieve set over a bowl.

Put the oil into a large, non-stick frying pan and set it over a medium-high heat. When hot, add the asafoetida and urad dal. As soon as the dal starts to pick up a little colour, add the mustard seeds, cumin seeds and the chillies. As soon as the mustard seeds start to pop, add the curry leaves (take care as they will splutter), then the onion, ginger and turmeric. Stir for a minute and add the potatoes. Stir and fry over a medium heat for 3–4 minutes, until the onion and potatoes are slightly browned. Sprinkle ¼ teaspoon of salt over the top. Mix gently, then gently stir in the beans.

Over a low heat, add all the poha, gently breaking up any lumps. Sprinkle in 1 teaspoon of salt, then the sugar and lime juice. Mix gently, using a flat spatula, lifting the ingredients from the bottom and folding them over. Keep tossing this way and cooking for about 3–4 minutes, or until the poha is heated through. Cover and set aside until you are ready to eat. Garnish with the fresh coriander and serve.

Jayanti Rajagopalan's
Bread Upma *Double Roti ka Upma*

If you come in from work and are tired and hungry, this upma can be prepared in no time. With it you could have a light salad, a bowl of soup or just a cup of hot tea. You can also serve it with eggs. It is a good way to use up day-old bread. I like to make my upma with wholemeal bread, but white bread will do as well.

SERVES 2–3

3 tablespoons olive or peanut oil

½ teaspoon urad dal

½ teaspoon whole brown
  mustard seeds

generous pinch of ground asafoetida

7–8 fresh curry leaves, lightly
  crushed in your hand

1 onion (140 g/5 oz), peeled
  and finely sliced

½–2 fresh hot green chillies,
  finely chopped

1 cm/½ inch piece of fresh ginger,
  peeled and very finely diced

generous pinch of ground turmeric

1 tomato (180 g/6 oz), chopped

salt

4 large slices of wholemeal bread,
  cut or broken into 1 cm/
  ½ inch cubes

2 tablespoons chopped fresh
  coriander

Put the oil in a medium, non-stick pan and set over a medium heat. When it is hot, add the urad dal. As soon as the dal begins to take on colour, add the mustards seeds and asafoetida. When the seeds start to pop, a matter of seconds, throw in the curry leaves (take care as they will splutter). A second later, add the onion, green chillies and ginger. Stir and sauté for about 3 minutes, or until the onion starts to soften. Add the turmeric and stir once. Now add the tomato and a generous pinch of salt. Reduce the heat to medium-low and cook, stirring now and then, until the tomato softens.

Add the bread and increase the heat to medium-high. Stir briskly until the spice mixture coats the bread and all the ingredients are well mixed. Cover, reduce the heat and cook over a low heat for another 2–3 minutes. Check the salt, adding more if needed. Sprinkle the fresh coriander over the top and serve.

Quinoa 'Upma' with Corn & Mint
Bhutta, Pudina aur Quinoa ka Upma

In South India, upmas are pilaf-like, well-spiced, savoury dishes that can be made with different grains, such as semolina (sooji) and flattened rice (poha). I have discovered, completely by accident, that they can also be made with Western grains, such as quinoa. This tiny, nutritious grain needs to be cooked first and then stir-fried with the chosen vegetables and seasonings. Here I have used corn and mint. I like to use fresh corn in the summer, but frozen cooked corn kernels may be used during the rest of the year.

This upma can be served as a snack at any time of the day with a cup of tea or coffee. It makes a perfect breakfast food or brunch item. For a light lunch, serve it with a green salad, to which you can add grapefruit or tomatoes, cucumbers and peppers.

SERVES 4

180 g/6 oz quinoa
3 tablespoons olive or peanut oil
generous pinch of ground asafoetida
½ teaspoon urad dal
½ teaspoon whole brown
   mustard seeds
½ teaspoon whole cumin seeds
1 dried hot red chilli
10–15 fresh curry leaves, lightly
   crushed in your hand
½ large onion, peeled and chopped
¼ teaspoon ground turmeric
150 g/5½ oz corn kernels, fresh
   (from 1–2 cobs), or frozen
   and cooked through
1–2 fresh hot green chillies,
   finely chopped
2 tablespoons chopped
   fresh coriander
1 tablespoon finely chopped
   fresh mint
salt and freshly ground black pepper
1 teaspoon sugar
1 tablespoon lime or lemon juice
lime or lemon wedges, to serve

Pour 475 ml/16 fl oz water into a pan and bring to the boil. Add the quinoa, stir and cover. Cook gently over a very low heat for 15 minutes. Turn off the heat and let the pan rest, covered, for another 15 minutes.

Put the oil into a large, non-stick frying pan and set it over a medium-high heat. When hot, add the asafoetida and the urad dal. As soon as the dal starts to pick up a little colour, add the mustard seeds, cumin seeds and the red chilli. When the mustard seeds start to pop and the chilli darkens, a matter of seconds, add the curry leaves (take care as they will splutter), then the onion and turmeric. Stir and fry over a medium heat until the onion is slightly browned, 3–4 minutes. Add the corn, green chillies, fresh coriander, mint and a generous pinch of salt. Stir and cook gently for about 2 minutes.

Add the cooked quinoa, gently breaking up any lumps, and sprinkle ¾ teaspoon of salt, a few grinds of pepper, the sugar and lime juice over the top. Cook over a very low heat for 3–4 minutes, tossing frequently by lifting all the ingredients from the bottom with a flat spatula and folding them over. When the quinoa is heated through, check the seasonings and make the necessary adjustments. Cover and set aside until you are ready to eat. Reheat with sprinklings of water. Serve with lime or lemon wedges.

Semolina Upma with Green Beans, Peas & Carrots *Sooji ka Upma*

This dish is from south Karnataka. It can be served as a snack or for breakfast with a sprinkling of lime juice and a yoghurt relish, or at lunch or dinner with a sambar (see page 150), as well as chutneys and relishes. I have also been known to serve it as first course with, quite heretically, a generous sprinkling of Parmigiano Reggiano cheese.

To reheat, add a generous sprinkling of water as you stir and mix, breaking up lumps with the back of a wooden spoon. You should do this on a medium or medium-low heat for 4–5 minutes, or until it is heated through and soft.

SERVES 3–4

180 g/6 oz semolina (see note on page 176)

2 tablespoons olive or peanut oil

½ teaspoon whole brown mustard seeds

1–2 hot red dried chillies

6–7 fresh curry leaves, lightly crushed in your hand

½ medium onion, peeled and chopped

1 fresh hot green chilli, finely sliced (optional)

85 g/3 oz green beans, cut into rounds 7.5mm/⅓ inch thick

85 g/3 oz fresh peas, or defrosted frozen peas

1 medium carrot, peeled and cut into 5 mm/¼ inch dice

salt

Put a wok or medium frying pan over a medium-high heat. When hot, add the semolina and stir it around for 3–4 minutes, or until you get a roasted aroma. The semolina should not change colour much. Transfer to a large bowl and set aside.

Clean out the pan and set over a medium heat. Add the oil and, when it is hot, add the mustard seeds and red chillies. Stir until the seeds pop and the chillies darken, a few seconds. Add the curry leaves (take care as they will splutter) and, a second later, the onion and green chilli (if using). Stir for a minute.

Add the beans, peas and carrot and sauté for 2–3 minutes. Add 4 tablespoons of water and ¼ teaspoon of salt. Cover and cook over a low heat for about 4 minutes, or until the vegetables are just done. Remove the lid and add 500 ml/ 18 fl oz water and ¾ teaspoon of salt. Bring to a simmer over a medium-high heat.

Pick up a fistful of semolina and begin adding it to the pan in a slow drizzle, stirring as you go. Keep doing this until all the semolina is used up. Never stop stirring. This will take about 5 minutes. Reduce the heat to medium-low and keep stirring and breaking up lumps for another 2 minutes. Continue to stir and break up lumps, now over a low heat, for another 3–4 minutes, or until the upma is soft and fluffy. Serve immediately, or cover and reheat as suggested above.

'Risotto' of Dal, Rice & Vegetables
Geeli Khichri

SERVES 6

200 g/7 oz moong dal (skinned and
split mung beans), already cooked
for stock as on page 15 (with the
1.2 litres/2 pints of liquid already
removed)

a 120 ml/4 fl oz measure of basmati
or jasmine rice, washed in several
changes of water and drained

1 teaspoon ground cumin

1 teaspoon ground coriander

½ teaspoon ground turmeric

¼ teaspoon nice red chilli powder

1 medium onion, peeled and
finely chopped

180 g/6 oz cauliflower,
finely chopped

130 g/4½ oz fresh peas or
defrosted frozen peas

1½ teaspoons salt

For the tarka

2 teaspoons olive or peanut oil
or ghee (clarified butter)

generous pinch of ground asafoetida

¼ teaspoon whole brown
mustard seeds

¼ teaspoon whole cumin seeds

2 dried hot red chillies

6 tablespoons tomato passata

Khichri is an ancient Indian dish made with the nutritious combination of dal and rice. If you add vegetables, it becomes a complete meal. It comes in a dry form, rather like rice, and a wet form, rather like a risotto or porridge. This is the latter.

I like to serve it spread out on an old-fashioned soup plate with a pat of butter or ghee, some lemon juice, some crisply fried shallot slivers, chopped green chillies, finely chopped fresh ginger and a few pinches of garam masala on the top. You can serve this as a first course in small portions, or as a main course.

I originally made this dish with the dal left over from making the stock for Red Pepper & Tomato Soup (see page 15). If you have not made the soup and still want to make the 'risotto', just combine the dal, rice, cumin, coriander, turmeric, chilli powder, onion, ginger, cauliflower, peas, and 3 litres/5¼ pints water in a big pan. Bring to the boil, cover partially and simmer gently for 1½ hours, adding boiling water as needed if the porridge gets too thick. Stir more frequently when the porridge thickens. Add the salt and mix it in. Do the tarka (see page 11) at the end.

Put the remaining dal in a large pan (the stock should already have been removed) and add all the other ingredients, apart from those for the tarka. Pour in 1.5 litres/2½ pints water and bring to the boil. Cover partially, lower the heat and simmer gently for 45 minutes, stirring frequently as the mixture thickens, and mashing the vegetables a bit.

To make the tarka, put the oil in a small frying pan over a medium heat. When hot, add the asafoetida and, a second later, the mustard seeds. As soon as they pop, add the cumin seeds and red chillies. Stir until the chillies darken, then add the tomato passata. Stir once or twice, then pour the contents of the pan over the khichri. Stir and serve as suggested above.

Grains:
Breads, Pancakes,
Savouries &
Noodles

Chapatis

Chapatis are the simplest of flatbreads. The name 'chapati' probably comes from the same source as the word chapat, which means 'to slap'. There is much slapping done as chapatis are made, and it is probable that initially the chapatis were not rolled out at all but slapped into shape. This is still done in many Indian villages.

Chapatis are made with finely ground wholemeal flour and eaten over a great area of north India. They can be thick or thin, small or large, depending upon who is making them. In villages they tend to be large and thick, and are often called 'roti'. Most people in little towns and big cities seem to like them small and very thin. This delicate version of the chapati is also known as 'phulka'.

I have been making my chapatis the same way for the last 60 years. It is the way they were made at our home in Delhi when I was growing up. But this year I happened to travel to Mysore, where a lady I met, Zubaida Vagh, told me that she had worked out a no-fail way to make chapatis. It did not involve any gadgets, such as chapati/tortilla presses – the chapatis were still rolled out by hand – but the dough did have a tiny bit of oil in it. The difference lay mainly in the timing after the chapati is slapped on to the tava or cast-iron griddle. I have used this new method here. My directions may be long but the process is quite fast and simple. A chapati cooks in a little over a minute.

Chapati flour is very finely ground. It is best to buy it from an Indian grocery, where it is also called 'ata' (pronounced 'ah-ta'), with many variations in the spelling, including 'atta'. You can put butter or ghee on the top of each chapati as soon as it is made, if you like.

Continued overleaf

MAKES 6

85 g/3 oz chapati flour, plus extra
    for dusting
1 teaspoon olive or peanut oil

Put the flour into a large bowl. Dribble in the oil and rub it into the flour until you have a breadcrumb-like texture. Slowly add water – you will need about 120 ml/4 fl oz water or a little bit less – mixing it to form a soft dough. Shape it into a ball and knead for 10 minutes, or until smooth. Form into a smooth ball, cover with a damp cloth and set aside for 30–60 minutes.

Knead the dough again for a few minutes, then divide into 6 equal balls. Flatten them slightly between your palms and cover them with a damp cloth.

Set a medium cast-iron frying pan or tava over a medium heat. Have a small wad of cloth handy, as well as a plate lined with a tea towel to put the chapatis in as they get made.

Dust your work surface with flour. Take one of the flattened balls, keeping the rest covered, and roll it out, flipping it over a few times and dusting it with flour whenever needed, until you have an even circle about 15 cm/6 inches in diameter. Lay it on one palm and then slap it on to the other palm to get rid of the excess flour. Now slap the chapati on to the hot pan for just 5 seconds. Using a fine-edged spatula, turn it over and leave for about 30 seconds, or until the bottom has a few, nice brown spots. Flip the chapati again, this time pressing down on it with the wadded cloth, and turning it slightly with each press. These will be quick motions – press and turn slightly, press and turn, and so on – lasting only about another 30 seconds. The chapati should puff up, but even if it does not, it will be delicious. Put the chapati on one half of the tea towel and cover with the other half.

Make all chapatis this way, turning the heat down to medium-low when you are doing the rolling, and turning it up again when you are almost ready to slap it on to the pan.

Plain Delhi Parathas
Dilli kay Tikaunay Parathay

Parathas are much richer than chapatis, so tend not to be eaten on a daily basis. They are not only layered with butter, oil or ghee, but also cooked in it, like pancakes. However, like pancakes, they are utterly delicious, and one does need to succumb to them every now and then. They can be eaten at breakfast with pickles, chutneys and relishes, or served at any meal with dals and vegetable dishes.

Parathas can be made plain, as in this recipe, or they can be stuffed with spiced potatoes, cauliflower, radishes and even eggs. Some recipes for these follow. In the Delhi tradition, these parathas are triangular and made with wholemeal chapati flour, also sold by Indian grocers as ata (see page 193 for more about this flour.)

MAKES 6

85 g/3 oz chapati flour, plus extra for dusting

⅓ teaspoon salt

3–4 tablespoons olive or peanut oil, melted butter or ghee (clarified butter)

Pictured on page 197

Put the flour and salt into a large bowl. Dribble in 2 teaspoons of the oil, butter or ghee and rub it into the flour until it has a breadcrumb-like mixture. Slowly add about 120 ml/4 fl oz water, working it into the flour. You are aiming for a ball of soft dough, so you might not need all the water. Once the ball is formed, knead it for 10 minutes, or until smooth. Shape it into a ball, oil or otherwise grease it and slip it into a plastic bag. Set aside for 30–60 minutes.

Knead the dough again for a few minutes, then divide into 6 equal balls. Flatten them slightly between your palms and cover them with a damp cloth.

Set a medium cast-iron frying pan or tava over a medium-low heat.

Meanwhile, dust your work surface with flour. Take one of the flattened balls, keeping the rest covered, and roll it out, flipping it over a few times and dusting it with flour whenever needed, until you have an even circle about 15 cm/6 inches in diameter. Brush it with about ½ teaspoon of the oil, butter or ghee and fold it in half. Brush again with ¼ teaspoon of oil, butter or ghee and fold in half again. Dusting with flour as

Continued overleaf

needed, roll the triangle into a larger triangle, about 15 cm/ 6 inches on each side. Lay it on one palm with your fingers spread out, then slap it on to the other palm to get rid of the excess flour.

Put 1 teaspoon of oil in the hot pan and slap the paratha right in the centre. Dribble ½ teaspoon oil over it and cook for 45–60 seconds, until the paratha has golden brown spots on the underside. Using a fine-edged spatula, turn it over and cook for another 45–60 seconds, until the second side has a few, nice brown spots too. Flip the paratha again, leave for 10 seconds, then flip again and leave for another 10 seconds. It should now be done – crisp on the outside and soft and layered inside. Transfer to a large plate and cover with an upturned plate.

Make all the parathas in the same way, taking the pan off the heat if it gets too hot as you do your rolling out, and then putting it back a little before you slap the next bread in.

Jayanti Rajagopalan's
Egg Parathas *Unday kay Parathay*

This is very similar to the previous recipe, except that this paratha is a bit larger and stuffed with spiced eggs. I love it for breakfast with Simple Yoghurt Dipping Sauce (see page 289), and a cup of hot tea.

MAKES 4

85 g/3 oz chapati flour, plus extra for dusting

salt

3–4 tablespoons olive or peanut oil, melted butter or ghee (clarified butter)

4 eggs

2–4 fresh hot green chillies, finely chopped

3 tablespoons peeled and finely chopped shallots

4 cherry tomatoes, chopped

2 tablespoons chopped fresh coriander

freshly ground black pepper

4 generous pinches of garam masala

Put the flour and ⅓ teaspoon of salt into a large bowl. Dribble in 2 teaspoons of the oil, butter or ghee and rub it into the flour until it has a breadcrumb-like texture. Slowly add about 120 ml/4 fl oz water, working it into the flour. You are aiming for a ball of soft dough, so might not need all the water. Once the ball is formed, knead it for 10 minutes, or until smooth. Shape it into a ball, oil or otherwise grease it and slip it into a plastic bag. Set aside for 30–60 minutes.

Knead the dough again for a few minutes and divide into 4 equal balls. Flatten them slightly between your palms and cover them with a damp cloth.

Break the eggs into 4 separate bowls and beat each one lightly. Put a quarter of the chillies, shallots, tomatoes and coriander into each bowl. Add some salt, pepper and garam masala and mix well.

Set a medium cast-iron frying pan or tava over a medium-low heat.

Meanwhile, dust your work surface with flour. Take one of the flattened balls, keeping the rest covered, and roll it out, flipping it over a few times and dusting it with flour whenever needed, until you have an even circle about 18 cm/7 inches in diameter. Brush it with about ½ teaspoon of the oil, butter or ghee and fold it in half. Brush again with ¼ teaspoon of oil, butter or ghee and fold in half again. Dusting with flour as needed, roll the triangle into a larger triangle, about 18 cm/ 7 inches on each side. Lay it on one palm with your fingers spread out, then slap it on to the other palm to get rid of the excess flour.

Put 1 teaspoon of oil in the hot pan and slap the paratha right in the centre. Dribble ½ teaspoon of oil over it and cook for 45–60 seconds, until the paratha has golden brown spots on the underside. Using a fine-edged spatula, turn it over and cook for another 30 seconds. Now lift the top flap of the paratha and pour 1 bowlful of egg mixture inside. It may not all fit, so keep the flap open and fold or scrape in the rest of the egg. Flip the paratha and leave for 20 seconds, then flip again and leave for 10 seconds. It should now be done. Transfer to a large plate and cover with an upturned plate.

Make all the parathas in the same way, taking the pan off the heat if it gets too hot as you do your rolling out, and then putting it back a little before you slap the next bread in.

Parathas with Ajowan Seeds & Red Chilli Flakes
Ajwain kay Parathay

Follow the recipe for Plain Delhi Parathas (see page 195), but with the following difference.

MAKES 6

pinch of ajowan seeds
dash of red chilli flakes

When you have rolled a paratha into a 15 cm/6 inch circle and brushed it with ½ teaspoon of oil, butter or ghee, sprinkle with the ajowan seeds and chilli flakes before folding the circle in half. Ajowan or ajwain seeds have a thyme-like taste and smell, so you can use fresh thyme leaves – about ½ teaspoon for each paratha – if you prefer.

Parathas Stuffed with Spiced Cauliflower *Gobi Paratha*

Great in the school lunchbox or as travel food, these parathas are also amongst my favourite Sunday breakfast dishes. All I need with them is Simple Yoghurt Dipping Sauce (see page 289) and some hot tea.

When grating the cauliflower, use the largest hole in the grater and grate just the florets, not the stems. Any bigger pieces that break and fall in can be finely chopped by hand.

MAKES 6

85 g/3 oz chapati flour, plus extra
   for dusting
salt
8 tablespoons olive or peanut oil,
   melted butter or ghee
   (clarified butter)
1 tablespoon peeled and finely
   chopped shallot or onion
180 g/6 oz grated cauliflower
   (see introduction above)
1–2 fresh hot green chillies,
   finely chopped
2.5 cm/1 inch piece of fresh ginger,
   peeled and very finely chopped
about 1 teaspoon garam masala
about ¼ teaspoon nice red
   chilli powder

Put the flour and ½ teaspoon salt into a large bowl. Dribble in 2 teaspoons of the oil, melted butter or ghee and rub it into the flour until it has a breadcrumb-like texture. Slowly add about 120 ml/4 fl oz water, working it into the flour. You are aiming for a ball of soft dough, so you might not need all the water. Once the ball is formed, knead it for 10 minutes or until smooth. Shape it into a ball, oil or otherwise grease it and slip it into a plastic bag. Set aside for 30–60 minutes.

Meanwhile, make the stuffing, by combining the shallot, cauliflower, green chillies and ginger in a bowl and mixing them together.

Knead the dough again for a few minutes and divide into 6 equal balls. Flatten them slightly between your palms and cover them with a damp cloth.

Set a cast-iron frying pan or tava over a medium heat.

Meanwhile, dust your work surface with flour. Take one of the flattened balls, keeping the rest covered, and roll it out, flipping it over a few times and dusting it with flour whenever needed, until you have an even circle about 14 cm/5½ inches in diameter. Brush it with about 1 teaspoon of the oil, butter or ghee. Put 2 heaped tablespoons of the cauliflower mixture in the centre and sprinkle with a little salt, garam masala and chilli powder. Make folds all around the edges to form a pouch. Pinch the folds together and give the top a twist for good measure. Dusting with flour as needed, and with the twisted side down, roll out the pouch until it is 14 cm/5½ inches in diameter. Lay the paratha on one palm and then slap it on to the other palm to get rid of the excess flour.

Put 1 teaspoon of oil in the hot pan and slap the paratha, folds side down, right in the centre. Dribble ½ teaspoon of oil over it, then press down with your spatula and cook for about 1 minute, until the paratha has golden brown spots on the underside. Turn it over, pressing down on it again, and leave for another minute or more or until the second side has a few nice brown spots too. Some of the cauliflower might get exposed but that often happens. Flip the paratha again, this time for 5 seconds, and then again for another 5 seconds. It should now be done. Transfer to a large plate and cover with an upturned plate.

Make all the parathas in the same way, taking the pan off the heat if it gets too hot as you do your rolling out, and then putting it back a little before you slap the next bread in.

Parathas with Rings
Lachchheydar Paratha

MAKES 6

85 g/3 oz chapati flour, plus extra
   for dusting

⅓ teaspoon salt

½ teaspoon sugar

about 6 tablespoons ghee (clarified
   butter) or olive or peanut oil

about 120 ml/4 fl oz warm milk, use
   only as much is needed to make a
   soft dough

This paratha is layered in rings.

Put the flour, salt and sugar into a large bowl. Dribble in 1 teaspoon of the ghee or oil and rub it into the flour until it resembles breadcrumbs. Slowly add the milk, mixing it in and gathering the flour into a ball. You are aiming for soft dough, so you might not need all the milk. Once the dough is formed, knead it for 10 minutes, or until smooth. Shape it into a ball, oil or otherwise grease it and slip it into a plastic bag. Set aside for 30–60 minutes.

Knead the dough again for a few minutes and divide into equal 6 balls. Flatten them slightly between your palms and cover them with a damp cloth.

Set a medium cast-iron frying pan or tava over a medium-low heat.

Meanwhile, dust your work surface with flour. Take one of the flattened balls, keeping the rest covered, and roll it out, flipping it over a few times and dusting it with flour whenever needed, until you have an even circle about 17 cm/6½ inches in diameter. Brush it with about ½ teaspoon of the ghee or oil, then dust it lightly with flour. Now pleat it tightly towards you, making 1 cm/½ inch folds, as if making a fan. Stand the pleated paratha on its long edge and roll into a tight pinwheel, tucking the end in firmly. Flatten the pinwheel, dust with flour as needed, and roll into a circle about 17 cm/6½ inches in diameter. Lay it on one palm with your fingers spread out, then slap it on to the other palm to get rid of the excess flour.

Put 1 teaspoon of the ghee or oil in the hot pan and slap the paratha right in the centre. Dribble ½ teaspoon of oil over it and cook for 35–45 seconds, or until the paratha has golden brown spots on the underside. Using a fine-edged spatula, turn it over and cook for another 35–45 seconds, or until the second side has a few nice brown spots too. Flip the paratha again, this time for 10 seconds, and then again for another 10 seconds. It should now be done, crisp on the outside and soft and layered inside. Transfer to a large plate and cover with an upturned plate.

Make all the parathas in the same way, taking the pan off the heat if it gets too hot as you do your rolling out, and then putting it back a little before you slap the next bread in.

From Vinita Pittie's home

Marwari Layered Griddle Breads
Marwari Tavey ki Roti or Batia

Very easy to make, this is really a layered paratha, only the
layers are circular. I like to serve it with Potatoes Cooked
in a Banarasi Style or Marwari Style (see page 100 or 102),
Cauliflower with Peas (see page 77), any simple dal and a
yoghurt relish. It is also a wonderful bread to take out on
picnics, carry on train journeys, and put into lunchboxes, as
Indians often do. All you need to add is a vegetable dish and
an Indian relish.

Marwaris (see page 102 for more about this community)
tend to make this bread with ghee, but you can use oil if you
prefer. I do.

MAKES 6

85 g/3 oz chapati flour, plus extra
    for dusting

⅓ teaspoon salt

¾ teaspoon ground cumin

1 or 2 generous pinches of nice
    red chilli powder

pinch of nigella seeds
    (kalonji, optional)

pinch of ajowan seeds (optional)

about 6 tablespoons olive or peanut
    oil or ghee (clarified butter)

Put the flour into a large bowl. Add the salt, cumin, chilli
powder and nigella and ajowan seeds (if using). Dribble in 1
teaspoon of the oil or ghee and rub it into the flour until it
has a breadcrumb-like texture. Slowly add about 120 ml/4 fl
oz water, working it into the flour. You are aiming for a ball
of soft dough, so you might not need all the water. Once the
ball is formed, knead it for 10 minutes, or until smooth. Shape
it into a ball, oil or otherwise grease it and slip it into a
plastic bag. Set aside for 30–60 minutes.

Knead the dough again for a few minutes and divide into
6 equal balls. Flatten them slightly between your palms and
cover them with a damp cloth.

Set a medium cast-iron frying pan or tava over a medium-
low heat.

Meanwhile, dust your work surface with flour. Take one
of the flattened balls, keeping the rest covered, and roll it out,
flipping it over a few times and dusting it with flour whenever
needed, until you have an even circle about 17 cm/6½ inches
in diameter. Brush it with about ½ teaspoon of the oil or ghee,
then roll it tightly inwards, forming a snake. Now roll the
snake into a tight pinwheel, tucking in the end firmly. Dusting
with flour as needed, roll out the pinwheel into a circle about
17 cm/6½ inches in diameter. Lay it on one palm with your
fingers spread out, then slap it on to the other palm to get rid
of the excess flour.

Put 1 teaspoon of oil in the hot pan and slap the bread right in the centre. Dribble ½ teaspoon of oil over it and cook for 35–45 seconds, or until the bread has golden brown spots on the underside. Using a fine-edged spatula, turn it over and cook for another 35–45 seconds, or until the second side has a few nice brown spots too. Flip the bread again, this time for 10 seconds, then again for another 10 seconds. It should now be done, crisp on the outside and soft and layered inside. Transfer to a large plate and cover with an upturned plate.

Make all the parathas in the same way, taking the pan off the heat if it gets too hot as you do your rolling out, and then putting it back a little before you slap the next bread in.

Puffed Fried Breads *Poori*

These very popular breads are reserved for special occasions
– festivals, weddings, picnics, train journeys and even Sunday
breakfasts! They are generally eaten with potatoes and other
vegetables, just as chapatis might be. As they are rich
(traditionalists cook them in pure ghee), they are not eaten
every day. Using full-fat milk rather than water to make the
dough keeps them nice and pliable, especially if you are taking
them to work or school, or are travelling with them.

These breads are always deep-fried in an Indian karhai,
which most resembles a wok, but is a bit deeper. It uses oil in
the most economical manner, but you can use a wok or a deep,
frying pan instead.

MAKES 12

180 g/6 oz chapati flour, plus extra
  for dusting
½ teaspoon salt
1 tablespoon olive or peanut oil,
  plus more for deep-frying

Put the flour and salt into a bowl and mix lightly. Dribble
in the oil and rub it into the flour evenly. Slowly add about
120 ml/4 fl oz water (or milk), working it into the flour. You
are aiming for a soft dough, so you might not need all the
liquid. Once the dough is formed, knead it for 10 minutes,
or until smooth. Shape it into a ball, oil or otherwise grease
it and slip it into a plastic bag. Set aside for 30–60 minutes.
You could even refrigerate it and hold it longer.

Shortly before you are ready to eat, pour a 4 cm/1½ inch
depth of oil into a karhai, wok or frying pan and set it over
a medium heat.

Meanwhile, knead the dough again and divide into 12 equal
balls. Flatten them slightly between your palms and cover them
with a damp cloth.

Dust the work surface very lightly with the flour. Take one
of the flattened balls, keeping the rest covered, and roll it out,
flipping it over a few times and dusting it with flour whenever
needed, until you have 14 cm/5½ inch circle. When the oil is
very hot, carefully lay the poori on the surface of the oil. It
may sink to the bottom, but will rise immediately and start
to sizzle. Using the back of a slotted spoon, push the poori
gently into the oil with tiny, swift strokes. In just seconds it
should puff up. Turn it over and cook the second side for a
few seconds. Remove with a slotted spoon and transfer to
a platter lined with kitchen paper.

Make all the pooris in the same way and serve them hot.
If you wish to serve them later, stack them and keep them
covered. When cool, place in an airtight tin or ziplock bag.

Puffed Fried Leavened Breads *Bhatura*

If you have ever eaten the 'fried dough' served by Native Americans, you will find this very similar. Bhaturas are a lot like pooris (see previous recipe), except that the leavening makes their texture a bit spongier. They are a speciality of the Punjab, where they are often served with chickpea dishes. Add a Tomato, Onion & Cucumber Koshambari (see page 299) and a yoghurt relish, and you have a fine lunch in front of you. I also love bhaturas with cauliflower and potato dishes.

Ideally, they should be eaten hot, as soon as they are made. If you cannot do that, line a plate with kitchen paper, stack the bhaturas one on top of the other as they are made and keep covered all the time by another upturned plate.

If you have children waiting impatiently as you are preparing dinner, give them a small piece of a bhatura dusted with a little caster sugar. It will bring smiles.

MAKES 8

200 g/7 oz plain flour, plus extra
    for dusting
½ teaspoon baking powder
¼ teaspoon bicarbonate of soda
½ teaspoon sugar
¼ teaspoon salt
1 teaspoon olive or peanut oil,
    plus extra for deep-frying
6 tablespoons natural yoghurt

Put the flour, baking powder, bicarbonate of soda, sugar and salt into a large wide bowl and mix lightly with your fingers. Add the teaspoon of oil and all the yoghurt. Mix until the dough is crumbly but still loose. Add about 2½ tablespoons of water and gather the dough together to make a smooth ball. Knead for a few minutes. Wash your hands, then put a little oil on them and rub it on the ball. Knead for another 8–10 minutes, until smooth. Rub a little more oil on the ball and slip it into a plastic bag. Set aside 40–60 minutes, or longer if you wish.

Shortly before you are ready to eat, pour a 4 cm/1½ inch depth of oil into a karhai, wok or frying pan and set it over a medium heat.

Meanwhile, knead the dough again and divide into 8 equal balls. Flatten them slightly between your palms and cover with a damp cloth.

Dust the work surface very lightly with the flour. Take one of the flattened balls, keeping the rest covered, and roll it out, flipping it over a few times and dusting it with flour whenever needed, until you have 13 cm/5 inch circle. When the oil is very hot, carefully lay it on the surface of the oil. It may sink to the bottom, but will rise immediately and start to sizzle. Using the back of a slotted spoon, push the bhatura gently into the oil with tiny, swift strokes. In just seconds it should puff up. Turn it over and cook the second side for a few seconds. Remove with a slotted spoon and transfer to a platter lined with kitchen paper.

Make all the bhaturas in the same way, taking the pan off the heat if it gets too hot as you do your rolling out, then putting it back a little before you slap the next bread in. Serve the bhaturas hot. If you wish to serve them later, stack them and keep them covered. When cool, place in an airtight tin or ziplock bag.

Sooji Pancakes *Rava Dosa*

These pancakes are soft, satiny and filled with tiny depressions. They are very similar to crêpes, but spongier and much easier to prepare. Excellent in their savoury form with a Potato & Onion Mélange (see page 98) stuffed inside them, they are just as good served as a dessert in their sweet form (see page 332). They may also be served plain for breakfast, with chutneys and a yoghurt relish. If you are going to stuff them, you do not need to add any seasoning other than the salt.

MAKES 12

120 ml/4 fl oz natural yoghurt

180 g/6 oz sooji (see page 176)

70 g/2½ oz rice flour (also called powdered rice)

2 tablespoons plain flour

1 teaspoon salt

about 4 tablespoons olive or peanut oil

2–3 tablespoons chopped fresh coriander (optional)

1 fresh hot green chilli, finely chopped (optional)

½ teaspoon whole cumin seeds (optional)

Empty the yoghurt into a bowl. Using a fork or whisk, beat it lightly until smooth and creamy. Slowly add 600 ml/1 pint water, mixing it well as you go.

Put the sooji, rice flour, plain flour and salt in a separate and larger bowl. Slowly add the yoghurt-water combination, mixing it in until everything is thoroughly blended and there are no lumps. Set aside for at least 1 hour. A little longer is fine too.

When you're ready to cook, put the oil in a small bowl and stick a teaspoon in it. Set a non-stick frying pan over a medium heat and add 1 teaspoon of oil. Meanwhile, add the coriander, chilli and cumin seeds to the batter and stir well. Measure 70 ml/2½ fl oz water into a ladle and mentally note the level to get an idea of how much batter you will need each time. Take a ladleful of the batter and pour it slowly into the pan, letting it expand into a circle about 15 cm/6 inches in diameter. This batter is very forgiving, so you can fill up any holes and round off the pancake to get the shape you want. Let it cook for a minute or so, until golden-red on the underside. Flip the pancake over and cook for another minute or so, until the second side is golden-red as well.

If you are serving the pancake plain and unstuffed, lift it with a spatula and slide it on to a plate. It is best eaten fresh.

If you are stuffing the pancake, flip it on to a plate, lay the stuffing on it slightly to one side, and roll it up like a 'wrap'.

Make only as many pancakes as you need, remembering to stir the batter thoroughly each time. The batter can be stored in the refrigerator for several days.

Rita D'Souza's

Rice Flour & Flattened Rice Pancakes
Rice Flour & Poha Dosas

I love all Indian savoury pancakes that can be included in the general category known as 'dosas'. And I am always looking for dosas that do not need fermentation, as they are far easier to make. Here is just such a dosa. It is made mainly with rice flour and can be eaten as a snack with chutneys, pickles and swigs of hot tea, of course, or like a chapati as part of a meal.

These dosas are made rather like crêpes. It is best to eat them as soon as they are made. Each takes less than 2 minutes to cook, so make a stack and then sit down to eat.

MAKES 7–8 SMALL DOSAS

140 g/5 oz rice flour (also called powdered rice)

120 ml/4 fl oz natural yoghurt

2 tablespoons flattened rice/thick poha (see page 174)

½ teaspoon salt

pinch of ground asafoetida

1 teaspoon peeled and finely grated fresh ginger

coarsely ground black pepper

1–2 very finely chopped fresh green chillies (such as bird's eye)

2–3 tablespoons chopped fresh coriander

about 1 tablespoon olive or peanut oil

Put the rice flour in a bowl and add the yoghurt, poha, salt, asafoetida and 175 ml/6 fl oz water. Mix well, then set aside for 15 minutes. Pour the mixture into a blender and whiz until smooth. Pour it back into a clean, dry bowl and add the ginger, black pepper, chillies and coriander. Mix, cover and set aside for 2 hours.

When you're ready to cook, check your batter. It should be a flowing, creamy mixture, rather like the one for crêpes. I usually need to add another tablespoon of water to it at this stage to thin it out a bit. Mix well.

Line two large plates with kitchen paper and place them near you. Pour the oil into a small bowl, stick a teaspoon in it and set that nearby too. Place a 15 cm/6 inch non-stick frying pan over a medium heat and brush it with a little oil. Measure 70 ml/2½ fl oz water into a ladle and mentally note the level to get an idea of how much batter you will need each time. When the pan is hot, dip your ladle into the batter, stir it round and pick up the measured amount. Pour the batter in the centre of the frying pan, quickly tilting it to make the batter flow to the edges. Let the dosa sit there for 45–60 seconds, until the top is set. Little bubbles may appear and the underside should get nice reddish spots. Pour a few drops of oil over it and around the edges, then turn and cook the second side for another 45 seconds. Using a spatula, transfer it to a prepared plate and cover with the other prepared plate.

Make all the dosas in the same way, stacking them on top of each other between the paper-lined plates. Serve immediately.

Rita D'Souza's
Rice Flour Pancakes *Rice Flour Dosas*

Eaten for breakfast or as a snack food, these are served with chutneys and pickles. You can also wrap them around any vegetable dish of your choice and serve them at lunch with a salad.

MAKES 8

120 ml/4 fl oz natural yoghurt

140 g/5 oz rice flour (also called powdered rice)

½ teaspoon salt

1–2 fresh hot green chillies, finely chopped

1 tablespoon peeled and finely chopped shallot

2 tablespoons finely chopped fresh coriander

about 3 tablespoons olive or peanut oil

Empty the yoghurt into a bowl. Using a fork or whisk, beat it lightly until smooth and creamy. Slowly add 350 ml/12 fl oz water, mixing it well as you go.

Put the rice flour and salt in a separate and larger bowl. Slowly add the yoghurt-water combination, mixing it in until everything is thoroughly blended and there are no lumps. Add the chillies, shallot and coriander and stir well. Set aside for 1–2 hours. A little longer is fine too.

When you're ready to cook, put the oil in a small bowl and stick a teaspoon in it. Set a non-stick frying pan over a medium heat and add 1 teaspoon oil. Meanwhile, add the coriander, chilli and cumin seeds to the batter and stir well. Measure 70 ml/2½ fl oz water into a ladle and mentally note the level to get an idea of how much batter you will need each time. Take a ladleful of the batter and pour it slowly into the pan, letting it expand into a circle about 15 cm/6 inches in diameter. This batter is very forgiving so you can fill up any holes and round off the pancake to get the shape you want. Let it cook for about 2 minutes, or until the underside is golden red. Flip it over and cook the other side for another 2 minutes or so, until it is golden-red as well. Pick up the pancake with a spatula and slide it on to a plate. You can fold it in half and then into quarters if you wish. Keep covered as you make the other pancakes in the same way, remembering to stir the batter thoroughly each time.

Make only as many pancakes as you need. The batter can be stored in the refrigerator for several days.

Savoury Wholemeal Pancakes
Wholemeal Dosas

These pancakes are similar to crêpes except that they are made with wholemeal flour, well spiced and eggless. Very popular in Maharashtra and along India's west coast, they are generally eaten for breakfast with chutneys, yoghurt relishes and pickles. They can also be served at lunch or dinner as flatbreads.

The pancakes are best served fresh, as soon as they are made, when they are both crisp and flexible. If you cannot manage that, stack them one on top of the other on a plate as you make them and keep them well covered with a second overturned plate. To freeze them, slip a layer of baking parchment or waxed paper between each pancake, allowing more of the paper for the top and the bottom, and let them cool completely. Slide the whole bundle into a ziplock bag and freeze flat. Defrost before reheating, then slap the pancakes, one at a time, on to a hot cast-iron griddle or frying pan, giving each a few seconds on both sides until nice and hot.

MAKES 7

85 g/3 oz chapati flour or ordinary wholemeal flour

¼ teaspoon salt

¼ teaspoon nice red chilli powder

½ teaspoon ground coriander

¼ teaspoon whole cumin seeds

½ medium tomato, finely diced

4 tablespoons peeled and finely chopped onion

1 fresh hot green chilli, finely chopped

3 tablespoons chopped fresh coriander

about 3 tablespoons olive or peanut oil or ghee (clarified butter)

Put the flour, salt, chilli powder and ground coriander into a bowl. Slowly add about 250 ml/8 fl oz water, mixing with a wooden spoon and breaking up lumps as you go, until you have a thinnish, smooth batter. Alternatively, whiz the ingredients in a blender, putting the water in first, then the flour and ground seasonings. Transfer to a bowl. Set the batter aside for 2 hours. Add all the other ingredients except the oil and stir to mix.

When you're ready to cook, put the oil in a small bowl and stick a teaspoon in it. Place a 15 cm/6 inch non-stick frying pan over a medium heat and add ½ teaspoon of oil. (The pan I use is 18 cm/7 inches at the widest part of the diameter, but narrows at the bottom.) Measure 70 ml/2½ fl oz water into a ladle and mentally note the level to get an idea of how much batter you will need each time. When hot, stir the batter from the bottom and pour a ladleful of it into the centre of the pan. Tilt the pan quickly in all directions until the mixture reaches the edges. Any holes may be quickly filled in with a little bit of extra batter. Cook for about 2 minutes, dribbling another ½ teaspoon oil over the top of the pancake. Peek underneath to see if the pancake has turned golden-red. Slide a fine-edged spatula all the way under the pancake to loosen it and flip it over. Cook the second side for another 1½–2 minutes, pressing down in the centre with the back of a spatula. This side should have many brownish-red spots. Turn the pancake over twice more, leaving it for just a few seconds each time. Put the pancake on a large plate and cover with an upturned plate.

Make all the pancakes in the same way and serve immediately, if possible.

Moong Dal Pancakes
Cheela, Poora

Made all over India, this savoury pancake is exceedingly popular in the north as a breakfast dish. My mother often made it for us on Sundays. It is eaten with chutneys, pickles and yoghurt relishes (see page 278). You could also have it instead of a chapati at lunch or dinner, with a cauliflower or potato dish and a raita.

The batter can be made a day in advance, covered and refrigerated. It can also be frozen.

MAKES ABOUT 9

200 g/7 oz moong dal (skinned and split mung beans), washed and soaked in water for 5–6 hours

1–3 fresh hot green chillies, chopped

2.5 cm/1 inch piece of fresh ginger, peeled and finely chopped

2 cloves garlic, peeled and chopped

¼ teaspoon ground turmeric

handful of fresh coriander, chopped

1 teaspoon salt

1 large shallot, peeled and finely chopped

about 6 tablespoons olive or peanut oil

Drain the dal and place in a blender. Add the chillies, ginger, garlic, turmeric, coriander, salt and 175 ml/6 fl oz water. Blend thoroughly, then empty into a bowl. Add the shallot, then stir in 3 tablespoons of water.

Put the oil in a small bowl and stick a teaspoon in it. Have two plates nearby to hold the pancakes as they are made. Measure 70 ml/2½ fl oz water into a ladle and mentally note the level to get an idea of how much batter you will need each time.

Set a medium non-stick frying pan over a medium-low heat and add a teaspoon of the oil. When hot, stir the batter from the bottom and pour a ladleful into the centre of the pan. Let it sit for a second or so, then lightly use the ladle or the back of a spoon to spread it outwards in a continuous spiral motion. When it is about 13 cm/5 inches in diameter, use a spatula to spread the batter outwards from the centre as if scraping it to the edges. Again, use a light touch so you do not disturb the bottom layer and spread evenly. Aim for a diameter of 18–20 cm/7–8 inches. Dribble a teaspoon of oil on the top and just outside the rim of the pancake, cover with a lid and cook for about 2 minutes, or until the underside has turned golden-red. Flip the pancake over and cook the second side, uncovered, for 1 minute. Put the cooked pancake on a plate and cover with an upturned plate.

Make all the pancakes in the same way, stirring the batter from the bottom each time you make a new one.

Chickpea Flour & Tomato Pancakes
Besan Tamatar Omlate

In western India, many vegetarians refer to this dish as an omelette, and eat it with toast and tea or coffee. It can be eaten for breakfast, or even as a snack. Chutneys are always offered on the side.

Follow the introduction to the preceding recipe for instructions on making these pancakes ahead of time.

MAKES ABOUT 7

115 g/4 oz chickpea flour (besan or gram flour)
¾ teaspoon salt
¼ teaspoon ground turmeric
¼ teaspoon nice red chilli powder
generous pinch of ground asafoetida
¼ teaspoon garam masala
180 g/6 oz tomato, finely diced
1 medium onion, peeled and finely diced
1 fresh hot green chilli, finely chopped (use more if you wish)
about 3 tablespoons olive or peanut oil

Sift the flour, salt, turmeric, chilli powder, asafoetida and garam masala into a bowl. Slowly add about 30 ml/1 fl oz water, mixing with a wooden spoon and breaking up any lumps as you go, until you have a thin, smooth batter. Alternatively, whiz the ingredients in a blender, putting the water in first, then the flour and ground seasonings. Transfer to a bowl. Set the batter aside for 2 hours. Add all the other ingredients, except the oil, and stir to mix.

When you're ready to cook, put the oil in a small bowl and stick a teaspoon in it. Place a 15 cm/6 inch non-stick frying pan over a medium heat and add ½ teaspoon of oil. (The pan I use is 18 cm/7 inches at the widest part of the diameter, but narrows at the bottom.) Measure 70 ml/2½ fl oz water into a ladle and mentally note the level to get an idea of how much batter you will need each time. When the oil is hot, stir the batter from the bottom and pour a ladleful of it into the centre of the pan. Tilt the pan quickly in all directions until the mixture reaches the edges. Any holes and empty spaces can be quickly filled with a little bit of extra batter. Cook for about 2 minutes, dribbling another ½ teaspoon of oil over the top of the pancake. Peek underneath to see if the pancake has turned golden-red. Slide a fine-edged plastic spatula all the way under the pancake to loosen it and flip it over. Cook the second side for another 1½–2 minutes, pressing down in the centre with the back of a spatula. This side should have many brownish-red spots. Turn the pancake over twice more, leaving it for just a few seconds each time. Put the pancake on a large plate and cover with an upturned plate.

Make all the pancakes in the same way and serve immediately, if possible.

From the Falaknuma Palace Hotel
Whole Mung Bean Pancakes
Pesarattu

One of the glories of Andhra Pradesh, these highly nutritious pancakes are made for breakfast with great flourish at the grand Falaknuma Palace Hotel in Hyderabad, right in front of the guests who order them. A ladleful of mung batter is dropped on to a massive oiled griddle. It is spread out quickly using the back of the ladle with a spiral motion, so it thins out like a crêpe into a very large oval. Finely sliced onions and peppers may be strewn over the top, and the crisp pancake served at once with a chutney such as Fresh Coriander, Ginger & Coconut Chutney (see page 271). Guests just gobble them up.

Pesarattus are equally popular with less affluent locals travelling on the highways of Andhra. A family of three riding on one motorbike may decide to jump off it as they get tempted by a pesarattu stand on the roadside. I never can resist one. Here several griddles are set up to take many different types of orders. You can have it plain, with chutneys and podis (dry chutneys) or slathered with a thin layer of semolina upma (a savoury, spicy porridge (see page 188) and folded over. One order came in for an egg pesarattu. For this, an egg was broken over the pancake and spread around, some podi sprinkled over the top and the pesarattu turned over to let the egg cook. I decided to try one too. It was delicious.

The batter for this plain pesarattu, as all others, can be made a day ahead, covered and refrigerated. It can also be frozen.

Continued overleaf

200 g/7 oz whole mung beans

15 or so whole fenugreek seeds

1–3 fresh hot green chillies, chopped

2 cm/¾ inch piece of fresh ginger, peeled and finely chopped

generous pinch of ground asafoetida

½ teaspoon ground cumin

handful of fresh coriander leaves

1 teaspoon salt

¼ teaspoon ground turmeric

1 tablespoon rice flour (also called powdered rice)

about 6 tablespoons olive or peanut oil

Put the beans and fenugreek seeds into a bowl and wash them in several changes of water. Drain, then cover generously in fresh water and soak for 5–6 hours. Drain and put into a blender. Add the chillies, ginger, asafoetida, cumin, coriander, salt, 175 ml/6 fl oz water and the turmeric. Blend for several minutes, pushing down with a spatula when necessary, until you have a pancake-like batter. It will not be smooth but the beans should be well ground. Add the rice flour, blend again and empty into a bowl.

Put the oil in a small bowl and stick a teaspoon in it. Have two plates nearby to hold the pancakes as they are made. Measure 70 ml/2½ fl oz water into a ladle and mentally note the level to get an idea of how much batter you will need each time.

Add about 3 tablespoons of water to the batter and mix well. It should now be like flowing cream but with a lot of texture.

Set a medium non-stick frying pan over a medium-low heat and add a teaspoon of the oil. When hot, stir the batter from the bottom and pour a ladleful into the centre of the pan. Let it sit for a second or so, then lightly use the ladle or the back of a spoon to spread it outwards in a continuous spiral motion. When it is about 13 cm/5 inches in diameter, use a plastic spatula to spread the batter outwards from the centre as if scraping it to the edges. Spread evenly, using a light touch so you do not disturb the bottom layer. Aim for a diameter of 18–20 cm/7–8 inches. Dribble a teaspoon of oil on the top and just outside the rim of the pancake, cover with a lid and cook for about 2 minutes, or until the underside has turned golden-red. Flip the pancake over and cook the other side, uncovered, for 1 minute. Either serve right away or put the cooked pancake on a plate and cover with the second plate.

Make all the pancakes in the same way, stirring the batter from the bottom each time you make a new one.

Whole Mung Bean Pancakes with Egg
Guddu Pesarattu

These pancakes are made exactly like those in the previous recipe except that they are topped with an egg. Serve with a fresh chutney.

MAKES ABOUT 9

1 quantity Whole Mung Bean
    Pancake batter (see page 220)
about 6 tablespoons olive or
    peanut oil, for frying

Topping per pancake
1 egg
¼ teaspoon Dry Chutney Made
    with Three Dals (see page 276),
    or a little salt, black pepper and
    nice red chilli powder

Follow the previous recipe until you have spread out the batter to the required 18–20 cm/7–8 inches. Now crack an egg and drop it on to the centre of the pancake. Break the yolk with one edge of your spatula and quickly spread the egg out over the whole pancake. Dribble 1 teaspoon oil over the top and along the outside of the rim. Sprinkle the dry chutney over the egg, then cover with a lid and cook for 2 minutes. Uncover, turn the pancake over and cook with the lid off for 1 minute. Serve immediately.

Whole Mung Bean Pancakes with Shallots & Peppers *Ulipaya Pesarattu*

MAKES ABOUT 9

1 quantity Whole Mung Bean
    Pancake batter (see page 220)
about 6 tablespoons olive or
    peanut oil, for frying

Topping per pancake
1 tablespoon finely sliced shallots
about 1 tablespoon finely julienned
    red peppers
¼ teaspoon Dry Chutney Made with
    Three Dals (see page 276), or
    Spicy Peanut Crumble (see page
    274), or a little salt, black pepper
    and chilli powder

Again, these pancakes are made exactly like the basic recipe for whole Mung Bean Pancakes, but are topped with finely sliced shallots and peppers. Those who like their food really spicy can add a few slivers of hot green chillies as well. Serve with a fresh chutney.

Follow the Whole Mung Bean Pancake recipe until you have spread out the batter to the required 18–20 cm/7–8 inches. Now spread the shallots and peppers evenly over the top and press them in with the back of a spatula. Dribble 1 teaspoon of oil over the top and along the outside of the rim. Sprinkle the dry chutney over the shallots and peppers, then cover with a lid and cook for 2 minutes. Uncover, turn the pancake over and cook with the lid off for 1 minute, pressing down on the pancake again. Serve immediately.

Nina Chandavarkar's
Four-dal Pancakes *Four-dal Dosas*

A very nutritious savoury pancake made with four different types of split peas and a little rice, all combined together. Each dal adds its own distinct texture and taste. As with most Indian savoury pancakes, these may be served at any meal, but are very commonly eaten for breakfast, accompanied by yoghurt relishes and chutneys. I also like to roll them around a dryish vegetable dish, such as Goan Potatoes or Cauliflower with Potatoes (see page 104 or 76), and serve them as 'wraps' with a fresh green salad for lunch.

75 g/2½ oz moong dal (skinned
   and split mung beans)

4 tablespoons plain toovar dal

4 tablespoons urad dal

4 tablespoons chana dal

4 tablespoons basmati rice

20–30 fresh curry leaves,
   finely chopped

large handful of fresh coriander,
   finely chopped

1½ teaspoons finely chopped fresh
   hot green chillies

1 teaspoon salt

about 120 ml/4 fl oz olive or
   peanut oil

Put the 4 dals and the rice in a large bowl and wash them in
in several changes of water, rubbing them between your palms.
Drain, cover generously with fresh water and soak overnight.

Drain the dals. Put 250 ml/8 fl oz water in a blender, then
add the dal mixture. Blend until you have a thick, grainy batter.
Empty into a bowl and add the curry leaves, coriander, chillies
and salt. Mix well. Add another 120 ml/4 fl oz water and mix
again. The batter should be like flowing cream but with a lot
of texture. If you later find it hard to spread out, you may
need to add another 3–4 tablespoons of water.

Put the oil in a small bowl and stick a teaspoon in it.
Have two plates nearby to hold the pancakes as they are made.
Measure 70 ml/2¾ fl oz water into a ladle and mentally note
the level to get an idea of how much batter you will need
each time.

Set a non-stick frying pan over a medium-low heat and
add a teaspoon of the oil. When hot, stir the batter from the
bottom and pour a ladleful into the centre of the pan. Let it
sit for a second or so, then lightly use the ladle or the back of
a spoon to spread it outwards in a continuous spiral motion.
When it is about 13 cm/5 inches in diameter, use a spatula
to spread the batter outwards from the centre as if scraping
it to the edges. Again, use a light touch so you do not disturb
the bottom layer, and spread evenly. Aim for a diameter of
18–20 cm/7–8 inches.

Dribble a teaspoon of oil on the top and just outside the
rim of the pancake, then cover with a lid and cook for about
2 minutes, or until the bottom has turned golden-red. Flip
the pancake over and cook the second side, uncovered, for
1½–2 minutes. Either serve right away or put the cooked
pancake on a plate and cover with the second plate.

Make all the pancakes in the same way, stirring the batter
from the bottom each time you make a new one.

Rice & Urad Dal *Pancake Dosa*

Times have changed since I first started writing cookery books in 1967. Many more of the ingredients for regional Indian cooking are now widely available, and with the Internet, everyone has access to everything. I struggled with the wrong rice for making dosas for decades. In India they are made with 'boiled rice', a parboiled, medium-grain rice that is now available in nearly all Indian shops.

Dosas are very nutritious as they contain a grain (rice), a legume (urad dal), and are generally eaten with a yoghurt-based chutney to make a perfect meal. They can be eaten for breakfast, lunch or dinner. Tomato, coriander and coconut chutneys are served on the side. Quick Yoghurt & Pickle Chutney (see page 278) is another choice. Dosas can also be folded over a stuffing of Potato & Onion Mélange (see page 98), or served with a bowl of sambar.

MAKES ABOUT 9

200 g/7 oz boiled rice (Indian parboiled rice)

15 or so fenugreek seeds

4 tablespoons urad dal

½ teaspoon salt

6 tablespoons olive or peanut oil

Wash the rice and fenugreek seeds, then cover generously in water and leave to soak overnight.

Wash the dal in several changes of water, then cover generously in water and leave to soak overnight.

Drain both the rice and dal and put in a blender along with 250 ml/8 fl oz water. Blend thoroughly for at least 5 minutes, pushing down with a spatula when necessary, until you have a smooth paste. It will feel very slightly gritty because of the tiny, sand-like granules of rice. Just remember that you have to keep going until the granules are, indeed, sand-like and not bigger.

Empty the batter into a bowl. Cover and leave to ferment in a warm place for at least 8 hours. I find that my batter takes about 24 hours. You will recognize when fermentation has occurred, as the batter will rise.

Stir the batter and add the salt and about 5 tablespoons of water to it. Mix well. It should be just a little thicker than crêpe batter.

Put the oil in a small bowl and stick a teaspoon in it. Have two plates nearby to hold the pancakes as they are made.

Measure 70 ml/2½ fl oz water into a ladle and mentally note the level to get an idea of how much batter you will need each time.

Set a medium non-stick frying pan over a medium-low heat and add a teaspoon of the oil. When hot, stir the batter from the bottom and pour a ladleful into the centre of the pan. Let it sit for a second or so, then lightly use the ladle or the back of a spoon to spread it outwards in a continuous spiral motion. When it is about 13 cm/5 inches in diameter, use a spatula to spread the batter outwards from the centre as if scraping it to the edges. Again, use a light touch so you do not disturb the bottom layer. Spread evenly, aiming for a diameter of 18–20 cm/7–8 inches. Dribble a teaspoon of oil on the top and just outside the rim of the pancake, then cover with a lid and cook for about 1 minute, or until the bottom has turned golden-red. Turn the pancake over and cook the second side, uncovered, for 1 minute. Transfer the cooked pancake to a plate and cover with the second plate.

Make all the pancakes in the same way, stirring the batter from the bottom each time you make a new one.

Cabbage & Onion Patties
Bandh Gobi ki Anglo-Indian Patty

The patty-man was such a welcome sight when I was growing up in India. I could spot his bicycle just as he turned into our gate and would watch him as he slowly came down our long, curving drive. There was a tin trunk attached to the back of his bike, and that is where my interest lay. This trunk contained a British-Indian speciality – patties. These were a little like pasties, except that they were made with puff pastry, they were spicy and came in both vegetarian and non-vegetarian forms. The vegetarian ones were always triangular, with a little yellow from the turmeric in the curry powder temptingly oozing out at the joints. They were usually made with potatoes, but I have changed the stuffing a bit, so this set of patties is stuffed with spicy cabbage and onions, and the next one is stuffed with a lovely potato mixture. Serve with chutneys at teatime, or for lunch with a green salad using Yoghurt Dressing (see page 289).

You can make your own puff pastry, but since this is an 'easy' book, I suggest that you buy it frozen from a supermarket. I get one sheet in each 400 g/14 oz packet, so I need two of them.

The recipe makes eight large patties. If you want just four, use only one pastry sheet and half the cabbage mixture. The cabbage can hold for several days in the refrigerator.

Discard the outer leaves of the cabbage, quarter what remains and remove the hard inner core. Now shred the cabbage as you would for coleslaw, either chopping by hand, using a mandoline or a food processor.

Put 1 tablespoon of the oil in a large saucepan set over medium-high heat. When hot, throw in the mustard seeds. As soon as they start to pop, a matter of seconds, add the cumin and fennel seeds. Two seconds later add the cabbage and onions. Stir and fry for 1–2 minutes, then cover and cook on a low heat for 5 minutes. The cabbage should wilt.

Add the ginger, chilli, curry powder, tomato purée and salt. Stir and cook for a minute.

MAKES 8 LARGE PATTIES

1 medium green cabbage
   (about 900 g/2 lb)
3 tablespoons olive or peanut oil
½ teaspoon whole brown
   mustard seeds
½ teaspoon whole cumin seeds
½ teaspoon whole fennel seeds
2 onions (about 285 g/10 oz in all),
   peeled and cut into fine half-rings
2 teaspoons peeled and finely
   grated fresh ginger
1 fresh hot green chilli,
   finely chopped
1 tablespoon hot curry powder
2 tablespoons tomato purée
2 teaspoons salt
flour, for dusting
800 g/1¾ lb frozen puff pastry
   (I buy the pastry in two 400g
   blocks), defrosted

Pour the remaining 2 tablespoons oil into a large, non-stick frying pan or wok and set over a medium heat. When hot, empty all the contents of the cabbage pan into the frying pan. Stir and fry for 15–20 minutes, or until the cabbage has browned a bit and is dry. Set aside to cool.

Preheat the oven to 220°C/gas mark 7. Line 2 baking trays with baking parchment.

Flour your work surface and the pastry. If you have bought the pastry in one block, cut the pastry in half. Roll out each piece so that you have a sheet that is 30 cm/ 12 inches square. Trim off any excess pastry. Cut each sheet into 4 squares so that you have 8 squares in total and prick each with the tines of a fork, going all the way down to your work surface. Divide the cabbage into 8 equal parts.

Take a square of pastry and, with one point facing you, fold it towards you into a triangle just to see where the fold will be. Open it up again and put 1 part of the cabbage mixture right at the fold line, spreading it evenly towards the two edges nearest you, but staying 2 cm/¾ inch away from the edges. Dip a finger in water and dab it generously on the two edges nearest you. Now fold the pastry into a triangle and seal the edges well by pressing down firmly with the balls of your fingers. Make all the patties in the same way.

Put the patties on the prepared baking trays and place in the oven for 15 minutes. Turn the heat down to 190°C/ gas mark 5 and cook for another 20 minutes, or until golden brown and cooked through. Serve hot, warm or at room temperature.

Potato Patties
Aloo ki Anglo-Indian Patty

Before making these patties, please read the introduction to the previous recipe (see page 226). The quantities below can easily be halved. Any leftover potatoes will keep for several days in the refrigerator, so can be used to make another batch of patties or eaten at a meal with Indian flatbreads.

MAKES 8 LARGE PATTIES

flour, for dusting
800 g/1¾ lb frozen puff pastry
   (I buy the pastry in two 400g
   blocks), defrosted
1 quantity Potatoes Cooked in a
   Banarasi Style (see page 100),
   made with 4 tablespoons of
   water rather than 120 ml/4 fl oz,
   and cooled

Preheat the oven to 220°C/gas mark 7. Line 2 baking trays with baking parchment.

Flour your work surface and the pastry. If you have bought the pastry in one block, cut the pastry in half. Roll out each piece so that you have a sheet that is 30 cm/12 inches square. Trim off any excess pastry. Cut each sheet into 4 squares so that you have 8 squares in total and prick each with the tines of a fork, going all the way down to your work surface. Divide the potatoes into 8 equal parts.

Take one square of pastry and, with one point facing you, fold it towards you into a triangle just to see where the fold will be. Open it up again and put 1 part of the potato mixture right at the fold line, spreading it evenly towards the two edges nearest you, but staying 2 cm/¾ inch away from the edges. Dip a finger in water and dab it generously on the two edges nearest you. Now fold the pastry into a triangle and seal the edges well by pressing down firmly with the balls of your fingers. Make all the patties in the same way.

Put the patties on the prepared trays and place in the oven for 15 minutes. Turn the heat down to 190°C/gas mark 5 and cook for another 20 minutes, or until golden brown and cooked through. Serve hot, warm or at room temperature.

From the Taj Mahal Palace and Tower Hotel
Bombay Sandwiches *Toasties*

These sandwiches are a newish addition to Bombay street food. They were certainly not around when I was a child. The sandwich-wallah today sits with other snack vendors, with his hand-held grilling cage held over an open fire. He is making India's version of a toasted sandwich, only it has many more ingredients than you would get in the UK: sweet peppers, potatoes, tomatoes, onions and the all-important green chutney, which is what makes the sandwich Indian. It is now so popular that the Taj Hotel's elegant Sea Lounge, where I went in the 1940s and 1950s for its delicate ham and cucumber tea sandwiches, now also offers spicy toasties. I love them with a cup of hot tea. You could also have them for lunch with a soup or salad. Make the toasties using a panini/sandwich-maker or cast-iron frying pan.

SERVES 2

2 waxy potatoes (about 225 g/8 oz in all), freshly boiled, cooled and peeled (do not refrigerate)

2 medium tomatoes

½ large green or red pepper

1 medium onion

butter

4 large slices of your favourite bread

salt and freshly ground black pepper

about 2 tablespoons Green Chutney (see page 268)

2 slices of cheese, such as Cheddar

Cut each of the potatoes lengthways into 5 ovals. Discard the rounded outer pieces. Slice the tomatoes, discarding the top and bottom slices. Cut off the top and bottom of the pepper and remove all the seeds. Cut the remaining flesh into thin, long slices. Peel the onion and cut into fine rings.

Butter the slices of bread. Working with just 2, arrange as many potato slices on them as will fit easily. Dust lightly with salt and pepper. Put as many of the tomato slices as will fit easily on top of the potatoes and dust lightly with salt and pepper. Top with the pepper slices and onion. Dribble the chutney over the top, using only what fits easily. Put the cheese over the chutney. Top with the reserved bread slices and press down.

If using a sandwich-maker, follow the manufacturer's instructions. Otherwise, set a heavy, preferably cast-iron, frying pan over a medium heat. When hot, melt about 1 tablespoon of butter in the centre, then lay the 2 sandwiches on top of it. Keep pressing down hard on them with a spatula until the underside is reddish-gold and the cheese has melted. Turn carefully, add a little more butter, and toast the second side in the same way.

Remove the sandwiches, cut into triangles and serve immediately.

A Note on Sevai

South Indians make their own sevai (thin fresh rice noodles) using all manner of wooden, brass and stainless steel presses to extrude rice dough, allowing the noodles to fall on to a lightly oiled plate set just below. They are then steamed and eaten with curries as a main meal, or just stir-fried with seasonings for a quick snack. They can also be doused with cardamom-flavoured fresh coconut milk and eaten for breakfast.

These noodles are known variously as 'idiappam' in Kerala, 'nuputtu' in Coorg and 'sevai' in most other places. Taking the easy way out, I use the east Asian dried rice noodles, known as rice sticks. Unfortunately, packets of rice sticks come in many different sizes and with a variety of cooking instructions – or no instructions at all, or incorrect instructions. My recipes call for about 140 g/5 oz noodles and serve 3–4.

A packet that declares its weight to be 150 g/ 5¼ oz is fine. For a packet marked 200 g/ 7 oz, you just have to break off a portion of the noodles while still dry and save them for another use. (They are wonderful in soups.)

How to prepare rice sticks
Bring a pan of water to a rolling boil. Drop in the folded rice sticks and boil rapidly for 3–7 minutes. Each brand is slightly different, and some cook in just a minute, so keep tasting until the noodles are soft, pliable and fully cooked. Empty them into a colander and run cold water over them. The noodles are now ready to be stir-fried or reheated with a sauce or a little water whenever you are ready for them. This second heating will help them relax and expand much more. Remember, they are not salted. Add the salt as you reheat. Plain noodles may be served with curries.

Thin Rice Noodles with Lemon & Peas *Sevai with Lemon & Peas*

This noodle dish may be eaten as a snack, or as part of a meal, or as the whole meal itself if you follow it with a salad with My Yoghurt Dressing (see page 289).

SERVES 3–4

150 g/5½ oz thin dried rice noodles,
generally sold as rice sticks

2 tablespoons olive or peanut oil

1 teaspoon urad dal

1 teaspoon whole brown
mustard seeds

8–10 fresh curry leaves, lightly
crushed in your hand

2 tablespoons peeled and finely
chopped shallots

1–3 fresh hot green chillies,
finely chopped

140 g/5 oz peas, parboiled and
drained if fresh, defrosted if frozen

1 teaspoon salt, or to taste

¼ teaspoon ground turmeric

2 teaspoons lemon juice

finely grated zest of 1 lemon

3 tablespoons chopped fresh
coriander

Bring a medium pan of water to a rolling boil. Drop in the noodles and let them cook until they are just tender. They should turn soft, pliable and slippery. This could take anywhere from 3–7 minutes, depending upon the brand. Bite into a noodle to check that it is cooked through. Drain and run under cold water, then set aside in the strainer.

Put the oil in a medium non-stick frying pan and set over a medium heat. When hot, add the urad dal. As soon as it begins to pick up a little colour, add the mustard seeds. When the seeds start to pop, a matter of seconds, add the curry leaves (take care as these will splutter), then the shallots and chillies. Stir and cook over a medium-low heat until the shallots have softened. Add the peas and stir for a minute.

Reduce the heat to low, then add the noodles, salt, turmeric, lemon juice and lemon zest. Stir gently and heat the noodles through, taking about 2–3 minutes to do so. The noodles should expand a bit more during this process. Taste for balance of seasonings and adjust as necessary. Add the fresh coriander and toss.

Thin Rice Noodles with Mushrooms & Tomatoes

Sevai with Mushrooms & Tomatoes

In Kerala, plain rice noodles are called 'idiappam' and often served with fiery fish curries. Here I have put them together with tomatoes and mushrooms to make a simple vegetarian dish.

I have used fresh shiitake mushrooms, now easily available. They are sold in different sizes, some being thin and small, and others quite large with thick, juicy tops. It is the large thick ones that I prefer here. I remove their stalks and quarter the caps. If you cannot find them, use whatever is available. You need chunky, 2.5 cm/1 inch pieces. White or cremini mushrooms can be used as a substitute, and in this case you do not have to remove the stems. Depending on their size, you can use them whole or cut into chunks.

SERVES 3–4

140 g/5 oz thin dried rice noodles, generally sold as rice sticks

3 tablespoons olive or peanut oil

1 teaspoon urad dal

1 teaspoon whole brown mustard seeds

2 dried hot red chillies

8–10 fresh curry leaves, lightly crushed in your hand

about 6 large, thick-capped fresh shiitake mushrooms (140 g/5 oz in all), stems removed and caps cut into 2.5 cm/1 inch chunks (see introduction above for alternatives)

1¼ teaspoons salt

2 tomatoes (315 g/11 oz in all), peeled and chopped

freshly ground black pepper

Bring a medium pan of water to a rolling boil. Drop in the noodles and let them cook until they are just tender. They should turn soft, pliable and slippery. This could take anywhere from 3–7 minutes, depending upon the brand. Bite into a noodle to check it is cooked through. Drain and run under cold water, then set aside in the strainer.

Put the oil in a medium non-stick frying pan and set over medium heat. When hot, add the urad dal. As soon as it begins to pick up a little colour, stir in the mustard seeds and red chillies. When the mustard seeds start to pop, a matter of seconds, add the curry leaves (take care as these will splutter) and, a few seconds later, the mushrooms and ¼ teaspoon salt. Stir and fry for about 4 minutes, or until the mushrooms appear wet and glossy.

Add the tomatoes, some generous grinds of black pepper, ½ teaspoon of salt and 120 ml/4 fl oz water. Stir and bring to a simmer, then cover and simmer over a medium-low heat for about 10 minutes, or until the tomatoes are soft and there are just a few tablespoons of sauce left. Reduce the heat if necessary.

Add the drained noodles and sprinkle another ½ teaspoon of salt over the top. Stir over a low heat until the noodles have heated through and thoroughly combined with the sauce, about 2–3 minutes. The noodles should expand a bit more during this process.

Eggs & Dairy

Jeffrey Dobbs, the Sun House in Galle, Sri Lanka
Chilli-fried Eggs from Sri Lanka
Chili Eggs

This is a simple, delicious version of fried eggs from Sri Lanka, inspired by those served at Sun House in Galle. Here I am using a new technique for frying eggs that I have recently learnt. It requires the eggs to be broken into a cold pan and uses much less oil.

The recipe can easily be doubled, in which case, use a medium frying pan instead of a small one. Serve the eggs with toast.

MAKES 2

4 teaspoons olive or peanut oil

4 tablespoons peeled and finely diced shallots

½–1 fresh hot green chilli, finely chopped

85 g/3 oz finely diced tomato

salt

2 eggs

Put 2 teaspoons of the oil in a small non-stick frying pan and set over a medium heat. When hot, add the shallots and chilli, and cook, stirring now and then, until the shallots start to soften, about 2 minutes. Add the tomato and a generous pinch of salt. Stir and cook for another 1½ minutes, or until the tomato is soft, turning the heat down a bit if necessary. Set the spicy mixture aside on a plate, taste for salt and add more if required.

Wash and dry the frying pan. Add the remaining 2 teaspoons of oil and break the eggs into the pan while it is still cold, letting them lie side by side. Cover the pan and place over a medium-low heat. Keep lifting the cover now and then to see if the eggs are done to your liking. I like my yolks soft and the whites completely set, which takes about 3 minutes to achieve. The yolks turn hard very quickly, so be vigilant.

Once ready, transfer the eggs to a serving dish and salt very lightly. Top with the spicy tomato mixture and serve immediately.

Simple Scrambled Eggs
Khichri Unda

These are the simplest scrambled eggs, soothing and satisfying, but also spicy or they would not be Indian. I make them without thinking, just the way I have been doing for the last 60 years. As I break the first egg, I go on autopilot.

In Indian towns and villages they are served either with flatbreads, such as Plain Delhi Parathas (see page 195), or with toasted or untoasted slices of bread. Pickles and chutneys may be offered on the side.

SERVES 2

4 eggs, broken into a bowl
salt
2 teaspoons olive or peanut oil
2 spring onions, cut into fine rings halfway up their green sections
2 tablespoons finely chopped tomatoes
1 hot fresh green chilli (or more if you wish), very finely chopped
2 tablespoons finely chopped fresh coriander
freshly ground black pepper

Beat the eggs until light and frothy, then sprinkle a generous pinch of salt over them.

Put the oil into a medium, non-stick frying pan and set over a medium heat. When hot, add the spring onions. Stir a few times, then add the tomatoes, chilli and coriander. Stir for a minute, then sprinkle a little salt and pepper over the top.

Pour in the beaten eggs and let the mixture flow to the edges. Begin to fold all the ingredients together, mixing them gently. When the eggs have set to the consistency you like, remove them quickly and serve.

Parsi Scrambled Eggs *Akoori*

Parsis are Zoroastrians whose ancestors, fleeing religious persecution, originally came to India from Iran during the 8th century. They have kept their culture and cuisine alive all these years. Eggs feature prominently in their everyday foods, and akoori, which is scrambled eggs, is a speciality that rises to the level of a main dish. It can be served at breakfast, lunch or dinner, with slices of bread, toast or Indian flatbreads. For lunch or a light dinner, a salad to follow is all you would need.

SERVES 2

4 eggs

2 tablespoons milk

salt and freshly ground black pepper

1 tablespoon butter, ghee (clarified butter) or olive oil

4 tablespoons peeled and finely chopped onions

⅛ teaspoon ground cumin

⅛ teaspoon ground turmeric

1–3 fresh hot green chillies, finely chopped

1 teaspoon peeled and finely grated fresh ginger

2–3 tablespoons chopped fresh coriander

4 medium cherry tomatoes, each cut into 8 pieces

Break the eggs into a bowl. Add the milk, ⅛ teaspoon of salt and some pepper. Beat until light and frothy, then set aside.

Put the butter, ghee or oil into a medium, non-stick frying pan and set over a medium heat. When hot, add the onions and fry for a minute. Add the cumin, turmeric, chillies, ginger and coriander. Mix well and cook for another 2–3 minutes. Add the tomatoes and ¼ teaspoon of salt. Stir for a minute.

Pour in the egg mixture, stirring gently inwards from the outside, forming large curds and cooking the eggs to a consistency that is just a little runnier than you like. Remove from the heat and continue to stir gently. The eggs will keep cooking. You are looking for soft, large curds. Serve immediately.

Omelette with Peas & Green Pepper
Matar aur Shimla Mirch ka Omlate

Here the omelette has a deliciously gingery stuffing of spicy peas and peppers. You can use just red peppers, or a mixture of green and red if you wish.

For serving suggestions, see previous recipe.

SERVES 2

4 tablespoons olive or peanut oil

scant ¼ teaspoon whole cumin seeds

2 tablespoons peeled and
finely chopped shallots

1 teaspoons peeled and finely
grated fresh ginger

1 fresh hot green chilli,
finely chopped

100 g/3½ oz peas, parboiled and
drained if fresh, defrosted if frozen

4 tablespoons diced green pepper,
seeds removed (the dice should
be the same size as the peas)

salt and freshly ground black pepper

2 tablespoons finely chopped
fresh coriander

4 eggs

Put 2 tablespoons of the oil in a medium, non-stick frying pan and set over a medium heat. When hot, add the cumin seeds. Let them sizzle for 10–15 seconds, then add the shallots and fry for a minute. Add the ginger and chilli and fry for 30 seconds. Stir in the peas and green pepper and cook for about 4 minutes, adding a light sprinkling of water if the pan gets too dry. Add ¼ teaspoon of salt and some black pepper. Taste for balance of seasonings and adjust as necessary. Stir in the coriander and take off the heat.

Break the eggs into two separate bowls and beat until frothy. Salt and pepper them lightly.

Put 1 tablespoon of oil in a medium, non-stick frying pan and set over a medium heat. Pour in one lot of beaten eggs and stir gently to scramble lightly, while tilting the pan to let the wet mixture to flow to the edges. When slightly set, spread half the pea mixture over half the omelette. Fold the plain half over it. Using a wide spatula, turn the omelette over and press down on it lightly. If no liquid egg oozes out, it is done. If not, keep over a low heat and turn a few more times. Make the second omelette in the same way and serve hot.

Spicy Cauliflower Omelettes
Gobi ka Omlate

Served with toast or crusty bread and a salad, these omelettes make a lovely light, East–West lunch or supper. You can also serve them the Indian way, with Plain Delhi Parathas (see page 195) and chutneys.

When grating the cauliflower, use the largest holes on the grater and grate just the flower part, not the stems. Any bigger pieces that break and fall in can be finely chopped by hand.

SERVES 2

about 4 tablespoons olive or peanut oil

¼ teaspoon whole brown mustard seeds

¼ teaspoon whole cumin seeds

5–6 fresh curry leaves, finely chopped (optional)

3 tablespoons peeled and finely chopped shallots

2.5 cm/1 inch piece of fresh ginger, peeled and finely chopped

115 g/4 oz finely grated cauliflower (see introduction above)

1–2 fresh hot green chillies, finely chopped

½ teaspoon garam masala

4 tablespoons finely diced tomato

3 tablespoons chopped fresh coriander

salt and freshly ground black pepper

4 eggs

Put 2 tablespoons of the oil in a medium frying pan and set over a medium-high heat. When hot, add the mustard seeds. As soon as they pop, a matter of seconds, add the cumin seeds. Let them sizzle for a second or two, then add the curry leaves (if using – take care as these will splutter), the shallots, ginger, cauliflower, chillies and garam masala. Stir and fry for 3–4 minutes, until the mixture is lightly browned. Add the tomato, coriander and black pepper. Stir and cook for a minute, then take off the heat.

Break the eggs into two separate bowls and beat until frothy. Salt and pepper them lightly.

Just before you wish to eat, add ¼ teaspoon of salt to the cauliflower mixture. Stir and taste. If you want more salt, add it now.

Put 1 tablespoon of oil in a medium, non-stick frying pan and set over a medium heat. Pour in one lot of beaten eggs and stir gently to scramble lightly, while tilting the pan to let the wet mixture to flow to the edges. When slightly set, spread half the cauliflower mixture over half the omelette. Fold the plain half over it. Using a wide spatula, turn the omelette over and press down on it lightly. If no liquid egg oozes out, it is done. If not, keep over a low heat and turn a few more times. Make the second omelette in the same way and serve hot.

Shobhana and Padma Reddy's

Simple Hard-boiled Egg Curry
Kodiguddu Masala Vepadu

This is the simplest of egg curries and is beloved in the Telengana region of Andhra Pradesh, where it is served with a khichri (see Rice with Moong Dal & Potato, page 165), tamarind rasam and crisp poppadoms.

　　You can increase the number of eggs and the amount seasoning. No real measurements are required here. You can easily improvise.

SERVES 2–4

4 hard-boiled eggs

1 tablespoon ghee (clarified butter) or unsalted butter

⅛ teaspoon ground turmeric

⅛–¼ teaspoon salt, or to taste

freshly ground black pepper

⅛ teaspoon chilli powder, or to taste

Peel the eggs, then cut 4–5 long slits in the whites going from somewhere near the top to somewhere near the bottom but not meeting.

　　Put the ghee or butter in a small frying pan and set over a medium heat. When hot, add the turmeric, salt, pepper and chilli powder. Stir together, then add the eggs and roll them around for about a minute, or until they are golden. Remove the pan from the heat and serve.

Eggs in a Mustard Sauce
Angrezi Mustard walay Unday

This recipe has been inspired by all the wonderful Bengali mustard sauces that I have enjoyed over the decades. For a meal, serve it with rice and other vegetables, such as spinach or peas. For breakfast, have it with slices of fresh Italian or French bread to soak up the good juices. Remember, as the sauce cooks, it loses most of its pungency.

SERVES 2

3 tablespoons English
   mustard powder
½ teaspoon ground turmeric
¼ teaspoon nice red chilli powder
1 fresh hot green chilli,
   finely chopped
1 teaspoon peeled and finely
   grated fresh ginger
salt
3 tablespoons tomato purée
2 teaspoons olive or peanut oil
generous pinch of whole
   mustard seeds
generous pinch of whole
   cumin seeds
generous pinch of whole nigella
   seeds (kalonji)
generous pinch of whole fennel seeds
4 hard-boiled eggs, peeled and
   cut in half lengthways

Combine the mustard powder, turmeric, chilli powder, green chilli, ginger, ½ teaspoon of salt and the tomato purée in a bowl. Slowly add 350 ml/12 fl oz water, mixing well and breaking up any lumps as you do so. Set aside.

Put the oil in a medium, non-stick frying pan and set over a medium heat. Meanwhile, put all the seeds in a small bowl. When the oil is hot, add all the seeds. When the mustard seeds start to pop, a matter of seconds, pour in the mustard sauce and bring to a simmer. Reduce the heat and simmer gently for 2–3 minutes.

Arrange all the egg halves in the sauce, yolk-side up, and spoon the sauce over them until they heat up. Transfer carefully to a serving dish, again with yolks facing up. Pour the sauce over them and serve immediately.

Mynah Pemmaiah's
Coorg-style Egg Curry with Potatoes
Mutta Curry

This is an excellent curry to serve at brunch or lunch with some plain rice. Some little relishes and chutneys would complete the meal.

SERVES 4

4 small red potatoes (about 180 g/
   6 oz in all), boiled and left to cool

2 tablespoons olive or peanut oil

½ teaspoon whole brown
   mustard seeds

½ teaspoon whole cumin seeds

5–6 fresh curry leaves, lightly
   crushed in your hand

1 onion (140 g/5 oz), peeled
   and chopped

4 cloves garlic, peeled and
   finely chopped

1 fresh hot green chilli,
   finely chopped

1 teaspoon ground coriander

1 teaspoon ground cumin

¼ teaspoon nice red chilli powder

2 tomatoes (about 200 g/7 oz in all),
   peeled and chopped

1 teaspoon salt, or to taste

250 ml/8 fl oz coconut milk,
   from a well-shaken can

4–8 eggs, as desired, hard-boiled
   and peeled

When the potatoes are cool, peel and quarter them. You need 2 cm/¾ inch pieces. Set aside.

Put the oil in a medium, wide pan and set over a medium heat. When hot, add the mustard seeds. As soon as they pop, a matter of seconds, add the cumin seeds and let them sizzle for 10 seconds. Add the curry leaves (take care as these will splutter) and, a few seconds later, the onion. Stir and fry for 5–6 minutes, or until the onion is lightly browned. Add the garlic and green chilli and stir for 2 minutes. Stir in the coriander, ground cumin and chilli powder. Now add the tomatoes, salt and 350 ml/12 fl oz water. Bring to a simmer, then cover and simmer very gently for 20 minutes.

Add the coconut milk, potatoes and eggs to the sauce. Bring to a simmer, then cook, uncovered, on a very low heat, for 3–4 minutes, stirring now and then. If the sauce seems too thick, add a few tablespoons of water.

Sanjeeda Shareef's

Eggs in a Hyderabadi Tomato Sauce
Tomato Kut

SERVES 4

6 eggs

3 tablespoons chickpea flour
(besan or gram flour)

350 ml/12 fl oz tomato passata

½ teaspoon tamarind concentrate
(sold in bottles)

salt

2 tablespoons olive or peanut oil

6–7 fresh curry leaves, lightly
crushed in your hand

2 teaspoons peeled and finely
grated fresh ginger

4 cloves garlic, peeled and crushed

½ teaspoon ground cumin seeds

¼–½ teaspoon nice red chilli powder

¼ teaspoon ground turmeric

For the tarka (see page 11)

2 tablespoons olive or peanut oil

¼ teaspoon whole brown
mustard seeds

¼ teaspoon whole cumin seeds

3–6 dried hot red chillies

2 cloves garlic, peeled and halved
lengthways, then cut into
lengthways slivers

6–7 fresh curry leaves, lightly
crushed in your hand

Pictured on pages 250–251

Hyderabadi cuisine developed in the courts of the rulers of
Hyderabad and in the homes of the mostly Muslim aristocratic
families who followed Moghul generals sent from the Delhi
imperial Moghul court to capture and then rule the southern
Hyderabad area.

In the heat of a new climate zone, the northern Moghul
cuisine began taking on southern accents. Wheat-eaters
became rice-eaters without quite giving up their naans and
kulchas and other baked goodies. The biggest changes were
in the seasonings. Mustard seeds and curry leaves, popular in
the south but unheard of in northern Muslim cuisine, became
constants, as did tamarind. In fact, the love affair with sour
foods, which aid digestion in hot climates, began early and
has never ended. Tamarind, tomatoes, green mango and limes
are used with the same frequency as they are by the original
inhabitants. The famous Hyderabadi 'Sour' Dal (see page
149) is really not all that different from the local sambar
(South Indian Dal with Vegetables, see page 150), and it too
is eaten with rice.

This tomato kut is another sour dish served with rice. It is
normally eaten at lunch or dinner, but I frequently serve it for
brunch. It is quickly devoured!

I have allowed 1½ eggs per person, but there is enough
sauce to increase the total to 8 eggs if you wish.

Hard-boil the eggs. Peel them under cold running water and
set them aside.

Put a small cast-iron frying pan over a medium-high heat.
When hot, add the chickpea flour and stir a few times until it
turns a shade darker. Transfer it to a medium bowl and leave
to cool.

When the flour is cold, slowly add 6 tablespoons of water,
stirring until you have a thick paste with no lumps. Now add
the tomato passata, the tamarind concentrate, 1½ teaspoons
salt and 600 ml/1 pint water. Mix and set aside.

Put the 2 tablespoons of oil into a medium, preferably non-stick frying pan and set over a medium heat. When hot, add the crushed curry leaves (take care as these will splutter), followed by the ginger and garlic. Stir a few times, turn the heat to low and add the ground cumin, chilli powder and turmeric. Stir a few times, then add the passata mixture. Place over a medium-high heat and bring to the boil, stirring constantly. Lower the heat and simmer gently for 10 minutes, stirring now and then. Check the salt. You might need to add another ¼ teaspoon or so.

To make the final tarka, put a small frying pan on a medium-high heat and add 2 tablespoons of oil. When it is very hot, put in the mustard seeds. As soon as they pop, a matter of seconds, add the cumin seeds and red chillies. When the red chillies darken, put in the garlic pieces. Let the garlic brown lightly. Throw in the curry leaves (take care as these will splutter) and quickly empty the contents of the pan evenly over the sauce.

To serve, find a shallow serving dish that can fit the egg halves in a single layer. Cut each of them in half again lengthways and arrange, yolk up, in the dish. Pour the sauce over them.

Malathi Srinivasan's
Yoghurt Rice *Curd Rice*

This is perhaps the simplest version of one of south India's most beloved dishes, usually offered at the end of the meal to soothe the fieriness of the foods eaten just preceding it. It is also offered in southern temples as holy, blessed food. Known variously as daddojanam (Andhra Pradesh), thayyir saadam (Tamil Nadu) mosaranna (Karnataka) and curd rice (by English speakers), it is eaten at the end of the meal with just pickles and chutneys, but it may be served with the meal as well, in individual bowls, like a salad. In fact, diced or grated cucumbers, grated carrots, diced grapes and pomegranate seeds are often added to it.

You will find the texture is perfect when the curd rice is initially made. If it sits for a few hours, it will thicken, so add more cold milk to thin it out. Grated cucumbers also help to keep it thinned out.

You can use 1–3 fresh hot green chillies, finely chopped, instead of the dry red chillies, adding them at the same time as the ginger. Or you can add both!

SERVES 4–8

a 250 ml/8 fl oz measure of
    jasmine rice
475 ml/16 fl oz natural yoghurt
120–250 ml/4–8 fl oz milk
2 teaspoons olive or peanut oil
2 tablespoons raw cashews,
    split in half lengthways
2 teaspoons chana dal
1 teaspoon urad dal or
    yellow split peas
1 teaspoon whole brown
    mustard seeds
½ teaspoon whole cumin seeds
2–3 dried hot red chillies,
    broken in half
6–8 fresh curry leaves, chopped
1 teaspoon salt, or to taste
2.5 cm/1 inch piece of fresh ginger,
    peeled and cut into minute dice
1–3 fresh hot green chillies,
    finely chopped (optional)
2–3 tablespoons chopped
    fresh coriander

Combine the rice and 600 ml/1 pint water in a small, heavy-based pan. Bring to the boil, then cover tightly and cook over a very low heat for 25 minutes.

Empty all the rice into a large, wide bowl and stir gently to cool it. Stir in the yoghurt, then mix in 120 ml/4 fl oz of the milk.

Put the oil in a small pan and set over a medium heat. When hot, add the cashews. Stir them around until they become golden, then remove them with a slotted spoon. Add the chana dal. As soon as it starts to colour, add the urad dal and, a few seconds later, the mustard seeds, cumin seeds and red chillies. As soon as the mustard seeds pop, a matter of seconds, add the curry leaves, then empty the contents of this pan over the rice mixture. Add the salt, ginger, green chillies (if using) and coriander. Stir well and taste for balance of seasonings. Garnish with the cashews just before serving. (If not serving straight away, see introduction above.)

A Note on Fresh Indian Cheese *Paneer*

Paneer means 'cheese', and in India there is basically just one kind – a very fresh variety that is generally made and consumed the same day. With refrigeration, it can be made to last a few more days.

The process of making the cheese is very simple. Milk is brought to the boil, then a curdling agent – lime juice or vinegar or day-old whey – is added. The curds are drained off and pressed into a wheel in a piece of muslin. That's it.

In India most people just buy paneer fresh from the market. In the West all good Indian grocers sell it, generally frozen into blocks.

Nonetheless, it is very good quality. All you have to do is defrost it, cut it into pieces of the size you want and you are ready to cook. If you are in a hurry, the defrosting can be done by immersing the plastic packet in warm water. If you have time, take the block out of the freezer a day before and refrigerate it. You could also leave it at room temperature for a few hours.

Some paneer recipes appear in the pages following. There is also a recipe for Spicy Paneer Slices on page 20.

Note that paneer gets hard as it sits. If it is heated, it becomes soft again.

Dell' Art Inde and Sarita Malhotra's

Fresh Indian Cheese Cooked Like Scrambled Eggs *Paneer ki Bhurji*

It is best if this dish is cooked just before it is served, and it helps to prepare all the ingredients in advance. If you wish to cook it fully ahead of time, cover the finished dish until needed. Then, just before you eat, add a little water, cover again, and set the pan on a low heat. Stir now and then until it is hot.

The original recipe was made without peas, and you can do so here if you wish.

In India, this bhurji is eaten all over the Punjab, from village homes to roadside truck stops. It is generally served with slices of bread or toast, or any plain flatbread. Pickles, chutneys and relishes are often served on the side.

SERVES 2

1 tablespoon olive or peanut oil

5 tablespoons peeled and finely chopped onion (about ½ a medium onion)

generous pinch of ground turmeric

1 fresh hot green chilli, finely chopped

1 teaspoon peeled and finely grated fresh ginger

4 medium cherry tomatoes, each cut into 8 pieces

200 g/7 oz fresh Indian cheese (paneer), crumbled into tiny pieces

3 tablespoons fresh cooked peas, or defrosted frozen peas

½ teaspoon salt, or to taste

freshly ground black pepper

2 tablespoons chopped fresh coriander

Put the oil in a medium non-stick frying pan and set over a medium heat. When hot, add the onion and fry for a minute. Add the turmeric and green chilli. Stir and fry for another 2–3 minutes, or until the onion has softened a bit. Add the ginger and stir a few times. Now add the tomatoes and stir for another minute.

Add the paneer, peas and salt and cook over a medium-low heat, stirring for 2–3 minutes. Everything should be heated through and the seasonings well mixed. Add the black pepper and fresh coriander and stir again. Taste for balance of flavours.

Stir-fried Fresh Indian Cheese with Green Pepper *Chilli Paneer*

Chilli Paneer is a Chinese-inspired Indian dish that has gained much favour over the past 20 years. It is generally made very hot and can be eaten as a snack or with a meal. Serve it with rice or Indian flatbreads.

You might need to add a little water when reheating.

SERVES 4–5

400 g/14 oz fresh Indian cheese
(paneer), cut into 2 cm/¾ inch
squares
1 tablespoon plain flour
salt and freshly ground black pepper
3 tablespoons olive or peanut oil
1 large green pepper, seeded and
cut into 2 cm/¾ inch squares
¼ teaspoon whole cumin seeds
1 onion (140 g/5 oz), peeled
and chopped
2 teaspoons peeled and finely
grated fresh ginger
3–4 cloves garlic, peeled and crushed
1 fresh hot green chilli,
finely chopped
1 teaspoon ground coriander
1 teaspoon ground cumin
¼ teaspoon nice red chilli powder
120 ml/4 fl oz tomato passata
1½ tablespoons soy sauce
½ teaspoon sugar
2–3 tablespoons chopped
fresh coriander

Put all the paneer pieces in a bowl. Sprinkle with the flour, ¼ teaspoon of salt and some black pepper and toss to mix.

Put the oil in a non-stick wok, karhai or frying pan and set over a medium heat. Add all the paneer in a single layer and fry until golden on all sides. Using a slotted spoon, transfer to a bowl.

Add the green pepper pieces to the oil left in the pan and stir-fry for about a minute. Sprinkle very lightly with salt, then use a slotted spoon to transfer to the same bowl as the cheese.

Keep the oil left in the pan over a medium heat and add the cumin seeds. Let them sizzle for 10 seconds, then add the onion. Stir-fry for 3–4 minutes, or until it looks glazed. Add the ginger, garlic and green chilli. Stir-fry for a minute, then add the coriander, ground cumin and chilli powder. Stir for a minute. Add the tomato passata, soy sauce, sugar, ¼ teaspoon of salt and 120 ml/4 fl oz water. Stir and bring to a simmer.

Fold in the paneer and green peppers and cook gently, stirring now and then, until the paneer is heated through. Sprinkle the fresh coriander over the top when serving. (You will need to add 4–5 tablespoons of water if the dish needs reheating.)

Fresh Indian Cheese with Peas & Mushrooms

Paneer, Matar aur Khumbi

This rich and satisfying dish is best eaten with Indian flatbreads, but you can serve it with rice if you prefer. A dal and some relishes may be served on the side.

SERVES 4

8 whole raw cashews

4 tablespoons tomato passata

1 teaspoon ground cumin

1 teaspoon ground coriander

¼ teaspoon ground turmeric

generous pinch of ground cloves

generous pinch of ground cinnamon

generous pinch of ground cardamom

2 tablespoons olive or peanut oil

generous pinch of ground asafoetida

½ teaspoon whole cumin seeds

7 medium mushrooms (about 115 g/
   4 oz in all), quartered lengthways

130 g/4½ oz fresh cooked peas,
   or defrosted frozen peas

1 teaspoon peeled and finely
   grated fresh ginger

200 g/7 oz fresh Indian cheese
   (paneer), cut into 2 cm/
   ¾ inch cubes

1 teaspoon salt

2 tablespoons double cream

Put the cashews, tomato passata and 4 tablespoons of water into a blender and add the first 6 ground herbs and spices in the order listed. Blend until smooth, then pour into a bowl. Rinse the blender with 120 ml/4 fl oz water and pour that into the bowl as well.

Put the oil into a medium, non-stick frying pan and set over a medium heat. When hot, add the asafoetida and cumin seeds. Let the seeds sizzle for 10 seconds, then add the mushrooms. Stir-fry them for a minute, or until they appear glossy. Add the peas and ginger and stir for a minute. Add the cheese cubes and the salt, stir for 2 minutes, then add the tomato mixture. Stir and bring to a simmer, then heat gently for about 3 minutes, until everything is warmed through and well mixed. Gently stir in the cream and serve.

Fresh Indian Cheese in a Butter-tomato Sauce *Paneer Makhani*

This is the vegetarian version of Chicken in a Butter-tomato Sauce, for which a tandoor-roasted bird is cut up and enfolded in a rich, creamy sauce. This vegetarian incarnation is much loved and generally eaten with Indian flatbreads, especially naans. There is no recipe for naans in this book, but you can buy them from grocers or Indian restaurants. Serve a chickpea dish or the Mixed Dal, Marwari Style (see page 141) on the side, along with a chutney or relish.

SERVES 4–6

250 ml/8 fl oz tomato passata

250 ml/8 fl oz double cream

2 teaspoons peeled and finely
    grated fresh ginger

1 teaspoon garam masala

2 teaspoons lemon juice

½ teaspoon sugar

1 fresh hot green chilli,
    finely chopped

1¼ teaspoons salt

¼ teaspoon nice red chilli powder

1 teaspoon ground roasted
    cumin seeds (see page 11)

1 tablespoon dried fenugreek leaves
    (kasuri methi), crumbled
    (optional)

400 g/14 oz fresh Indian cheese
    (paneer), cut into 2 cm/
    ¾ inch squares

freshly ground black pepper

2 tablespoons unsalted butter plus
    1 tablespoon olive or peanut oil

¼ teaspoon whole cumin seeds

2–3 tablespoons chopped
    fresh coriander

Combine the tomato passata, cream, ginger, garam masala, lemon juice, sugar, green chilli, 1 teaspoon of the salt, chilli powder, ground roasted cumin and dried fenugreek leaves (if using) in a bowl. Stir thoroughly and set aside.

Put the cubed cheese into another bowl. Add ¼ teaspoon of salt and some black pepper. Toss well to mix.

Put the butter, oil and cumin seeds in a medium, non-stick pan and set over a medium heat. Put all the cheese cubes in the pan in a single layer and brown them very lightly on at least two sides. Pour the tomato sauce over the top and stir to mix. Bring to a simmer, then heat very gently for 4–5 minutes, stirring with a light hand as you do so. Sprinkle the fresh coriander over the top before serving.

Spinach with Fresh Indian Cheese
Saag Paneer

There are dozens of recipes for saag paneer in the Punjab, where dairy products are a mainstay of the diet and where this dish originated. Here is one of the simplest. It is generally served with Indian flatbreads and a dal.

The size of the paneer cubes you cut will depend partly upon the size of the block you buy.

SERVES 4–5

285 g/10 oz fresh spinach, well washed and lightly drained

1 good-sized tomato (about 180 g/6 oz), chopped

2 generous handfuls of fresh coriander leaves

1–2 fresh hot green chillies, chopped

2 tablespoons dried fenugreek leaves (kasuri methi), crushed between your palms or fingers into a powder

3 tablespoons olive or peanut oil

1 medium onion (140 g/5 oz), peeled and finely chopped

1 tablespoon peeled and very finely grated fresh ginger

2 cloves garlic, peeled and crushed

¼–¾ teaspoon chilli powder

2 teaspoons ground coriander

1 teaspoon ground cumin

¼ teaspoon ground turmeric

1 teaspoon salt, or to taste

400 g/14 oz fresh Indian cheese (paneer), cut into 2 cm/ ¾ inch cubes

Bring a large pan of water to a rolling boil and drop all the spinach into it. As soon as it wilts, drain in a colander and run cold water over it. Set aside to drain for another 5 minutes. Do not try to squeeze any more water out of it.

Put the tomato, spinach, fresh coriander, green chillies and dried fenugreek leaves into a blender in the order listed and blend until smooth. Set aside.

Pour the oil into a medium, non-stick frying pan and set over a medium heat. When hot, add the onion and fry for 7–8 minutes, or until soft and golden. Add the ginger and garlic and continue to stir-fry for another 2–3 minutes. The onion should pick up a little colour. Stir in the chilli powder, ground coriander, cumin and turmeric. Now pour in the mixture from the blender, adding the salt, cheese and 120 ml/4 fl oz water. Stir and bring to a simmer, then cook over a low heat for about 10 minutes, stirring gently now and then.

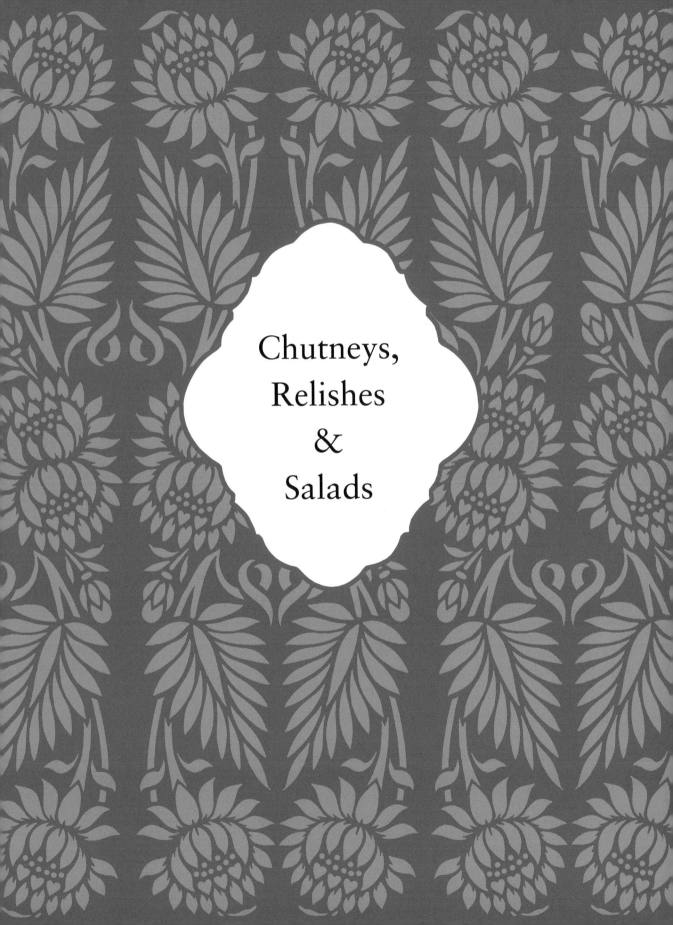

Chutneys,
Relishes
&
Salads

Green Chutney *Hari Chutney*

This is the simplest version of the green chutney that all northern Indians eat in their homes. It is dribbled over snack foods, used as a dip for fritters, and many a child, including me, has been known to take a green chutney and cheese sandwich to school in his or her lunchbox. You can also spread it on a Chapati (see page 193), along with leftovers of a cauliflower or potato dish, and roll it up for lunch or a snack.

Being a fresh chutney, this keeps only for a few days, though it can be frozen. Its bright green colour seems to bear witness to its health-giving properties – basically, lots of vitamins – as it includes fresh coriander, lime juice, green chillies and ginger. It is hot and sour and totally unlike any preserved chutney.

MAKES ABOUT
250 ml/8 fl oz

1 good-sized bunch fresh coriander,
    the greenest you can find
1 tablespoon lime juice
2–3 fresh hot green chillies,
    sliced into fine rings
2.5 cm/ 1 inch cube of ginger,
    peeled and finely chopped
1 tablespoon natural yoghurt
scant ½ teaspoon salt

Cut off the leaf-free stalks of the coriander. Wash and drain the remaining stalks and leaves. You should have 70 g/2½ oz. Chop well, as this will help in the blending.

Put the lime juice in your blender first, followed by the chillies, then the ginger, yoghurt and 4 tablespoons of water. Blend, then add the chopped coriander. Whiz to a smooth paste, pushing down the mixture as needed. Pour the chutney into a small bowl, add the salt and mix it in.

Rita D'Souza's
Simple Coconut Chutney
Nariyal Chutney

SERVES 4–6

Made in less than 5 minutes, this chutney can be served with most meals. A coconut chutney is nearly always served with Indian dosas, the savoury pancakes for which you will find many recipes in this book. The coconut powder used here is dry, unsweetened and easy to store.

30 g/1 oz fine coconut powder
1–2 fresh hot green chillies, chopped
1 teaspoon sugar
½ teaspoon salt
4 teaspoons lime or lemon juice

Combine all the ingredients in a blender along with 120 ml/ 4 fl oz water. Blend until smooth. Refrigerate until needed. Coconut powder tends to thicken as it sits, so add a little more water before serving if you need to.

Fresh Coriander & Yoghurt Chutney
Dahi aur Haray Dhaniyay ki Chutney

SERVES 6

A simple, everyday chutney that could be served with most meals. It is also good drizzled over soups.

250 ml/8 fl oz natural yoghurt
1 tablespoon lime or lemon juice
60 g/2 oz fresh coriander, chopped
2–3 fresh hot green chillies, chopped
¼ teaspoon salt, or to taste

Put 4 tablespoons of the yoghurt plus all the remaining ingredients into a blender and whiz until smooth, pushing down with a rubber spatula if necessary. If your blender seems to stick, add a little more of the yoghurt.

Empty the remaining yoghurt into a bowl. Beat lightly with a fork or a whisk until smooth and creamy. Add the mixture from the blender and stir until well mixed.

Rajul Gandhi's
Fresh Coriander, Ginger & Coconut Chutney
Gujarati Hari Chutney

Similar fresh chutneys exist throughout western and southern India. This particular one comes from the Jains of Palanpur. For more information about them, see page 77.

You can serve this chutney with any Indian meal. It is particularly good with stuffed flatbreads and the dosa family of savoury pancakes.

For this recipe it is best to buy a large bunch of coriander and pick off the required weight of leaves with the small stems attached to them.

SERVES 6–8

60 g/2 oz small leafy stems
   of fresh coriander
1 cm/½ inch piece of fresh ginger,
   peeled and finely chopped
½–3 fresh hot green chillies,
   chopped
7–8 fresh curry leaves, chopped
¼ teaspoon salt, or to taste
30 g/1 oz fine coconut powder
1 teaspoon olive or peanut oil
¼ teaspoon urad dal
generous pinch of ground asafoetida
¼ teaspoon whole brown
   mustard seeds

Wash the fresh coriander and drain, then chop well. Place in a blender along with the ginger, green chillies, curry leaves (if using), salt and 120 ml/4 fl oz water. Blend together, then add the coconut powder and blend again. Transfer to a small bowl. Check the salt, adding more if you wish.

Put the oil in a small frying pan set over a medium-high heat. When hot, add the urad dal and asafoetida. As soon as the dal begins to change colour, put in the mustard seeds. When the mustard seeds start to pop, a matter of seconds, pour the contents of the frying pan into the bowl of chutney and stir to mix.

This chutney will keep for several days in the refrigerator.

Simple Tamarind Chutney
Aasaan Imli ki Chutney

Tamarind chutney is an essential component of many Indian snack foods. It is used as a dip for fritters and samosas, and it can be dribbled over such disparate things as sliced bananas, seasoned potato patties and yoghurt relishes. It is sour, sweet, hot and quite delicious. It can be made by soaking tamarind, squeezing out its pulp and then seasoning it. Today the quicker option is to use a ready-made paste or concentrate, which seem to be the same thing, though there is a dizzying variety available. I use the concentrate, sold under the name Tamicon, because of its uniformity.

Put the tamarind concentrate in a smallish bowl, removing as much of it as possible from the measuring spoon with the help of another spoon or your finger. Add 3 tablespoons of boiling water and mix thoroughly. Add the sugar, salt, roasted cumin and chilli powder and mix again. Add either or both of the optional ingredients if you want them, and mix thoroughly.

You will now have a very thick chutney, good for dribbling on bananas, but too thick to use as a dip for fritters, samosas and other snacks such as the Salad of Puffed Rice, Cucumbers, Onions & Tomatoes (see page 50). In any recipe that requires it, I indicate how much to thin it out.

MAKES ABOUT
120 ml/4 fl oz

2 tablespoons tamarind concentrate (sold in bottles)

4 tablespoons sugar

¾ teaspoon salt

½ teaspoon ground roasted cumin seeds (see page 11)

¼ teaspoon nice red chilli powder

¼ teaspoon ground ginger (optional)

¼ teaspoon finely crushed dried mint or ½ teaspoon very finely chopped fresh mint (optional)

Smita Kulkarni's

Spicy Peanut Crumble
Shenga Hindi

Not all chutneys are wet and flowing. There are many, particularly in the southern half of India, that take the form of a powder or coarse crumble. This chutney, from northern Karnataka, resembles breadcrumbs, some quite fine and some a little bit coarser. Northern Karnataka and Maharashtra grow a lot of peanuts (and sesame seeds) and all the local people, more so vegetarians, commonly use them to add protein to their meals. This particular chutney may be strewn over rice or sprinkled over bread and savoury pancakes.

MAKES ABOUT
250 ml/8 fl oz

85 g/3 oz roasted, unsalted peanuts
⅓ teaspoon salt
1 teaspoon nice red chilli powder
(or more if you like)

Put all the ingredients in a grinder and grind until you have a mixture of coarse and fine 'crumbs'. Empty into a screw-top jar and store in a cool place.

Smita Kulkarni's
Spicy Peanut & Garlic Crumble
Shenga Hindi

MAKES ABOUT
250 ml/8 fl oz

1 tablespoon olive or peanut oil

4 cloves garlic, peeled and chopped

85 g/3 oz roasted, unsalted peanuts

⅓ teaspoon salt

1 teaspoon nice red chilli powder
  (or more if you like)

This chutney is very much like the previous one, except that it includes garlic. I find it very delicious. It too may be strewn over rice or sprinkled over bread and savoury pancakes.

Put the oil and garlic in a small frying pan and set over a low heat. Let the garlic slowly turn golden and crisp, stirring now and then. Lift the garlic out with a mesh spatula or slotted spoon and spread on kitchen paper to cool and become even crisper. (The leftover oil can be used for salad dressings or to cook vegetables.)

Put the garlic and all the remaining ingredients in a grinder and grind until you have a mixture of coarse and fine 'crumbs'. Empty into a screw-top jar and store in a cool place.

From Sayi Rani in Vishakhapatnam
Dry Chutney Made with Three Dals
Kandi Podi

Here is another dry chutney, this time made with three dals, all of which need to be slightly roasted first. It is very typical of Andhra Pradesh in south India, where such dry chutneys are known as 'podis' (or gunpowder!), and eaten with savoury pancakes and rice dishes.

This chutney can also be used as a seasoning for quick-cooked vegetables, such as aubergine, okra and bitter gourds. Generally speaking, the method is as follows: you put some oil in a pan and make a tarka (see page 11) with urad dal, mustard seeds, cumin seeds and curry leaves (take care as these will splutter). Then you add a cut vegetable and sauté it until cooked through. Finally, you sprinkle some dry chutney over the top.

MAKES 250 ml/8 fl oz

4 tablespoons chana dal
4 tablespoons plain toovar dal
2 tablespoons urad dal
½ teaspoon whole cumin seeds
4–6 dried hot red chillies
3 cloves garlic, peeled and sliced
generous pinch of asafoetida
8–10 fresh curry leaves, lightly
   crushed in your hand
salt

Set a small, cast-iron frying pan over a medium-low heat. When hot, add the chana dal and roast it, stirring, for about a minute. Add the toovar dal and keep roasting for another minute. Now add the urad dal, reduce the heat to low and roast until the dals are all a golden-red colour, about 5–6 minutes in all. Empty the dals into a bowl.

Put the cumin seeds, chillies, garlic, asafoetida and curry leaves into the empty frying pan, still over a low heat. (Take care as the curry leaves will splutter.) Stir and roast until the chillies darken and the curry leaves dry up, about 5–6 minutes. Add these seasonings to the bowl of dals and set aside to cool.

Pour the contents of the bowl into a grinder, add ½ teaspoon of salt and grind as finely as you can. The chutney will look like powder but be slightly granular. Taste for salt. It should be a little saltier than your normal food, so adjust as necessary. Store in a screw-top jar in a cool place.

Quick Yoghurt & Pickle Chutney
Dahi aur Achaar ki Chutney

I just made up this recipe one day when I was searching around for something simple and spicy to eat with my Moong Dal Pancakes (see page 216). I used what I had lying around in the kitchen, including something labelled Mango Thokku, which I had bought from the pickle section of my local Indian store. Any paste-like pickle will do. As long as it has no big chunks, it will work fine. Aubergine pickle is generally paste-like, as are many others. Some that are not, like most lime pickles, can be chopped finely to become paste-like. I just add a little of this pickle to yoghurt and I am ready to eat. You could serve it with any of the pancakes in this book.

The day I made this chutney for the first time, my lunch was a big green salad from the produce in my garden, a moong dal pancake (two, if truth be told) and this chutney, which acted as a kind of dip. It was delicious. (This is also very good as a dip for crisps.)

SERVES 1

120 ml/4 fl oz natural yoghurt
1 teaspoon (or more, if desired) any ready-made paste-like Indian pickle

Put the yoghurt in a small bowl and beat lightly with a fork until smooth and creamy. Add the pickle and mix it in thoroughly.

Tomato & Ginger Chutney
Tamatar-Adrak ki Chutney

SERVES 4

2 tomatoes (340 g/12 oz in all),
   peeled, cored and very finely
   chopped

2 teaspoons peeled and finely
   grated fresh ginger

2 cloves garlic, peeled and crushed

¼ teaspoon salt

¼ teaspoon nice red chilli powder

2 tablespoons olive or peanut oil

¼ teaspoon urad dal

¼ teaspoon whole mustard seeds

5–6 fresh curry leaves, lightly
   crushed in your hand

Here is a hot, savoury chutney, which can be eaten with almost any Indian meal. It comes from a south Indian Muslim cook in Albany, New York! He served it to me in the back of a small grocery store and I just guessed at what might be in it. A dollop of it in a soup, rather like a French rouille, perks it right up.

Combine the tomatoes, ginger, garlic, salt and chilli powder in a small bowl.

Put the oil in a small, non-stick frying pan and set over a medium-high heat. When hot, add the urad dal. As soon as it starts to colour, add the mustard seeds. When they pop, a matter of seconds, add the curry leaves (take care as these will splutter) immediately followed by the contents of the small bowl. Stir continuously and fry for about 7–8 minutes, or until you have a dark, thick paste. When cool, remove the curry leaves.

Red Chutney from the Konkan Coast
Konkani Lal Chutney

The pretty, fertile Konkan coast slithers down the western side of India from just north of Bombay all the way south to Mangalore, partially covering the narrow coastal plains of two states, Maharashtra and Karnataka. That is where this lovely chutney comes from. It has dozens of variations and may be eaten at all meals, including breakfast, when savoury pancakes and steamed savoury cakes are served in villages along the coast with hot coffee sweetened with liquid jaggery (raw brown sugar) stored in round-bottomed terracotta pots.

SERVES 6

4 dried hot red chillies or
6–7 genuine Kashmiri or byadgi chillies, if you can get them
⅓ teaspoon salt
½ teaspoon dark brown sugar
8 tablespoons fresh grated coconut, or defrosted if frozen
¼ teaspoon ground roasted cumin seeds (see page 11)
2 teaspoons sweet red paprika (not needed if using genuine byadgi chillies)
1 tablespoon olive or peanut oil
generous pinch of ground asafoetida
¼ teaspoon whole brown mustard seeds
5–6 fresh curry leaves, lightly crushed in your hand

Put the chillies in a small bowl and pour 120 ml/4 fl oz boiling water over them. Let them soak for 2–4 hours, until very soft. Lift them out of the water, remove the seeds and chop the flesh. Save the water.

Put the chillies, salt, sugar and reserved water into a blender. Add another 4 tablespoons of water and blend until smooth. Add the coconut, cumin and paprika (if using) and blend again until the mixture is as fine as you can get it. Scrape the chutney into a bowl.

Put the oil into a small frying pan and set over a medium-high heat. When hot, add the asafoetida, quickly followed by the mustard seeds. As soon as the seeds start to pop, a matter of seconds, throw in the curry leaves (take care as these will splutter). Quickly pour the contents of the pan into the chutney and mix well.

This chutney will keep for about 3 days in the refrigerator, but can also be frozen. It tends to get thicker as it sits, so feel free to add a little water to thin it out.

Sweet Green Mango Chutney
Aam ki Meethi Chutney

Green, unripe mangoes, sour and rich in pectin, are used throughout India to make all manner of sour pickles and sweet chutneys. Many of the latter are like preserves and can be kept for a long time. But mangoes can also be made into fresh chutneys, such as this one, which needs to be eaten within a day or two. However, it is so delicious, it will hardly last you a few hours! The recipe comes from a Bengali village, where my friend, the documentary film-maker Kavery Kaul, was served it as a penultimate course, just before the sweets, by farmers returning home from a morning of tilling. In Bengal such chutneys are often eaten all by themselves in meals that start with fried foods, such as fritters (see pages 23–26), go on to the rice, dal and vegetable course, then to the chutney and finally to the sweetmeats, which Bengalis love and specialize in.

My mangoes were large, so I needed just two. You will find sour green mangoes in Indian groceries, especially from April to August. You might need to adjust the salt and sugar as the amount of flesh and the sourness of mangoes can vary according to the variety and the time of picking.

SERVES 6–8

675 g/1½ lb green, unripe
   sour mangoes
salt
2 teaspoons olive or peanut oil
¼ teaspoon whole brown
   mustard seeds
2 hot dried red chillies
3 tablespoons sugar, or to taste

Peel the mangoes, then cut the flesh off the stone and chop into rough dice. Put the dice into a medium saucepan, adding 250 ml/8 fl oz water and ¼ teaspoon of salt. Bring to the boil, then cover and simmer gently for 7–8 minutes, or until the mango pieces are very soft. Drain in a sieve.

Wash and dry the pan and set it over a medium-high heat. Add the oil and, when hot, the mustard seeds and chillies. As soon as the seeds pop and the chillies darken, add the cooked mango. Stir in ¼ teaspoon of salt and the sugar, then mash up the mangoes as they cook for another 5–6 minutes. Taste for the balance of sugar and salt, adding more of whatever is needed. Serve at room temperature.

Gingery Cranberry Chutney with Mustard Seeds

Cranberry ki Chutney

This chutney is very easy to prepare. I make it with two cans of jellied cranberry sauce so no chopping or cutting is required. During the Holiday Season, I make enough to fill several jars that I take as gifts for friends. You may serve it at meals or on oatcakes or other savoury biscuits with tea. Indians love the combination of hot tea with something a bit sweet, sour and spicy.

MAKES ABOUT
900 ml/2 lb

2 x 400 g/1 lb tins of jellied cranberry sauce
2 teaspoons olive or peanut oil
1 teaspoon whole yellow or brown mustard seeds
250 ml/8 fl oz cider vinegar
1 tablespoon peeled and very finely grated fresh ginger
8 tablespoons sugar
½ teaspoon salt
¼ teaspoon nice red chilli powder (or more if you wish)

Place the cranberry sauce in a large bowl. Mash it as best as you can with a potato masher, or push it through a sieve or potato ricer. It will still be a little lumpy but that is fine.

Put the oil in a medium saucepan and set over a medium heat. When hot, add the mustard seeds. They should pop within seconds. Quickly pour in the vinegar and add the ginger, sugar, salt and chilli powder. Stir, then simmer vigorously on a medium heat for 12–15 minutes, stirring every now and then, until the liquid has reduced by about half. Stir in the cranberry sauce and bring to a simmer, then simmer gently for 10 minutes, stirring frequently.

Let the sauce cool a little bit, then spoon it into sterilized jars. When the sauce has cooled completely, seal with lids and refrigerate. The sauce should be good for 2 weeks or more.

Rifat Rahman's

Green Mango Relish with Mustard Sauce *Aam Makha*

Many Indian villages have mango trees that, as they grow larger, provide ample shade for whole families to spread cots (rope beds) under them and rest in the afternoons. Throughout the early summer, they also provide hard, sour (unripe) green mangoes that can be made into quick, refreshing salads. Here is one such relish/salad from Bangladesh, given to me by my physical therapist. Similar relishes can be found in the Indian state of West Bengal. They are eaten as part of the meal or as a snack. Kasundi, the spicy mustard sauce used to dress the relish, comes in a bottle and can be bought in some Indian and Bangladeshi shops. In case you can't find it, I have provided a quick version of my own (see Home-made Mustard Sauce, page 285).

Approximate seasonings are given for the relish because the sourness of mangoes can vary hugely. The amount of sugar used is really a matter of taste as well.

SERVES 4–6

2 large hard, sour green mangoes (about 675 g/1½ lb in all)

1 teaspoon salt

1 tablespoon sugar

1–2 fresh hot green chillies, finely chopped, or ¼–¾ teaspoon nice red chilli powder

1–2 tablespoons Home-made Mustard Sauce (see page 285)

Peel the mangoes and grate them on the coarsest part of your grater. Place in a bowl, add all the other ingredients and mix well.

Home-made Mustard Sauce
Kasundi

In the West it is very hard to find a bottle of kasundi, the Bengali mustard sauce used in West Bengal, India and Bangladesh as a dressing and a dip for all manner of sour fruit and vegetables (see my recipe for Green Mango Relish with Mustard Sauce on page 284). Use it anywhere a grainy mustard is required.

I do not exactly make the mustard sauce from scratch. I buy a bottle of wholegrain mustard and then add seasonings so it tastes and looks almost exactly like the real thing.

MAKES ABOUT 120 ml/4 fl oz

1 teaspoon white wine vinegar
½ teaspoon ground cumin
¼ teaspoon ground turmeric
1 teaspoon sugar
3 tablespoons ready-made
   wholegrain mustard

Put 5 tablespoons of water in a small pan. Add the vinegar, cumin, turmeric and sugar and bring to a gentle simmer over a low heat. Stir and simmer gently for a minute, then set aside to cool.

Spoon the mustard into a small bowl. Slowly add the cooled contents of the pan, stirring to mix. Store in a screw-top jar in the refrigerator.

Simple Seasoned Yoghurt, North Indian Style
Dahi ka Saada Raita

This is the simplest of generic north Indian yoghurt relishes. It is also the base to which you might add vegetables (parboiled and chopped spinach, roasted and mashed aubergine, boiled and diced potatoes, chopped tomatoes and grated cucumbers, etc.) and cooked legumes (chickpeas, urad dal dumplings, etc.). It can be served with all Indian meals, especially northern ones.

SERVES 4

250 ml/8 fl oz natural yoghurt
¼ teaspoon salt
½ teaspoon ground roasted cumin
   seeds (see page 11), plus a
   little extra for sprinkling
¼ teaspoon nice red chilli powder,
   plus a little extra for sprinkling

Put the yoghurt, salt, cumin and chilli powder in a serving bowl. Beat lightly with a whisk or fork until smooth, creamy and thoroughly mixed. Sprinkle a generous pinch each of cumin and chilli powder lightly over the top.

Simple Seasoned Yoghurt, South Indian Style
Mosaru Pacchadi/Perugu Talimpu

This is the simplest of generic south Indian yoghurt relishes. At the Windflower Resort in Mysore it appears on the table with all orders of Indian food.

SERVES 4

250 ml/8 fl oz natural yoghurt

¼ teaspoon salt

1 teaspoon olive or peanut oil

½ teaspoon urad dal or yellow split peas

¼ teaspoon whole brown mustard seeds

2 hot dried red chillies

5–6 fresh curry leaves

Put the yoghurt and salt in a serving bowl. Beat lightly with a whisk or fork until smooth and creamy.

Put the oil in a small pan and set over a medium-high heat. When hot, add the dal. As soon as it changes colour, add the mustard seeds. When they pop, a matter of seconds, add the chillies, rolling them until they darken all over. Quickly add the curry leaves (take care as these will splutter), then pour the contents of the pan over the yoghurt. Do not stir – leave the seasonings on top as decoration.

S. Sampoorna's

Simple Seasoned Yoghurt, Telengana Style *Perugu Pachadi*

From Andhra Pradesh, this dish was part of a meal that
S. Sampoorna cooked for me (see page 148).

Here the yoghurt is left in a rough state, not whisked until
smooth. It can be served with Toovar Dal with Spinach & Sorrel
(see page 148), some rice and Stir-fried Carrots (see page 71).

SERVES 4

250 ml/8 fl oz natural yoghurt

¼ teaspoon salt

2 tablespoons peeled and finely
chopped shallots

1–2 fresh hot green chillies,
finely chopped

generous pinch of ground turmeric

1 tablespoon oil

¼ teaspoon whole brown
mustard seeds

¼ teaspoon whole cumin seeds

generous pinch of ground asafoetida

2 dried hot red chillies,
one broken in half

6–8 fresh curry leaves, lightly
crushed in your hand

Put the yoghurt in a bowl. Add the salt, shallots and chillies.
Stir roughly to mix, then place the turmeric on top of the
yoghurt, right in the centre.

Put the oil in a small pan and set over a medium-high
heat. When it is very hot, add the mustard seeds, cumin seeds
and asafoetida. As soon as the mustard seeds pop, add the
chillies and stir for a few seconds until they darken. Add the
curry leaves (take care as these will splutter), then quickly
pour the contents of the pan over the yoghurt, aiming to
cover the turmeric so that it gets 'cooked'. Mix and serve.

Simple Yoghurt Dipping Sauce
Dahi ki Chutney

SERVES 2–4

250 ml/8 fl oz natural yoghurt
¼ teaspoon salt
freshly ground black pepper
generous pinch of nice red
  chilli powder

A simple yoghurt sauce, this is particularly good with spicy or stuffed Indian flatbreads and pancakes. It can also be served with a meal.

Put the yoghurt in a bowl and beat lightly with a fork or whisk until smooth and creamy. Add all the other ingredients and mix well.

My Yoghurt Dressing for Salads
Dahi ki Dressing

MAKES ENOUGH TO
DRESS A SALAD FOR 4

350 ml/12 fl oz natural yoghurt
½ teaspoon salt, or to taste
freshly ground black pepper
generous pinch of nice red chilli
  powder (optional)
½ teaspoon ground roasted cumin
  seeds (see page 11, optional)
1½ teaspoons white wine vinegar
2 tablespoons extra virgin olive oil

Yoghurt (and other dairy foods) often completes the nutrition balance of vegetarian Indian meals, but sometimes I just want a 'wrap' made with an Indian pancake or bread and a crunchy green salad to accompany it, an East–West mixture that seems to have become part of my repertoire. I still need some dairy in the meal for its food value, so I have taken to dressing salads of crisp greens with a yoghurt dressing that I have created. Use just enough to coat the leaves lightly. The dressing can also be used as a dip.

Place the yoghurt in a bowl. Add the salt, black pepper, chilli powder and cumin (if using). Beat lightly with a fork or whisk until smooth and creamy. Beat in the vinegar and olive oil, then taste for balance of seasonings and adjust as necessary.

Spinach Raita *Saag ka Raita*

Here is a simple northern raita that can be served with nearly all Indian meals. You could also make a light meal of it for two people by adding two handfuls of cooked, drained chickpeas to it.

SERVES 4–6

115 g/4 oz raw spinach

475 ml/16 fl oz natural yoghurt

¼ teaspoon salt, or to taste

¼ teaspoon nice red chilli powder

1 or 2 generous pinches of
  ground roasted cumin seeds
  (see page 11), plus a little
  extra for sprinkling

Drop the spinach into a small pan of boiling water and let it wilt. Drain and refresh under cold running water. Squeeze out the water and chop the spinach.

Put the yoghurt in a bowl. Add the salt, chilli powder and cumin. Beat with a fork or whisk until smooth and creamy. Stir in the spinach, then sprinkle a little roasted cumin over the top.

Mynah Pemmaiah's
Yoghurt with Cucumber, Kodava Style *Chauthe Pachadi*

Mynah lives in Siddapur in southern Coorg, Karnataka. The front of her house faces miles of open fields – she raises her guinea hens there – and at the back are the forests where she forages for mushrooms, wild fruit and wild greens, as all people in Coorg seem to love to do. She made a magnificent meal for me in her outdoor kitchen. This is the yoghurt relish she served, along with Simple Kodava Mushroom Curry (see page 87), fiddlehead ferns, young colocasia leaves (still furled up), the lightest of rice flatbreads and egg curry. For more on Mynah and the people of Coorg, see the introduction to her Kodava Mushroom Curry with Coconut (page 84).

SERVES 4

3 tablespoons fresh grated coconut, or defrosted if frozen

1–2 fresh hot green chillies, finely chopped

generous pinch of English mustard powder

70 g/2½ oz piece of peeled cucumber, cut into 5 mm/ ¼ inch dice

1 teaspoon olive or peanut oil

¼ teaspoon whole brown mustard seeds

1 dried hot red chilli

5–6 fresh curry leaves, lightly crushed in your hand

250 ml/8 fl oz natural yoghurt

¼ teaspoon salt, or to taste

2 tablespoons finely chopped fresh coriander

Put the coconut, green chillies and mustard powder into a mortar and pound with the pestle until you have a coarse paste. Alternatively, whiz these ingredients in a small grinder.

Place the cucumber in a bowl. Add the coconut mixture and mix thoroughly.

Pour the oil into a small pan and set over a medium-high heat. When hot, add the mustard seeds. As soon as they start to pop, a matter of seconds, add the red chilli. When it darkens, add the curry leaves (take care as these will splutter). Quickly pour the contents of the pan over the cucumber.

Put the yoghurt into a serving bowl. Add the salt and whisk until the yoghurt is smooth and creamy. Stir in the coriander, then fold in the cucumber mixture. Taste for balance of seasonings, and adjust as necessary.

Carrot Raita *Gajar ka Raita*

SERVES 6

350 ml/12 fl oz natural yoghurt

½ teaspoon salt

freshly ground black pepper

2 teaspoons sugar

1 fresh hot green chilli, finely
   chopped, or ¼ teaspoon
   nice red chilli powder

1–2 tablespoons chopped
   fresh coriander

2–3 medium carrots, peeled
   and coarsely grated

2 teaspoons olive or peanut oil

½ teaspoon whole mustard seeds

½ teaspoon whole cumin seeds

This raita has a slightly sweet and sour taste. If you wish, you can add a tablespoon of sultanas, but soak them first in boiling water for 30 minutes and drain them. Add them at the same time as the carrots.

Put the yoghurt in a bowl. Add the salt, pepper, sugar and green chilli or chilli powder. Mix with a small whisk or fork until creamy. Add the coriander and carrots and mix well. Set a small frying pan over a medium-high heat and add the oil. When hot, add the mustard seeds. When they start to pop, a matter of seconds, add the cumin seeds. Let them sizzle for 5 seconds, then pour the contents of the pan over the yoghurt. Stir to mix.

Yoghurt Raita with Tomato, Shallots & Cucumber
Tamatar aur Kheeray ka Raita

SERVES 6

450 ml/16 fl oz natural yoghurt

½ teaspoon salt

¼ teaspoon nice red chilli powder
   or 1 fresh hot green chilli, finely
   chopped (add more if desired)

¾ teaspoon ground roasted cumin
   seeds (see page 11)

2 large cherry tomatoes, each
   cut into 8 pieces, or 4 smaller
   ones, quartered

2 tablespoons peeled and finely
   chopped shallots

4 tablespoons finely diced cucumber

2 tablespoons chopped fresh
   coriander leaves

Here is a raita that is almost a salad. You can eat it all by itself or as part of a meal.

Put the yoghurt in a bowl. Beat lightly with a fork or whisk until smooth and creamy. Add the salt, chilli powder and cumin and mix well. Fold in all the other ingredients, then taste for salt and adjust as necessary.

Yoghurt & Pineapple Salad, Kerala Style *Pineapple Pachadi*

Pineapples came to India in the late 15th century with Portuguese traders. They first landed in Kerala, where locals disdainfully declared them to be 'the jackfruit of the donkey'. They travelled all over the country, going as far north as the Moghul court in Delhi, where they were considered a wondrous curiosity. The British in India began to grow them, along with bananas and mangoes, on the lower reaches of their coffee and tea plantations. For their Sunday club lunches, they loved to combine hot curries with sweet fruit chutneys and relishes. The people of Kerala too began to use them in the same manner, as they did with some of their other fruit, either eating them fresh or incorporating them into their everyday foods. The pineapple yoghurt salad or relish is one such dish. Southern pachadis, rather like northern raitas, can be served with most meals.

SERVES 4

225 g/8 oz fresh pineapple chunks, cut into 7 mm/⅓ inch dice (save any juice)

2–3 fresh hot green chillies, finely chopped

generous pinch of ground turmeric

¼–½ teaspoon nice red chilli powder

salt

1 tablespoon unsweetened coconut powder

2 teaspoons sugar

250 ml/8 fl oz natural yoghurt

2 teaspoons olive or peanut oil

¼ teaspoon whole brown mustard seeds

1–2 dried hot red chillies

5–6 fresh curry leaves, lightly crushed in your hand

1 medium shallot, peeled and cut into fine slivers

Put the pineapple and its juice into a medium, preferably non-stick frying pan set over a medium-high heat. Add the green chillies, turmeric, chilli powder, ¼ teaspoon of salt, coconut powder, sugar and 120 ml/4 fl oz water. Stir, bring to a simmer and cook until all the liquid has been absorbed. Set aside to cool.

Place the yoghurt in a bowl. Add ¼ teaspoon of salt and whisk until smooth and creamy. Stir in the cooled pineapple.

Put the oil into a small frying pan set over a medium-high heat. When hot, add the mustard seeds. As soon as they pop, a matter of seconds, add the red chillies. When they darken, add the curry leaves (take care as these will splutter). A second later, add the shallot. Stir and fry over a medium heat until it starts to brown at the edges.

Empty the contents of the pan over the pineapple salad. Leave the spices on top, like a decoration, and stir them in at the table.

Usha Machaiah's

Yoghurt with Fresh Mango
Mango Pajji

In the north we call yoghurt relishes 'raita'. In the south a yoghurt 'pachadi' or 'pajji' is very similar. This is a Kodava recipe from Coorg. (For more about that area, see Mushroom Curry with Coconut, page 84.) Naturally, this delicious sweet-and-sour relish has southern flavours, such as those that come from coconut and curry leaves.

Usha served this dish to us in her grand ancestral home, known as Chamaraja Villa in Coorg's capital city, Madikeri (also called Mercara), filled with handsome Anglo-Indian furniture and objects. Coorg was an independent state until it merged with Karnataka in 1956. The British, who went on to build large coffee plantations here and who loved its hills, mists and hunting and fishing traditions, could not pronounce the name of the land, Kodagu, so they began calling it Coorg. Now both names are used.

You can eat this yoghurt dish by itself as a snack, but it is normally served with meals, as a relish. It is good with both north Indian and south Indian foods.

SERVES 4

250 ml/8 fl oz natural yoghurt

¼ teaspoon salt

2 teaspoons sugar, or to taste

¼ teaspoon tamarind concentrate
  (sold in bottles)

2 packed tablespoons fresh grated
  coconut, or defrosted if frozen

1–3 fresh hot green chillies,
  finely chopped

2 teaspoons olive or peanut oil

¼ teaspoon whole brown
  mustard seeds

5–6 fresh curry leaves, lightly
  crushed in your hand

½ medium onion, peeled and
  finely chopped

1 clove garlic, peeled and
  finely chopped

1 ripe mango, peeled, sliced neatly
  and cut into 1 cm/½ inch dice

Put the yoghurt in a medium bowl and add the salt, sugar and tamarind. Beat lightly with a whisk until smooth and creamy, and well mixed.

Put the coconut and chillies into a mortar. Pound with the pestle until you have a rough paste.

Put the oil in a medium frying pan set over a medium heat. When hot, add the mustard seeds. As soon as they pop, a matter of seconds, throw in the curry leaves (take care as these will splutter). Add the onion a second later and fry for about 2 minutes.

Reduce the heat to low, add the garlic and cook for another 2 minutes. Add the coconut paste from the mortar and stir for a minute. Now tip the contents of the pan into the bowl of yoghurt and mix well. Add the mango and mix again. Taste to check the balance of seasonings and add whatever you think is needed. Cover and refrigerate until you are ready to serve.

A Note on the Maharashtrian/North Kannada Salad Known as Kosambir, Koshambir, Kosmir, Kosambari or Koshambari

I first had this salad in a Saraswat Brahmin home in Maharashtra at a formal meal served on a silver thali (platter), which contained all the dishes for our lunch. It had its special place, which was on the left. If it were to be served in a village on a banana leaf, it would still be on the left.

There are hundreds of versions of this salad (it is often eaten as a snack as well), which can be found all over Maharashtra and northern Kannada. It may be prepared with raw vegetables, such as carrots, cucumbers and tomatoes, or cooked vegetables, such as green beans, beetroot and potatoes. It can also include roasted nuts, such as peanuts, for added protein. It is always sour, made so with lime juice, though it could be tamarind water.

It could have a slight sweetness from adding grated coconut. When it is served at weddings and festivals, it always has either soaked mung dal or sprouted mung beans in it. These are offered to God in the morning, then combined with the salad at mealtime for everyone to share the holy blessings.

What most of these salads have in common is a tarka (see page 11). Once the major ingredients have all been put together, oil is heated in a small pan and seasonings, such as whole mustard seeds, a bit of urad dal, asafoetida and curry leaves, are allowed to splutter for a few seconds before being emptied over the salad. It is this that gives each salad its regional flavour.

Nina Chandavarkar's
Green Bean Salad *Kosambari*

Here the beans are cut and steamed before being dressed. Every home in western and southern India has at least one steamer in the kitchen. They used to be made out of wood and bamboo, but those are now for collectors to find and marvel at. The best of today's steamers are made of stainless steel and are used for rice noodles, rice cakes, split pea savouries and vegetables.

This salad is generally served at room temperature, though it could be refrigerated and served cold. Add the lime juice at the last minute so that the beans do not lose their colour.

SERVES 4

250 g/9 oz green beans (round or flat), cut crossways into 5 mm/¼ inch pieces

3 tablespoons peeled and finely chopped shallots

1–3 fresh hot green chillies, very finely chopped

4 tablespoons fresh grated coconut, or defrosted if frozen

2 tablespoons chopped fresh coriander

½ teaspoon salt, or to taste

1 teaspoon olive or peanut oil

½ teaspoon whole brown mustard seeds

1 tablespoon lime juice

Steam the beans for about 10 minutes, until tender but with a hint of crispness. (You could also parboil and then drain them.) Refresh with cold water, then pat dry. Place in a bowl, then mix in the shallots, green chillies, coconut, coriander and salt.

Put the oil in a small frying pan and set over a medium-high heat. When hot, add the mustard seeds. As soon as they pop, a matter of seconds, pour the oil and seeds over the beans. Stir to mix.

Add the lime juice just before serving and toss again.

Carrot Salad with Peanuts
Koshambir

SERVES 4–6

3 large carrots (about 425 g/15 oz
   in all), peeled and grated
1 tablespoon lime or lemon juice
½ teaspoon sugar
½ teaspoon salt
1 fresh hot green chilli,
   finely chopped
3 tablespoons chopped
   fresh coriander
4–5 tablespoons roasted peanuts,
   crushed
1 teaspoon olive or peanut oil
½ teaspoon whole brown
   mustard seeds
2 tablespoons sultanas (optional)

Here we have a light salad that can be served with most meals.

Combine the carrots, lime juice, sugar, salt, chilli, coriander
and peanuts in a bowl.

Put the oil in a small frying pan and set over a medium-high
heat. When hot, add the mustard seeds. As soon as they pop,
a matter of seconds, add the sultanas (if using). Immediately
pour the contents of the pan over the carrots and stir well. Taste
for balance of seasonings, adding whatever you think is needed.

Tomato, Onion &
Cucumber Koshambari
Koshambari

Adjust the salt and lemon juice in the recipe according to the tartness of the tomatoes. It is best to combine all the vegetables in a bowl but add the seasonings shortly before you serve.

SERVES 4

1 medium tomato, diced

1 medium onion, peeled and diced

1 small cucumber, peeled and diced

1 teaspoon olive or peanut oil

½ teaspoon whole brown
   mustard seeds

1–1¼ teaspoons salt

1 or 2 generous pinches of
   nice red chilli powder

1–1½ tablespoons lemon juice

Put the tomato, onion and cucumber into a bowl.

Pour the oil into a small pan and set over a medium-high heat. When hot, add the mustard seeds. As soon as they pop, a matter of seconds, pour the contents of the pan over the salad. Toss to mix.

Just before serving, add the salt, chilli powder and lemon juice and toss well. Taste to check the balance of flavourings, and adjust as necessary.

Salad with Indian-style Beansprouts
Koshambir/Kosambari

There are many possible variations of this nutritious, everyday salad from Maharashtra in western India. This version is the first one I ever ate, and I still love it.

The salad can be served with most meals, or by itself as a light lunch. You can add some natural yoghurt to it if you wish.

It is best to use small, firm cherry tomatoes here as they hold their shape best when cut.

SERVES 4

about 285 g/10 oz medium cherry tomatoes, cut into 5 mm/ ¼ inch dice

2 medium cucumbers with small seeds (about 200 g/7 oz in all), cut into 5 mm/¼ inch dice

1 medium carrot, peeled and coarsely grated

60 g/2 oz Indian-style mung beansprouts (see page 132)

½–2 fresh hot green chillies, chopped, or 1–2 generous pinches of nice red chilli powder

freshly ground black pepper

2 teaspoons olive or peanut oil

1 teaspoon whole brown mustard seeds

1 teaspoon salt

1½ tablespoons lemon juice

2 tablespoons chopped fresh coriander

Combine the tomatoes, cucumbers, carrot, beansprouts, chillies and black pepper in a bowl.

Put the oil in a small frying pan and set over a medium-high heat. When hot, add the mustard seeds. As soon as they start to pop, a matter of seconds, pour the contents of the pan over the salad ingredients. Toss well.

Just before eating, add the salt, lemon juice and fresh coriander. Toss again.

Nepalese 'Pickled' Potatoes
Aloo Achaar

More a salad than a pickle, albeit a very spicy one, this recipe comes from Nepal. It is traditionally made with mustard oil, which gives it a unique pungency that I just love, but if you find that a bit strong, use a very good virgin olive oil instead. Serve it as you would any potato salad.

In Nepal, this salad is made with sesame seeds that are roasted and ground. You can do so by adding 3 tablespoons of them, in which case you might need to use more oil later on. I have taken the easy way out and used tahini.

SERVES 4

500 g/1 lb 2 oz waxy potatoes, boiled and cooled, but not refrigerated
3 tablespoons tahini (sesame paste)
¼ teaspoon nice red chilli powder
generous pinch of ground turmeric
½–2 fresh hot green chillies, finely chopped
2 tablespoons mustard oil
1½ tablespoons lemon juice
2–3 tablespoons chopped fresh coriander
¾–1 teaspoon salt

Peel the potatoes and cut them into 2.5 cm/1 inch pieces.

Put the tahini in a good-sized bowl. Slowly add 4 tablespoons of very hot water, mixing to a smooth paste as you go. Add the chilli powder, turmeric, chillies, mustard oil, lemon juice, coriander and salt (starting with ¾ teaspoon). Mix well so you have a smooth paste. Taste for the balance of seasonings, adding more salt if you wish.

Add the potatoes and gently mix them in. Serve at room temperature or cold.

Simple South Indian Tomato Sauce
Tamatar Pacchadi

This is a wonderfully spicy sauce that can be thrown over pasta or rice noodles, spread over grilled aubergine or courgette slices, or used as a dip for a variety of crisp and crunchy Indian fritters, chips and pancakes.

As I use this sauce so often, I like to freeze it and always have it on hand. This way I can defrost it whenever the need arises.

MAKES ABOUT 650 ml/22 fl oz

800 g/1¾ lb ripe tomatoes, chopped

1 onion (70 g/2½ oz), peeled
  and chopped

1–2 fresh hot green chillies, sliced
  crossways into thin rounds

generous handful of fresh
  coriander tops, chopped

1 teaspoon salt

½ teaspoon tamarind concentrate
  (sold in bottles)

¼–½ teaspoon nice red chilli powder

¼ teaspoon ground turmeric

2 teaspoons olive or peanut oil

½ teaspoon urad dal

¼ teaspoon whole mustard seeds

¼ teaspoon whole cumin seeds

8–10 fresh curry leaves, lightly
  crushed in your hand

Put the tomatoes into a bowl and crush them as much as you can with your hand to release their moisture. Add the onion, green chillies, coriander, ½ teaspoon of the salt, the tamarind, chilli powder and turmeric.

Set a medium pan over a medium heat and add the oil. When really hot, add the urad dal. As soon as it starts to turn reddish, add the mustard seeds. When they start to pop, a matter of seconds, add the cumin seeds. Let them sizzle for a few seconds, then throw in the curry leaves (take care as these will splutter). Add the tomato mixture, reduce the heat to medium-low and bring to a gentle simmer. Simmer uncovered, stirring now and then, until the sauce has thickened, about 20–25 minutes. Taste, adding the other ½ teaspoon of salt if needed. Cool a bit, then blend to a thick sauce and serve.

Fresh Peach Salad
Aru ka Salaad

Somewhere between a salad and chaat (spicy snack food), this dish and others like it always remind me of my mother, who made them for us as a treat. In the bazaars of Delhi, similar salads were served in bowls made of large leaves stitched together with twigs. Simple wooden toothpicks took the place of cutlery. At home we had the salad on plates, though my mother always added the toothpicks to get some of the feel of the wild bazaar.

Peaches were never used in the bazaar as they were expensive. Starfruit, bananas, roasted white yams and guavas were much more common.

Serve this salad with lunch or as a snack. It should be made just before being eaten because it gets very watery as it sits.

Combine all the ingredients in a bowl. Taste for the balance of seasonings, adding more of anything you wish.

SERVES 2–3

2 ripe peaches, peeled and each
   cut into 10–12 slices
⅓ teaspoon salt
freshly ground black pepper
½ teaspoon roasted and ground
   cumin seeds (see page 11)
⅛ teaspoon chilli powder,
   or more as desired
1 teaspoon lime or lemon juice
2 teaspoons finely chopped
   fresh coriander

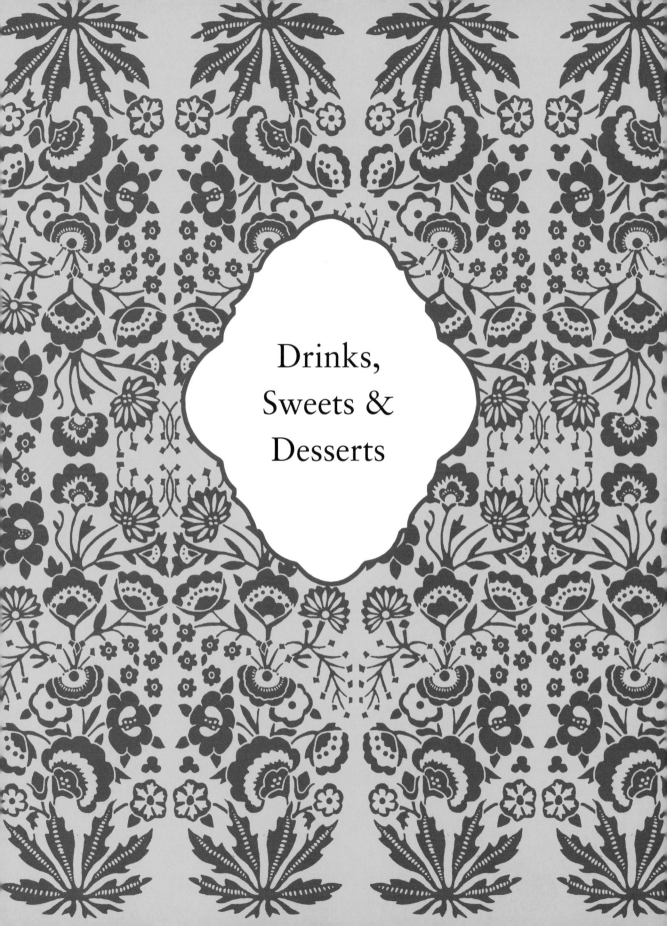

Drinks, Sweets & Desserts

A Pomegranate & Mint Drink
Anaar ka Ras

When I arrived at the Falaknuma Palace Hotel in Hyderabad recently, they offered me a pomegranate mojito. I wasn't quite ready for a proper drink, so I asked if I could just have the pomegranate juice. This is how they serve it. You could try it with a gin or vodka if you like.

This recipe may easily be doubled. I used organic, pure pomegranate juice that is easily available in healthfood stores. At the hotel, they simply squeeze out fresh juice. If you have a juicer, you could do the same.

SERVES 1

250 ml/8 fl oz pomegranate juice

15 fresh mint leaves, crushed,
   plus a mint sprig for garnish

2 teaspoons lime juice

4–5 teaspoons honey, or to taste

5–6 ice cubes, plus extra for serving

Combine the pomegranate juice, mint leaves, lime juice, honey and ice cubes in a shaker or jug. Shake or stir well and strain into a glass. Serve garnished with the mint sprig and with a few extra cubes of ice.

Sri Lankan Lemonade Flavoured with Ginger & Lemon Grass
Sri Lanka ki Lemonade

I had this drink in Sri Lanka, at a very elegant ladies' lunch in Colombo, where they also served a marvellous ginger beer. Both were offered before the grand, multi-course lunch.

SERVES 6

2 sticks of lemon grass
20 cm/8 inch piece of fresh ginger, peeled and chopped
200 g/7 oz sugar
200 ml/7 fl oz fresh lime juice
ice cubes

Cut off the very top of the lemon grass sticks, retaining the bottom 20 cm/8 inches. Lightly smash the bulbous end. Now cut the lemon grass crossways into very fine slices. Place in a medium pan with the ginger, sugar and 250 ml/8 fl oz water and bring to the boil. Reduce the heat and simmer, uncovered, for 15 minutes. Strain and set aside to cool, then store the syrup in a small jug or screw-top jar.

Whenever you wish to make a glass of lemonade, put 4 tablespoons of the flavoured syrup into a glass followed by 3 tablespoons of fresh lime juice and 120 ml/4 fl oz water. Stir to mix, then drop in 6–7 ice cubes and stir again. Taste and adjust the sweetness or sourness as needed. The syrup will make up to 6 glasses in this way.

Ginger Mint Tea
Adrak ki Chai

SERVES 4

7.5 cm/3 inch piece of fresh
   ginger, peeled and cut into
   thin round slices
20 fresh mint leaves
honey, preferably unboiled, to serve
   (unboiled honey is available from
   healthfood stores)

A wonderful tea to have on a cold day, or when you have a cold.

Put the ginger and 1 litre/1¾ pints water into a saucepan and bring to the boil. Lower the heat and simmer gently for 15–20 minutes, then strain into a warmed teapot. Discard the ginger.

    Crush the mint leaves lightly in your hand and throw them into the teapot. Cover and leave to steep for 5 minutes. Serve the tea with honey.

Heera Nandi's
Yoghurt & Cucumber Drink
Southekai Majjige

SERVES 1–2

250 ml/8 fl oz natural yoghurt,
   nice and cold
200 g/7 oz cucumbers (3 smallish
   ones), peeled and chopped
   (I like the seedless Persian
   or Armenian ones)
1 teaspoon peeled and finely
   chopped fresh ginger
2 teaspoons lime juice
½ fresh hot green chilli, chopped
   (optional)
¼ teaspoon salt, or to taste
2 tablespoons chopped fresh
   coriander or 1 tablespoon
   chopped fresh mint
ice cubes (optional)

This is a very cooling and refreshing drink.

Put all the ingredients in a blender in the order listed and blend until smooth. Strain through a fine sieve, pushing out all the liquid, and pour into a glass. Add an ice cube or two if you wish.

From Rohit Gandhi in Bombay

Yoghurt Drink with Curry Leaves, Fresh Coriander & Cumin *Chaas*

Rohit's family believes that curry leaves help to lower cholesterol. This is another simple, nutritious and cooling drink that can be served with meals or by itself. 'Chaas' is a common north Indian name for yoghurt and buttermilk drinks. It is only in the state of Punjab that these drinks are known as 'lassi', a name that seems to have taken over.

SERVES 2

4 tablespoons chopped
   fresh coriander
about 30 fresh curry leaves
1 fresh hot green chilli, chopped
475 ml/16 fl oz natural yoghurt
½ teaspoon salt, or to taste
1 teaspoon ground roasted
   cumin seeds (see page 11), plus
   extra for serving

Put 250 ml/8 fl oz water into a blender, add the coriander, curry leaves and chilli and blend thoroughly. Add the yoghurt, salt and cumin and blend again. Strain into a jug through a fine sieve, pushing out as much liquid as possible. Refrigerate until needed.

To serve, pour into two glasses, adding a few ice cubes to each one and dust with a little extra ground cumin seeds.

Curry Leaf-flavoured Yoghurt Drink
Chaas

SERVES 2

A simple, nutritious and cooling drink that can be served with meals or by itself.

475 ml/16 fl oz natural yoghurt
about 30 fresh curry leaves
1 fresh hot green chilli, chopped
½ teaspoon salt, or to taste
ice cubes

Put all the ingredients into a blender along with 250 ml/ 8 fl oz water. Blend thoroughly. Strain into a jug through a fine sieve, pushing out as much liquid as possible. Refrigerate until needed.

To serve, pour into two glasses, adding a few ice cubes to each one.

Sweet Cardamom-flavoured Yoghurt Drink *Meethi Chaas*

SERVES 2

A sweet, cooling drink that can be served with meals or by itself.

475 ml/16 fl oz natural yoghurt
3 tablespoons sugar, or to taste
1 teaspoon ground cardamom seeds

Put all the ingredients into a blender, add 250 ml/8 fl oz water and blend thoroughly. Refrigerate until needed.

To serve, pour into two glasses, adding a few ice cubes to each one.

A Note on Rasam

'Rasam' is the Tamil name for a watery, soupy dish that is eaten all over south India. It is known as 'saaru' in Kannada and 'chaaru' in Telegu, but it also has numerous other names, including 'pulusu', 'pulichaar' and 'satamudhu'. Most of the names imply a juice, an essence or an infusion of some sort.

A rasam is always sour and hot, and those characteristics initially came from tamarind and black pepper. But since India was introduced to tomatoes and red chillies in the 15th century, these have happily been added to the earlier ingredients. Stock can also be used in a rasam. This is not a meat stock but the water that comes from cooked split peas, which is utterly delicious.

At a traditional meal in Tamil Nadu, where all courses are served with rice, prayers come first, then rice with ghee, followed by rice with sambar (see page 150) and assorted vegetables, then rice with rasam and, finally, rice with yoghurt, pickles, and so forth. Everything is eaten with the right hand. No utensils are used, even for the soupiest of dishes.

If you have ever eaten a mulligatawny soup, you should know that its origins lie centuries back in a rasam. The British perhaps mispronounced the words milagu tannir, which mean 'black pepper water'. Milagu tannir was just one kind of rasam made with an infusion of black pepper and tamarind. And, of course, the British wanted to eat the 'soup' with a spoon, so the rasam was thickened, a little rice was added (instead of the rasam being added to the rice) and a spoon provided.

And that brings me to the question of serving and eating rasams in the West. It has now become quite customary, even in India, to serve rasam in a small glass or cup, or even a wine glass (if the liquid is at room temperature) as a drink. The only problem is that there are all manner of bits and bobs in a rasam. Some float to the top, others sink to the bottom, some hover in the middle. So, ideally, a small spoon has to be offered for stirring. You should stir the rasam from the bottom as you serve it, and stir it before you take a sip. Any curry leaves, chillies, etc. that float up should be put to the side as elegantly as you can. You could also try removing them before you serve.

I have yet another way to serve my rasams. I ladle them into old-fashioned soup plates and put an ice-cream scoop of hot rice in the centre. And yes, I offer soup spoons.

You will find four very different rasams in this chapter – one made with tamarind, another with yoghurt, a third with tomatoes and a fourth with the 'stock' from toovar dal and tamarind water. Serve them as a small drink or a soup, however you wish.

Tamarind Rasam *Pachi Pulusu*

Like most rasams, this can be served in a glass as a drink, and often is, but its main function is to be eaten with rice (see Note on page 315). In the Telengana region of Andhra Pradesh, where this dish originates, it is often combined with roasted and ground sesame seeds that thicken it slightly. If you wish to do that, roast 2 teaspoons of sesame seeds in a small cast-iron frying pan set over a medium heat, stirring them until they are a shade darker and emit a roasted aroma. Allow to cool, then grind them and stir into the rasam. Also, some people like to roast the green chillies over a fire or in a hot cast-iron pan and crush them into the tamarind juice. I have done that here, but it is not essential.

There are many types of tamarind available. It is best to buy the kind that comes packed in blocks with most of the seeds removed. I like the blocks from Thailand best, as they are much softer and easier to handle.

In the summer this dish can be served cold, either in a small glass or cup. You could also serve it in a soup plate with a scoop of hot Rice with Moong Dal & Potato (see page 165) in the centre. In Andhra Pradesh they serve this combination with Simple Hard-boiled Egg Curry (see page 246) and some crisp poppadoms as a light meal.

SERVES 3–4

1 ball of tamarind, about 4 cm/
 1½ inches in diameter

½ teaspoon salt

3 tablespoons peeled and very finely
 chopped onion

1–2 fresh hot green chillies, lightly
 roasted, then mashed

2 tablespoons finely chopped fresh
 coriander leaves

1 teaspoon sugar

2 teaspoons olive or peanut oil

1 teaspoon whole brown
 mustard seeds

½ teaspoon whole cumin seeds

1–2 dried hot red chillies, broken
 in half

1 clove garlic, peeled and crushed

6–7 fresh curry leaves, lightly
 crushed in your hand

Break the tamarind into small pieces and place in a medium bowl. Add 700 ml/24 fl oz boiling water and set aside for 30 minutes. Rub the tamarind pieces with your fingers to release all the pulp. Strain into another bowl and add the salt, onion, green chillies (one at a time to gauge the heat), coriander and sugar. Stir to mix and taste for balance of seasonings.

Put the oil in a small frying pan and set over a medium heat. When hot, add the mustard seeds. As soon as they pop, a matter of seconds, add the cumin and red chillies. When the chillies darken, add the garlic and stir once or twice. Add the curry leaves (take care as they will splutter) and quickly pour the contents of the pan over the tamarind mixture. Stir and set aside for 30 minutes. Serve at room temperature.

Yoghurt Rasam *Mor Rasam*

The yoghurt used in this south Indian dish needs to be quite sour. Some of the acidophilus yoghurts sold by healthfood stores are perfect for this dish. Indian grocers also sell good yoghurt, often calling it 'dahi', its north Indian name. Try to get as natural a yoghurt as you can, then leave it unrefrigerated for 24 hours: that should sour it.

The dry red chillies in the tarka (see page 11) may be broken in half before dropping them into the oil. This will make the rasam hotter.

Serve with plain rice or as a drink with the meal or before it. Stir as you drink it.

SERVES 2–3

250 ml/8 fl oz sour natural yoghurt
(see introduction above)

pinch of ground turmeric

½ teaspoon salt

2 teaspoons plain toovar dal

½ teaspoon whole black peppercorns

1 teaspoon whole cumin seeds

2 teaspoons olive or peanut oil

½ teaspoon whole brown
mustard seeds

2–3 hot dried red chillies

pinch of ground asafoetida

6–7 fresh curry leaves, lightly
crushed in your hand

Put the yoghurt in a medium pan and beat lightly with a whisk until smooth and creamy. Slowly add 250 ml/8 fl oz water, whisking as you go. Add the turmeric and salt and whisk them in too.

Put a small, cast-iron frying pan over a medium heat. When hot, add the toovar dal, peppercorns and cumin seeds. Stir and roast until the dal is a shade darker and the cumin smells roasted. Transfer to a plate to cool, then grind to as fine a powder as you can manage. Whisk this powder into the yoghurt mixture. Set the yoghurt over a medium-low heat, whisking lightly. Just before it comes to the boil, take it off the heat.

Put the oil in the frying pan used for roasting the spices and set over a medium heat. When hot, add the mustard seeds and red chillies. As soon as the seeds start to pop, a matter of seconds, add the asafoetida and curry leaves (take care as they will splutter). Quickly pour this mixture over the yoghurt, then stir together. Serve warm or at room temperature, always stirring from the bottom first.

Tomato Rasam *Thakaali Rasam*

Made mainly with tomatoes, this is a lovely rasam (see Note on page 315) that can be served hot, warm or at room temperature. If you wish it to remain only as spicy as it is just after you make it, remove all the chillies when you finish cooking. In south India this dish is always very hot, making a perfect contrast with bland rice.

SERVES 4

1 ball of tamarind, about 2.5 cm/
1 inch in diameter (for the best
type, see page 316)

3 tomatoes (about 370–400 g/
13–14 oz in all), peeled and
finely chopped

3 cloves garlic, peeled, crushed
and finely chopped

2–3 fresh hot green chillies,
slit open lengthways

1¼ teaspoons salt

1¼ teaspoons sugar

¼ teaspoon ground turmeric

1 teaspoon ground cumin

1 teaspoon ground coriander

1 teaspoon freshly ground
black pepper

2 teaspoons olive or peanut oil

½ teaspoon whole brown
mustard seeds

2 dried hot red chillies, broken
in half if you want the dish
really hot

pinch of ground asafoetida

7–8 fresh curry leaves, lightly
crushed in your hand

2 tablespoons fresh coriander leaves

Break the tamarind into several pieces and soak in 250 ml/ 8 fl oz boiling water for 30 minutes. Rub the tamarind with your fingers to release all the pulp, then strain the tamarind water into a medium pan. Add the tomatoes, garlic, green chillies, salt, sugar, turmeric, cumin, coriander, black pepper and 1 litre/1¾ pints water. Stir and bring to the boil, then lower the heat and simmer very gently for 30 minutes. Taste for balance of sugar and salt, adding whatever is needed.

Put the oil in a small frying pan and set over a medium heat. When hot, add the mustard seeds. As soon as they pop, a matter of seconds, add the red chillies and asafoetida. When the chillies darken, add the curry leaves (take care as they will splutter). Stir once and pour this mixture over the rasam. Stir again, then sprinkle the fresh coriander over the top.

Rasam *Saaru or Chaaru or Rasam*

This is the most traditional rasam served, with slight variations, in many south Indian homes in Tamil Nadu, Andhra Pradesh and Karnataka (see Note on page 315). The base of this drink is the water that comes from boiling toovar dal. This is the 'stock'. There are several little steps involved in getting this rasam right. None of them is hard to do, and the results are most gratifying.

SERVES 4–5

100 g/3½ oz plain toovar dal

1 ball of tamarind, about 2.5 cm/
 1 inch in diameter (for the best
 type, see page 316)

1 medium tomato, peeled and
 finely chopped

1 medium onion, peeled and
 finely chopped

1 fresh hot green chilli,
 finely chopped

1 clove garlic, peeled and crushed

¼ teaspoon nice red chilli powder

1 teaspoon ground coriander

¼ teaspoon ground turmeric

1 teaspoon salt

½ teaspoon sugar

1 tablespoon plain toovar dal

½ teaspoon black peppercorns

1 teaspoon whole cumin seeds

For the tarka

2 teaspoons ghee (clarified butter)
 or olive oil or peanut oil

½ teaspoon urad dal

½ teaspoon whole brown
 mustard seeds

1–2 dried hot red chillies

pinch of ground asafoetida

5–6 fenugreek seeds

7–9 fresh curry leaves, lightly
 crushed in your hand

1 clove garlic, peeled and crushed

Wash the dal in several changes of water, then drain and place in a medium pan. Add 1.5 litres/2½ pints water and bring to the boil. Skim off the froth, then cover partially and simmer for 1 hour. Strain into a large pan, getting at least 1 litre/ 1¾ pints of liquid. If there is not enough, add a little water. Save the cooked dal for other purposes.

While the dal is cooking, break the tamarind ball into pieces and soak in 250 ml/8 fl oz boiling water for at least 30 minutes. Rub the tamarind with your fingers to release all the pulp, then strain the tamarind water into the pan of dal stock. Add the tomato, onion, green chilli, garlic, chilli powder, ground coriander, turmeric, salt and sugar.

Put a small, cast-iron frying pan over a medium heat. When hot, add the toovar dal, black peppercorns and cumin seeds. Stir and roast until the dal is a shade darker and the cumin smells roasted. Transfer to a plate to cool, then grind to as fine a powder as you can manage. Add this powder to the pan of rasam and bring to the boil. Reduce the heat to medium-low and simmer vigorously for 30 minutes, or until reduced by about 20 per cent. Taste for balance of seasonings, making adjustments as needed.

To make the tarka (see page 11), put the ghee into a small, cast-iron frying and set over a medium heat. When hot, add the urad dal. As soon as it starts to colour, add the mustard seeds, red chillies and asafoetida. When the seeds pop and the chillies darken, a matter of seconds, add the fenugreek seeds, curry leaves (take care as they will splutter) and garlic. Stir once or twice, then empty the contents of the frying pan into the rasam. Simmer gently for another 10 minutes. Stir from the bottom before serving.

I like to serve this hot, in an old-fashioned soup plate with a scoop of hot, plain rice in the centre.

A Note on Jaggery

Jaggery is a form of raw sugar. My father once managed a sugar factory that made refined sugar and candy. Our house at that time was set in the middle of acres upon acres of sugar cane. The cane was cut, juiced and then boiled. As the juice solidified, it was called jaggery. You could get it fairly molten in the early stages, but then it got harder. As India has always had sugar cane, jaggery has been used since ancient times and is as popular today as it ever was. It is used in many sweet dishes and brittles.

There are really two types of jaggery in India. Along the coast it is made from both palm sugar and sugar cane, but inland only sugar cane jaggery is available.

Indian grocers in the West sell jaggery in various shapes – cones, pebbles or big rocks – and in colours ranging from dark brown to light brown and everything in between. Sometimes it is crumbly and at other times it is very hard. For the recipes in this book, look for light-coloured jaggery that is soft and crumbly. You can use light brown sugar as a substitute, but it will not have the true jaggery flavour.

Melon Balls with Mint
Pudina Kharbooja

A lovely summery dessert, this needs to be made ahead of
time and refrigerated.

   The melon should be very sweet. If you have a double-
ended melon-baller, use the larger end of the scoop.

   Kewra water has an aroma very similar to that of the
South-east Asian paandaan leaf, a lovely tropical fragrance.
Rose water or orange blossom water may be substituted.

SERVES 4–5

1 large melon, about 1.7 kg/3¾ lb

1 teaspoon ground cardamom seeds

6 tablespoons sugar

about 35 fresh mint leaves,
   very finely chopped

2 tablespoons lime juice

2–3 teaspoons kewra water, rose
   water or orange blossom water

Cut the melon in half and discard all the seeds. Using a
melon-baller, scoop out the flesh and place in a serving bowl.
Sprinkle with the cardamom and mix well.

   Put the sugar in a small bowl. Add the mint leaves and
rub them into the sugar with your fingers. Add the lime juice
and your choice of fragrant water. Mix well and pour over
the melon balls. Mix, cover and refrigerate, stirring every
now and then. Serve cold in small dishes with the juices.

Meera Prasad's
Melon Payasam *Kharbooja Payasam*

Meera Prasad cooked what can best be described as a banquet for us in Bangalore, at the end of which, she presented this melon payasam. Nothing could have been nicer. Payasam, in south India, is a pudding, generally made with grains or beans and sometimes with fruit. I love fruit desserts, as they tend to be lighter and somehow perfect after a spicy Indian meal. This is served cold, so for me it is doubly perfect – cooling and refreshing. I have been serving it frequently, and now you can do the same. I like to serve this in an ice-cream dish with a spoon, as it is fairly watery.

I have used jaggery, a raw Indian sugar here (see Note, page 321). I buy the palest variety and grate it on the coarsest part of the grater. You can use light brown sugar instead, but taste as you go because you will need much less of it.

I bought a large melon that weighed about 1.7 kg/3¾ lb. After removing the skin and seeds and chopping it, I got 900 g/2 lb finely chopped flesh. For chopping the melon into a kind of mush just short of pulverization, I use a large knife. I am careful to preserve all the juices and then add them to the melon. You could also put larger pieces of melon into a food processor and chop them very small by pulsing in short bursts.

SERVES 4–5

900 g/2 lb very finely chopped
   melon (green or orange flesh)
315 g/10½ oz pale-coloured jaggery,
   grated
175 ml/6 fl oz coconut milk,
   from a well-shaken can
½ teaspoon ground cardamom
   seeds, plus a little extra
   for sprinkling

Place all the ingredients in a bowl and stir together. Cover and chill in the refrigerator. Dust with a little ground cardamom before serving.

Cardamom-flavoured Butter Biscuits
Naan Khatai

These are my favourite Indian biscuits, and very easy to put together. I have loved naan khatai since I was a child. They are light and crumbly and also slightly chewy, with a texture somewhere between that of shortbread and a macaroon.

MAKES 24

50 g/1¾ oz plain flour

60 g/2 oz sooji (Indian semolina, see page 176)

60 g/2 oz chickpea flour (besan or gram flour)

¼ teaspoon baking powder

½ teaspoon ground cardamom seeds

115 g/4 oz soft unsalted butter, plus a little extra for greasing

140 g/5 oz sugar

1 tablespoon chopped flaked almonds

1 tablespoon chopped raw pistachios

Preheat the oven to 190°C/gas mark 5.

Combine the flour, sooji, chickpea flour, baking powder and cardamom in a medium bowl. Mix together with a fork or dry whisk.

Put the butter and sugar in a large bowl. Using an electric beater, cream the two together until light and frothy. Add the flour mixture, then use your hands and a light touch to combine them and form a ball of dough. Break the ball into 24 equal parts and roll each into a ball. Make sure there are no cracks in the balls. Flatten the balls very slightly between your palms.

Grease a baking sheet with butter. Lay the slightly flattened balls on it about 4 cm/1½ inches apart. Cut shallow lines in the pattern of a noughts and crosses grid on top of each biscuit without going right to the edge. Place a mixture of the nuts in the central square, pushing them down a bit so they do not roll off. Bake for 12–14 minutes (they will still be very soft), then set aside to cool on the sheet for 5 minutes. Using a fine spatula, carefully transfer them to a wire rack to cool completely. Store in a flat, airtight container.

Caramelized Bananas
with Sesame Seeds
Kelay Ka Meetha

SERVES 2–4

1 teaspoon sesame seeds

30 g/1 oz ghee (clarified butter)
  or ordinary butter

2 tablespoons sugar

2 ripe but very firm bananas

120 ml/4 fl oz double cream, lightly
  whipped to soft peaks (optional)

A simple sweet or dessert that could be made hastily for
a hungry child or grown-up.

Put a small, cast-iron frying pan over a medium heat. When
hot, add the sesame seeds and roast them for a minute or so,
stirring until they are a shade darker and smell roasted. They
might fly about, in which case, cover loosely but keep stirring.
Transfer to a small bowl when done. (This can be done ahead
of time.)

Put the ghee or butter in a medium, non-stick frying pan
and set over a low heat. When it has melted, sprinkle in the
sugar evenly. Stir and let the sugar start to caramelize. Peel
the bananas and cut them in half crossways, then lengthways.
Place them in the pan in a single layer and cook over a medium-
low heat for about 1½ minutes on each side, or until they are
golden and coated with the caramel.

Transfer the bananas to a serving dish and sprinkle the
sesame seeds over the top. Serve hot, offering the whipped
cream separately (if using).

Fried Stuffed Dates
Khajoor ka Meetha

A long time ago, when I was working on my very first cookbook, I wrote a recipe for simple fried dates that I had learnt from my sister, Kamal, who had learnt it from her Gujarati Bohra in-laws. It was a sticky, chewy and easy-to-make sweetmeat, and I just loved it. So, apparently, did Elizabeth David. When my book was published, she wrote me a little note to say so. That made my day! I have been cooking those dates for several decades, but over time I have added this or that to them. Here is my newest variation. I serve it at the end of the meal with coffee, along with Cardamom-flavoured Butter Biscuits (see page 325), and squares of Sooji Halva (see page 331), both of which I make in advance. The dates, though, have to be made at the last minute, but they could be stuffed well ahead of time and kept covered.

Note that the nuts need to be chopped to a fairly small size so they can be stuffed into a date, but not so small that they turn into crumbs.

MAKES 16 DATES

16 medium-sized dates, stoned
about 3 tablespoons chopped
    raw pistachios and walnuts
3 tablespoons ghee (clarified butter)
250 ml/8 fl oz double cream,
    whipped to a soft foam

If the dates have been stoned by making a slit down one side, open them up slightly, one at a time, and stuff about ½ teaspoon of the nuts inside them. If the stones have been pulled out from the top, you will have to push the nuts in from the top and bottom of the date. Cover the stuffed dates with cling film and set aside until you are ready to eat them.

Put the ghee in a medium, non-stick frying pan and set over a medium heat. When hot, add the dates and stir them around for 10–20 seconds. Using a slotted spoon, quickly transfer them to a dish and serve immediately. Offer the cream separately to put on top of the dates.

From the Highway Gomantak
restaurant in Bombay

Sooji Pudding with Coconut Milk
Sooji Kheer

From the Goa region of western India, this dish is one of those soothing, calming puddings that would make toddlers as happy as grown-ups. It is similar to rice pudding, except it is made with sooji (Indian semolina, see page 176), not rice. It is somewhat like the next recipe for halva, but kheers are less dense and a bit more flowing. Besides, this has the lovely coastal taste of coconut and cashews.

In India, some fresh coconut, ground so it is satiny-smooth, is added to the kheer. I can never get mine to the right texture, so I have just left it out and used only coconut milk, which is also called for. This kheer gets thicker as it sits, so you might need to thin it with water or coconut milk if you do not eat it immediately.

SERVES 6

4 tablespoons ghee (clarified butter)

4 tablespoons coarsely chopped raw cashews

4 tablespoons sultanas

100 g/3½ oz sooji

115 g/4 oz light brown sugar (taste and add more, if desired, when the kheer thickens)

½ teaspoon ground cardamom seeds

1 x 400 ml/14 fl oz can coconut milk, well shaken

Put the ghee in a medium, non-stick deep frying pan and set over a medium-low heat. When hot, add the cashews and stir until they turn golden. Using a slotted spoon, quickly transfer the nuts to a plate.

Add the sultanas to the ghee remaining in the pan. They will plump up almost immediately. Remove them with the slotted spoon and put next to the cashews.

Put the sooji into the remaining ghee and fry over a low heat for 6–7 minutes, stirring now and then, until it is golden. Add the sugar and mix well. Add 600 ml/1 pint water, the ground cardamom, and most of the reserved nuts and sultanas (save some for the decoration). Bring to a simmer over a medium-low heat, then stir and cook over a low heat for 4 minutes. Add the coconut milk, stir and cook for 5–6 minutes, until the kheer has thickened. Turn off the heat and keep stirring gently until the kheer has cooled a bit. It will also get thicker. Cover the kheer with cling film in such a way that it touches the whole surface of it. This will prevent a skin forming on the top.

Serve hot, warm or at room temperature, decorated with the remaining nuts and sultanas.

Sooji Halva

Sooji, an Indian semolina made with soft wheat (see page 176) may be used to make quick savoury dishes, but it makes equally quick sweet dishes as well. The most popular amongst them is probably this halva, enjoyed equally by the poorest villager and the richest industrialist in north India. As it is always offered to the gods at temples on religious occasions, then given back to people praying at the temples as prashad (blessed food), it carries with it an air of holiness even when it is cooked at home.

Sooji halva is cooked in ghee and very easy to prepare. It is often eaten by itself as a sweet dish or dessert. You can eat it just the way it comes out of the frying pan, hot and soft, or you can put it into a square or rectangular cake tin, press down on it and then cut it into squares. These have a cake-like texture and are perfect with a cup of tea.

But there is another way sooji halva is served. At Sunday breakfasts it is frequently offered, nice and hot, with Pooris (see page 206) and spicy potatoes, such as Potatoes Cooked in a Banarasi Style (see page 100). The combination of something sweet and something spicy is quite enticing.

My halva is lightly sweetened, just the way I like it. If you want it sweeter, add another 1–2 tablespoons of sugar.

SERVES 4–5

4 tablespoons ghee (clarified butter)

2 tablespoons flaked almonds

2 tablespoons raw, shelled pistachios, cut into long slivers

90 g/3 oz sooji (Indian semolina)

70 g/2½ oz sugar

¼ teaspoon ground cardamom seeds

Put the ghee in a medium, non-stick frying pan and set over a medium-low heat. When hot, add the almonds and pistachios, and stir just until the almonds turn golden. Using a slotted spoon, quickly transfer the nuts to a plate.

Put the sooji into the ghee remaining in the pan and fry over a low heat for 6–7 minutes, stirring now and then, until it is golden. Add the sugar and mix well. Add 350 ml/12 fl oz water, the ground cardamom and the reserved nuts, and bring to a simmer over a medium-low heat. Stir and cook over a very low heat for 2–3 minutes, then turn off the heat and stir for another minute. Serve hot.

If you prefer, you could put the halva into an 18 x 18 cm/ 7 x 7 inch cake tin or similarly shaped dish. Press down lightly and flatten the surface, then cut into 4 cm/1½ inch squares. When it has cooled to room temperature, place cling film directly on the surface of the cake to stop a skin forming. Serve immediately or later, as you would any cake.

Sooji Crêpes Stuffed with Caramelized Apples, Coconut & Walnuts
Sooji ki Bharva Pancake

SERVES 6

120 ml/4 fl oz natural yoghurt

180 g/6 oz sooji (Indian semolina)

85 g/3 oz rice flour (also called
powdered rice)

2 tablespoons plain flour

¼ teaspoon salt

1 tablespoon sugar

about 2 tablespoons olive or
peanut oil

For the stuffing

115 g/4 oz unsalted butter

4 large Granny Smith's or
other sour, firm apples

½ teaspoon ground cardamom

2 tablespoons chopped walnuts

2 tablespoons chopped
raw pistachios

2 tablespoons chopped
flaked almonds

70 g/2½ oz finely shredded fresh
coconut, or defrosted if frozen

195 g/6½ oz sugar

For serving

250 ml/8 fl oz double cream

1 tablespoon sugar

¼ teaspoon ground cardamom

In Goa, pancakes are often stuffed with a sweetened coconut and nut mixture. I have added apples to it to make a stuffing of my own. The crêpes are very similar to the Sooji Pancakes on page 210, but instead of spices, they have a bit of sugar in them.

The filling and the crêpes may be made a few hours ahead of time, but do not refrigerate them. Put the filling in a covered dish, then stack the crêpes, interleaved with sheets of waxed paper or baking parchment, and wrap the bundle in foil. Shortly before serving, put the dish of stuffing and the foil bundle into a warming oven to reheat. Serve warm, not hot.

Place the yoghurt in a bowl and beat lightly with a fork or whisk until smooth and creamy. Slowly add 600 ml/1 pint water, mixing well as you go.

Put the sooji, rice flour, white flour, salt and sugar in a large bowl. Slowly add the yoghurt combination, mixing until thoroughly blended and you have a batter free of lumps. Set aside for at least 1 hour.

To make the stuffing, put the butter into a medium, non-stick frying pan and set over a very low heat to melt. Meanwhile, peel and core the apples and slice them straight into the butter, folding them in as you do so. I get about 6 thinnish slices from each apple quarter. Add the cardamom, all the nuts, the coconut and sugar. Stir gently and cook over a medium-low heat for about 4 minutes, until the sugar has completely dissolved. Increase the heat to medium-high and continue cooking, stirring gently now and then, until the mixture has caramelized a bit, about 7–8 minutes. Turn off the heat and set aside, covered.

Put the oil in a small bowl and stick a teaspoon in it. Have two plates nearby to hold the pancakes as they are made. Measure 70 ml/2½ fl oz water into a ladle and mentally note the level to get an idea of how much batter you will need each time.

Place a non-stick frying pan over a medium heat and add 1 teaspoon of oil to it. When hot, stir the batter from the bottom and slowly pour a ladleful into the pan in an expanding circle about 15 cm/6 inches in diameter. This batter is very forgiving, so you can fill up any holes and round off the pancake to get the shape you want. Let the pancake sit for a minute or so, until the underside is golden-red.

Slide a spatula underneath and flip the pancake over. Cook for another minute or so, until the other side is also golden-red. Transfer to a plate.

Make at least another 6 pancakes in the same way; the first one rarely turns out perfectly, so you might be making 7 or 8. Remember to stir the batter thoroughly each time from the bottom. Place a sheet of waxed paper or baking parchment between each pancake and cover the stack with an upturned plate. Leftover batter can be stored in the refrigerator for several days.

Whip the cream into soft peaks, adding the sugar and the cardamom. Refrigerate until needed.

To serve, lay a pancake, best-side down, on a plate. Place as much stuffing as will fit easily on half of it, then fold the uncovered half over it. Put a good-sized dollop of cream on top. (Leftover stuffing can be refrigerated and used later.)

Mangoes Mumtaz
Aam Mumtaz

It has never been easy for me to decide what the dessert should be after one of my more formal Indian dinners. I like light, fruity desserts, but India seems to have a shortage of them (we tend to eat fresh fruit instead), so I have taken to creating my own. This is one of them. I have been serving it in different versions over the last 20 years, and this is the latest incarnation.

I was to attend the Mango Festival in Florida one year, and shortly before it a reporter from the *Miami Herald* came to interview me in New York. She turned out to be an old friend, Maricel Presilla, the most knowledgeable wizard of Latin American cooking. I made a lunch for her that ended with this dessert. 'What is it called?' she asked as she took notes. 'I don't know,' I answered. 'It is just something I make.' 'You can't have no name for it. Let's call it…' And so Maricel named it 'Mangoes Mumtaz'.

The best mango purée you can use is one that comes from canned, sweetened Alphonso mangoes. Indian grocers sell it.

First make the praline. Preheat the oven to 180°C/gas mark 4. Grease a small baking sheet with oil.

Spread the pistachios in a baking tin and put them into the oven. Stir every few minutes until lightly toasted. Set aside.

Put the sugar into a small, heavy-based saucepan and set over a medium-high heat. Keep swirling the pan as the sugar melts and then starts to caramelize. As soon as it becomes light brown, add the toasted pistachios and the ground cardamom seeds. Let the mixture bubble for a few seconds as you stir. Quickly take the pan off the heat and spread the praline on the oiled baking sheet. Allow 10 minutes for it to cool and harden, then break into pieces and either crush in a mortar or whiz in a blender. Keep it in a screw-top jar and use as needed.

The rest of the dessert should be made just before serving. Whip the cream with the sugar until it forms soft peaks. Add the ground cardamom and pistachios, plus 1–2 tablespoons of the praline and fold together. Pour in the mango purée and fold lightly so you can see swirls of both white and orange.

Scoop the mixture into four serving bowls. Divide the diced mango between the bowls, mixing it in lightly. Decorate each bowl with a teaspoon of the praline and serve immediately.

SERVES 4

250 ml/8 fl oz double cream

3 tablespoons sugar

½ teaspoon ground cardamom seeds

60 g/2 oz chopped unsalted, raw pistachios

175 ml/6 fl oz canned, sweetened Alphonso mango purée

165 g/5½ oz fresh mango flesh, preferably Alphonso, neatly diced

For the praline

olive or peanut oil, for greasing

60 g/2 oz chopped unsalted, raw pistachios

100 g/3½ oz sugar

½ teaspoon ground cardamom seeds

Chapter Recipe Lists

SOUPS, APPETIZERS & SNACKS

VEGETABLES

DALS: DRIED BEANS & LEGUMES

EGGS & DAIRY

CHUTNEYS, RELISHES & SALADS

DRINKS, SWEETS & DESSERTS

Index

A

Acknowledgements

I would like to thank the following for helping me to make this book possible: Vikram Doctor, Rita D'Souza, Fatma Zakaria, Sunita Nair, the Taj Hotel in Bombay, Shashikala Potnis and Sanjali Potnis at the Highway Gomantak restaurant in Bombay, Rajul Gandhi, Boman Kohinoor at Britannia & Company, Usha Subramaniam, Rohit, Sarita, Kapil and Yogesh Malhotra at Dell' Arte Inde, Ravi Gandhi at Gazdar, Aziz Javeri at Joy Shoes, Kalini Kodial, Suman Kodial, Simran Lal and Anita Lal from Good Earth, Meera Kumar, Cecelia Kerketta, Mugdha Savkar, Janaki Shirgaonkar, Tarini Bahadur, the Chinmaya Mission in Delhi, the Aurobindo Ashram in Delhi, Saraswathy Ganapathy and Girish Karnad, Geetha Rao, Malathi Srinivasan, Nina Bopiah, Kaveri Ponnapa, Nina Chandavarkar, Tara Chandavarkar, Shantha Gersappe, Sarvanna, Dr Meera Prasad, Chef Selveraju at Vivanta by Taj in Bangalore, Varukaranam Usha Rani, K.P. Uthappa and Vani Uthappa, Chhoti and Kiran Machaiah, Mynah Pemmaiah, Heera Nandi, Zubeda Vagh, Chef Srinivasan at the Windflower Resort and Spa in Mysore, Swarnalatha and Rajalaxshmi, Andrew, our driver, Usha Ramakrishna, Vinita Pittie, Geeta Devi, Falaknuma Palace Hotel, Rehana, Anwar Alikhan and his family, Sanjeeda Shareef, D. Lalitha, Smita Kulkarni, Shobhana Reddy, Padma Reddy, the Babai Hotel in Vijaywada, S. Sampoorna, the Taj Gateway Hotels in Vijaywada and Vishakapatnam, P. Posaiah and P. Ramanna, fisherfolk on Edilamma Lanka in the Godavari River, Jayanti Rajagopalan and her mother, Hotel Vasavi in Rajahmundry, Sayi Rani, Kaveri Kaul, Yasmeen Tayebbhai, Mehreen Khosla, Juji and Viru Dayal, Bhargavi Menon.